Pelican Books

The Politics of Secrecy

James Michael was born in the state of Oklahoma, U.S.A., in 1940, and grew up in Oklahoma and Kansas. He attended Northwestern University in Illinois on a scholarship, and received a B.Sc. in 1962. After three years' military service as a signals officer in the U.S. Marine Corps (which included positive-vetting for access to top secret cryptographic material) he studied at Georgetown Law Center in Washington, D.C. for his J.D., and was admitted to the District of Columbia Bar. He worked as an editor with *U.S. Law Week*, and was staff counsel with the National Commission on Product Safety before joining Ralph Nader's Center for Study of Responsive Law, where he edited (with Ruth Fort) *Working on the System*, a guide to government agencies for pressure groups.

He moved to London in 1972, initially to work for the Public Interest Research Centre, a Nader-inspired British group. He has an LL.M. from the London School of Economics and is now a senior lecturer in law at the Polytechnic of Central London. He spent the 1979–80 academic year doing research on government information and privacy law at Stockholm University.

James Michael

THE POLITICS OF SECRECY

Penguin Books

Penguin Books Ltd, Harmondsworth,
Middlesex, England
Penguin Books, 625 Madison Avenue,
New York, New York 10022, U.S.A.
Penguin Books Australia Ltd, Ringwood,
Victoria, Australia
Penguin Books Canada Ltd, 2801 John Street,
Markham, Ontario, Canada L3R 1B4
Penguin Books (N.Z.) Ltd, 182–190 Wairau Road,
Auckland 10, New Zealand

First published 1982

Copyright © James Michael, 1982
All rights reserved

Made and printed in Great Britain by
Hazell Watson & Viney Ltd, Aylesbury, Bucks.
Set in Baskerville by
Rowland Phototypesetting Ltd
Bury St Edmunds, Suffolk

Contents

Introduction

This book is not about what most people still think of as 'official secrets': information about espionage, surveillance, and other things done in the name of 'national security'. This is deliberate, because it is still too readily assumed that any 'official secret' is kept secret in order to protect the country from foreign and domestic enemies. The emphasis here is on the more routine secrecy of British government, why it is thought that secret government is good government, and what might be done about it.

There is a need for much more public and Parliamentary scrutiny of the British security apparatus. It is now subject to almost no supervision at all, presenting opportunities not only for its oppressive use against the British people, but also for corruption and inefficiency in carrying out its legitimate functions. But there are other writers who are specifically interested in secrecy of that sort.

This is mostly about secrecy of a less dramatic kind, from the secret meetings and accounts of local authorities to the secret system of Cabinet committees. The book has both a bias and a commitment to specific changes in the law affecting government information. The bias is in the liberal-democratic tradition, believing that the governed should know as much as possible about how they are governed. It assumes that their informed consent is essential in a democracy, and not just because of the British constitutional doctrine that political, if not legal, sovereignty is based on popular support. It also rests on the proposition that competition in the market-place of information, as well as that of ideas, is at least very useful in determining how a society should be run, and that publicity is an important safeguard against maladministration.

It is not enough for the law to be neutral about information, allowing the greatest possible circulation of opinion. Even if that was sufficient when it was argued for by the pamphleteers of the seventeenth and eighteenth centuries, it no longer is. Modern government has expanded until it touches all of our lives every day, but this has not been accompanied by any greater openness about how the decisions of such a government are taken. If anything, it has been accompanied by a concentration of information within government about all sorts of things and people. And the reflex of any government is to keep such information to itself.

James Callaghan explained it to the Franks Committee (on section 2 of the Official Secrets Act) in 1972 by pointing out that government 'is not like a cricket club where on the whole all the members belonging to the club want it to go on, provided it wins games'. Instead, 'frankly half the people in this country are concerned to find things that will redound to the discredit of the Government, every day. It is inevitable in this case that a Government is going to have some defensive reaction and say, "We are not going to tell you anything more than we can about what is going to discredit us . . ."'

It was a candid expression of a common attitude in government that near-absolute control over information about how power is exercised is a natural part of office. Information may not be power itself, but it is a very important adjunct to it. Political debate over subjects ranging from the safety of food additives to matters of high national policy is inevitably one-sided when it is between those who know the facts and those who do not. And one consequence of disclosing those 'facts' is that critical scrutiny may show that they are just not true.

The law can protect government information, be neutral, or actually compel greater openness. In Britain it is now almost entirely protective, with the all-encompassing section 2 of the Official Secrets Acts as the best-known illustration. It is neutral in the sense of allowing fairly free expression of opinion. It is also neutral about 'briefing', but punitive in tracking down 'leakers' of official information. James Callaghan explained the difference to the Franks Committee: 'Leaking is what you do and briefing is what I do.'

Other countries, Sweden and the United States in particular, have tried to make the law a force for open government by generally requiring governments to make records available to the public. It is the sort of legislation usually described as 'freedom of information' or 'open government' laws. The details of definitions, exemptions, and enforcement can be extremely complicated, but the principle is simple: people should have the right to know as much as possible about how they are governed.

Chapter One

The Secretive State

From top to bottom, from the present machinery of government to the archives of the past, from silly examples of bureaucratic intransigence to hard cases of law enforcement and national defence, Britain is about as secretive as a state can be and still qualify as a democracy. The working assumption at all levels is that secret government is good government, and that principle is enshrined in the Official Secrets Act.

That Act, and some of the other reasons for the reflex secrecy in the government of this country, will be considered later. But a few examples may illustrate some of the pervasive reticence. And, as an Australian writer commented in a book on the similar secrecy in his country, it is the extent of secrecy which is the greatest secret of all.

It is still said, however, as the Franks Committee did in 1972, that Britain is not really much more secretive than other countries. The simplest answer to that is to consider information, specifically British information, that is only available in other countries.

British Secrets from U.S. Files

British researchers and journalists have in recent years got into the habit of going to the United States and using the Freedom of Information Act there to find out more about their own country. Charles Medawar, the director of a British pressure group called Social Audit, was able to get information about British companies only by going to Washington.

He found that foreign producers who want to export cooked meat products to the U.S. must be inspected and approved by U.S. authorities. He asked for, and got, reports on sanitary conditions in several British plants, and not all the reports were good ones.

Two Scottish plants were struck off the approved list in 1975 after failing inspections. Robert Wilson & Sons of Kilwinning, Ayrshire, failed their inspection in September 1975. Among other things, the report said that their walls were mouldy, equipment was broken and rusty, the roof was leaking, and an employee was seen picking meat off the floor and putting it back on the processing table. The W. A. Baxter company in Morayshire was failed for poor sanitation, with rusty equipment and paint flaking into the cooking vats. American officials making these inspections are often accompanied by British inspectors. The reports are passed on to local authorities, but are not available to the public here.

Pharmaceutical manufacturers in this country who export to the U.S. must also be approved by U.S. inspectors and Charles Medawar got reports on I.C.I., Beechams, and Cyanamid. They were more reassuring than the meat plant reports. All three of the companies passed with only minor discrepancies, although the Gosport Cyanamid plant was given a formal notice after inspection in April 1976 for deficiencies in their records of batch-testing.

The U.S. Civil Aeronautics Board also maintains public registers of complaints made by passengers about airlines. On request, the C.A.B. sent a huge pile of complaints made about British airlines. Most of them were travellers' horror stories of oversold flights, of delays, lost baggage, rudeness, and assurances made but not kept.

The Consumer Product Safety Commission in Washington has a very efficient computer index of accident reports involving products, and it includes the country of manufacture. Selecting one of the products from the computer print-out sent on request, I asked for, and received, a thick file on a British bicycle manufacturer, Lamberts, that exported thousands of defective cycles to America before going bankrupt.

Both Britain and the U.S. ban some food additives as unsafe.

The decisions are based on laboratory tests, usually made on animals. In 1977 an American pressure group was readily allowed to see the laboratory tests on several food colourings, and used them as evidence in their petition to the U.S. Food and Drug Administration to have the colourings banned as unsafe. The Ministry of Agriculture, Fisheries, and Food in this country refused a request to see similar files here because the information was 'treated on a basis of confidentiality . . . and it therefore cannot be offered for inspection'. This is particularly ludicrous, because the same information is available not only in the U.S., but also in technical journals and United Nations publications.

Charles Medawar was also sent copies of reports made by public health inspectors on cruise ships calling at U.S. ports. In 1976–7 they showed that many British ships, including the *Queen Elizabeth II*, were regularly failing their inspections. When this was published by the *Sunday Times* in November 1977 there was a crude attempt at financial retaliation by the owners of some British ships, who threatened to withdraw all advertising. (See Chapter 5 for further details.)

Although it is not specifically British information, there is a direct parallel between plans in the United States for evacuation of areas around nuclear power plants in case of accidents and similar plans in this country. For years, Mrs Kathleen Rogers, who lives near the nuclear plant at Hinckley Point in Somerset, has been trying to find out what she and others are supposed to do if something happens to go wrong there. Until very recently she was given nothing more than reassurances that the plans were well in hand, and that everything would be taken care of in case of an accident. In the United States such plans have regularly been made available. One result is that many of them have been shown to be inadequate, and in one case the inadequacy of the evacuation plan was enough to convince a federal judge to stop construction of a plant.

It is also possible to learn more in America about British corporate standards of behaviour than it is here. Information from such companies as British Petroleum and I.C.I. about bribes and 'questionable payments' to get foreign contracts is available from the U.S. Securities and Exchange Commission. And the S.E.C. is adopting even more stringent rules about requiring companies to make such reports in future.

A B.B.C. television producer went to Washington in early 1979, where he was shown defect reports on automobiles, including some made by British Leyland. This was included in a documentary broadcast in April, but there was retaliation of a sort. The accuracy of the information was not denied, but B.L. appealed to the patriotism of the B.B.C., and was able to have a repeat of the programme stopped, even after a special reply by the company had been filmed to be included. The specific information was about a defective hub assembly. B.L. knew about it, but did not bother to tell car owners. A passenger in one B.L. car was permanently disabled when the hub assembly disintegrated.

It was a dramatic illustration that what you don't know *can* hurt you, and the same producer, Michael Barnes, had used other British examples of how routine government secrecy can have deadly results in a 1974 programme called 'The Right to Know'. It included case histories of asbestos workers who were crippled and dying from the substance they had worked with for years. The factory inspector, who was also interviewed, had known of the danger, but felt that the Official Secrets Acts kept her from telling the employees.

The Real British Disease?

The term was a favourite one of the late Richard Crossman to describe the obsession with secrecy and confidentiality in this country. It was fitting that the last thing he did before dying was to arrange for publication of the diaries he kept as a Cabinet Minister, which was to lead to one of the major legal battles over government secrecy in recent years. It is now more widely recognized that an official secret is not always something that is vital to national security. M.P.s and journalists are also beginning to be more aggressive about following up refusals to disclose information of all sorts.

Some of these have turned into running battles. For years, Frank Field, first as a director of Child Poverty Action Group and now as Labour M.P. for Birkenhead, has urged the Department of Health and Social Security to publish the rules on welfare benefits, commonly called the A-Codes and described only as guidelines for the exercise of discretion. He was still repeating his requests in December 1979, although the year before the Minister of State had presented the slightly curious argument that they were leaked so widely that they weren't really secret, but he still wasn't going to make them public officially.

The existence of secrets usually turns up almost by accident, and journalists need to have a fair idea of what the 'secret' information is before it becomes a story. The justifications for keeping information secret are considered in more detail later, but they often are similar to the words of Ibsen's mayor: '. . . it is a matter of the greatest concern to me that your report [that the public baths were contaminated] must be withheld for the good of the community. Later on, I shall bring up the matter for discussion, and we shall deal with it as best we can – discreetly. But nothing of this dangerous business – not a single word – must become known to the public.' The official in *An Enemy of the People* would have felt at home with the authorities in Bath in 1977. The springs had become contaminated, but there was no publicity about it until a young woman died of meningitis.

The list of specific examples ranges from local authorities to ministries to the nationalized industries. Some of them have their sillier aspects. For several years a German flower-seller kept writing to British Rail asking about the practice of depositing the contents of railway lavatories onto the tracks. British Rail replied that it presented no danger to public health at all. They had done a study in 1958 which established that. But when he asked if he might read the study they replied that it was 'confidential'.

Some examples are particularly serious to people like the family of Paul Bramwell, who died in a quarry accident in 1976. He had taken every possible precaution when he went into a pit under a conveyor belt to repair the steel plating. But someone replaced the fuse he had removed, took down the 'Danger' sign he had put up, and started the belt, which dumped a 431-lb block of ice on him.

Compensation has been paid, and the family have been told that safety standards were tightened up, but they still want to see the report prepared by an Inspector of Mines and Quarries. But, like most such reports, it is 'confidential'. They are angry that the company was not prosecuted, and feel that a fine might have been more of an incentive for that company and others to tighten up on safety than the 'persuasion and guidance' that the Minister said was preferred to prosecution. They were lucky enough to have an M.P. who pressed the matter to an adjournment debate in the House of Commons, but release of the report to them would still, as it was explained, be 'inappropriate'.

Local Government: Thatcher's Law

Local government secrecy is the best evidence that the Official Secrets Act is only a symptom of the disease. The only local authority officers who are bound by it are police officers. But secrecy persists (as in some of the examples already given), and in spite of open government provisions in the Local Government Act 1972.

One of these provisions, requiring local authority meetings to be open, was the creation of Margaret Thatcher as a newly elected M.P. She drew a high place in the ballot for private members' bills on her first try, and decided to make the most of it. Instead of the usual uncontroversial maiden speech for a new M.P., she gave hers to introduce a bill of her own in the face of opposition from her government front-bench. She emphasized the £1,600 million spent every year by local authorities, asserted that the public should have a right to know how it was spent, and quoted the 1957 Franks Report on Tribunals and Inquiries that 'publicity is the greatest and most effective check against any arbitrary action'.

She steered the bill through committee, more or less successfully, and it became the Public Bodies (Admission to Meetings) Act 1960. But both as an open government measure and a private member's bill, it was something of a preview for Clement Freud's open government bill nearly twenty years later. The arguments against it were that it would cost money and inhibit the necessary candour. She had intended to include a clause setting forth acceptable reasons for holding local authority meetings in secret, but was persuaded to accept a provision allowing secrecy if the council thought that it would be 'prejudicial to the public interest' otherwise. That was the first mistake. The second was that there was no machinery to enforce the measure, and no penalties for its evasion.

That is why the *U.K. Press Gazette* still regularly runs short items about local reporters being excluded from meetings held in secret, why a random survey of fifty authorities reported in *The Times* in 1963 revealed that over half of them excluded the press and public from committee meetings, and why, despite some modest improvement in the 1972 Local Government Act, a 1979 survey of local authorities in Kent showed much the same pattern.

There is only one public-access provision in the Local Government Act that does have penalties, and it has been used successfully at least once. The law requires the accounts to be open to local electors just before the annual audit, and there is a fine for non-compliance. In 1976 some Hillingdon ratepayers took legal action to enforce it, and the recalcitrant authority was fined £10 – but also had to pay about £5,000 in costs for the appeal against conviction. (See Chapter 6 for further details.)

Secret History: Archives

Historians as well as journalists and researchers have been able to find out more about Britain from U.S. files than they can from the Public Record Office here. Professor Geoffrey Warner, of the University of Leicester, used the American Freedom of Information Act for his research on Belgium at the end of the Second World War.

He was fortunate in knowing the specific files he wanted, if only because he had tried to get them here and had been turned down. The American authorities were reluctant to let the records out at first, saying that British permission would be required. But when they were reminded that classification could be appealed to the courts they handed over nearly all that he had asked for.

When the Public Records Act 1968 established a general 'fifty-year' rule for archives it was considered a great advance towards openness, and the 1977 reduction of that period to thirty years was presented as another liberalization. But the system still has so many loopholes that it would be more accurate to describe it as a 'thirty-year, if nobody concerned has any serious objection and if we can manage to sort them' rule.

The decision to withhold records for longer than thirty years is taken formally by the Lord Chancellor, but in practice it is the government departments that decide. For example, records of field executions during the First World War are still withheld, ostensibly to protect from embarrassment the families of those who were shot.

Occasionally the 'weeders' of archives nod, and documents become public records, only to be turned back into official secrets if they become embarrassing. In 1977 the Home Office hurriedly recalled some files that had been in the Public Record Office for eleven years, after some historians began to write about them. They included Special Branch reports on the hunger marchers of the 1930s, with statements from informers about the leaders of the march. Some of the reports, apart from being inaccurate about what the marchers were doing, were highly defamatory about one of the leaders who was still alive, Will Paynter. In the midst of the government reclassification muddle he brushed aside suggestions that he should sue for libel.

Harder Cases: Defence and National Security

Even information about defence and national security, kept secret in Britain, is readily available in other countries. Although there are obviously legitimate reasons for keeping some military information secret, it is incongruous to keep secret information that is published in the U.S. For example, a 1976 report of the House of Commons Sub-committee on Defence had some evidence about the 'Hot', 'Tow', and 'Hawkswing' missiles deleted. It read: 'the

range of these three missile systems is all roughly the same, ***.'
At about the same time the chairman of the U.S. Joint Chiefs of
Staff was volunteering to the Senate Armed Services Committee,
and anyone else who cared to read his published statement, that
the range was about 3,000 metres. The British report also stated
that the 'Dragon' missile had a 'range of only ***'. But the
American Senate committee, and the public, were told that the
missile was 'medium-range (60 to 1,000 metres)'.

The arguments about what the law should be on information
relating to defence and national security are considered elsewhere. But this sort of compulsive secrecy, of which the best-
known example is that the names of the heads of M.I.5 and 6
(Sir Howard Trayton Smith and Sir Arthur Franks, as every
foreign spy certainly knows) are not published, means that the
British public is kept in far greater ignorance about matters of
defence and security than any potential enemy.

Chapter Two

'Nanny Knows Best' and Other Reasons

'Decent Reticence' and 'Garish Publicity'

It is difficult, though not impossible, to compare governments in terms of their relative openness. The Franks Committee made a stab at it in their 1972 report, and generally concluded that most of the countries they considered were pretty much the same. There certainly was, in the Committee's opinion, no 'stark contrast, drawn by a few witnesses, between an obsessively secret system in this country and gloriously open systems in some other countries'.

While few would go so far as to describe the Swedish and American systems as 'gloriously open', it is still true that things which are kept secret in Britain are not secret in other countries. The clearest demonstration of this has already been given: British information that British researchers could only get from American files. An Israeli political scientist[1] came to a similar conclusion in a comparative study. After considering law and practice in ten countries, he placed Britain firmly in the category of those in which the government's privilege to conceal was valued above the public's right to know.

The impulse to secrecy is certainly common to all governments. (Max Weber thought it was one of the sociological characteristics of bureaucracy.) But in Britain it is positively indulged. This is certainly the case when British statutes are considered. Quite apart from the Official Secrets Act, the Franks Committee totted up sixty-one other laws with provisions making it an offence to disclose various kinds of information without authorization, and there are now eighty-nine such laws. On the other side, there are only about six statutes giving citizens legally enforceable rights to any sort of information. Most of these are of recent origin, and many of them so qualified as to be of little effect.

But the Franks Committee was not inclined to place much emphasis on laws in considering openness in government. Law was 'by no means the most important influence . . . [and] in some countries it is not even a major one'. Other factors, such as 'constitutional arrangements, political tradition, and national character, habits and ways of thought . . .' were equally, if not more, important.

The 1979 Civil Service Department report[2] had an even longer list of all the things that made open government such a 'complicated subject':

A comprehensive examination of all its various aspects would require a study in depth of the history and culture of most western democracies; their constitutions; the ways their legislatures, executives and judiciaries operate; the methods whereby official information is disclosed; the sources of pressure for such disclosures and their causes; the political climate; the attitude of the media and how they conduct their business; the ways in which information held by government about individuals is protected and controlled; how grievances are redressed; how national and trade secrets are safeguarded; how documents are classified; and how archives are kept and revealed. There is a very large body of specialist literature on all of these aspects.

The C.S.D. report did not attempt 'such a comprehensive examination'; nor does this book. But that limitation did not inhibit the mostly factual C.S.D. report from commenting on these other aspects, usually to explain why open government legislation might be right for them but not for us. (They seemed in particular to assume that such laws might be acceptable in small countries, but wouldn't do for such a large one as Britain.)

Other chapters in this book comment on some of the other named aspects, at least in this country. But having already described some of the many specific examples of government secrecy in Britain, it may be useful to consider why government is so secretive here. And the Franks list of other factors seems as good as any to start with.

'Constitutional arrangements' is a nice way of describing the untidy mixture of statutes and conventions that make up the uncodified constitution of the United Kingdom of Great Britain and Northern Ireland. Its democratic characteristics are still very much wine of recent vintage poured into an ancient royal flask. Professor Finer (in *Comparative Government*) sums up British constitutional history as the story of a continuous struggle for control of the executive machinery.[3] The machinery is, historically and characteristically, authoritarian. With some exceptions, the thrust of British development towards democracy has been to have a greater voice in choosing between wise masters every five years or so rather than having much say in what they do in between.

Whatever say there is between elections is through two general channels. The first, and constitutional, one is Parliament. But the Parliamentary voice is not only muted by the various devices through which the Commons is kept in ignorance, as described in Chapter 4; there are basic political constraints as well. ('Muted' is not quite the right word; it frequently seems that shrillness in argument is a direct function of ignorance, often unavoidable, about the subject.)

The basic political constraint is the fusion of the executive and legislative functions. It is taken as given that those with the job of government must also have whatever new legislative tools they want. The law-making function of Parliament is almost entirely devoted to making minor adjustments to proposals that have emerged from the government machine. If the government cannot have whatever laws it wants, it is 'weak' and must be replaced by another which is strong.

The other group of voices listened to by the government between elections is that of the civil service and what Professor Finer calls 'pressure groups'. If there is a set of values shared by civil servants in any political sense, it is likely to be a dedication to what is practical and sensible. Any incoming minister will be presented with papers showing how well civil servants understand what he has promised to do, how he can go about doing it, and also which parts of his campaign promises are clearly impractical and why.

The civil service is more of an interest than a pressure group. It is a large organization with the function of carrying out the policies of the government of the day. It also has, and it would be surprising if it did not, a basic interest in securing its own position. That is why the introduction of even a handful of temporary advisers by some ministers was bitterly resented, and has largely been thwarted. It is also why the intrusiveness of the 'think tank', the Central Policy Review Staff, was resisted, and occasionally blocked. The C.P.R.S. was set up by Edward Heath as a body of experts from outside with the job of inquiring into whatever the Cabinet (in theory) or the Prime Minister (in fact) wanted looked at. All of this is perhaps best understood as a high-level demarcation dispute. The job of advising ministers and the Cabinet belonged to career civil servants, not to a flighty bunch of outsiders who hadn't done their apprenticeships.

Another basic interest of the civil service as a whole is that they should be seen to be as neutral politically as they are constitutionally. They must be seen so by the general public, which is just as powerful an argument as the 'candour' one for keeping advice to ministers confidential. They must also be seen to be neutral by their new ministers, which is why the minister will not be allowed to see the papers containing advice given to his predecessor. 'Allowed' is perhaps too stark a word. The rule, as the Head of the Civil Service explained to the Select Committee on Parliamentary Questions in 1972, is a 'self-denying ordinance' observed by successive governments. He also observed that 'It is occasionally necessary for civil servants to draw the attention of Ministers to this . . .' [4] It was hardly known at all before then, at least outside the civil service, but has recently been restated by Margaret Thatcher in the House of Commons.

The other 'pressure groups' which influence government between elections are very far from the likes of Friends of the Earth, the National Council for Civil Liberties, the National Association for Mental Health (Mind) and others. They are probably more accurately described as 'interest groups' which exist largely to secure the economic interests of their members. The Confederation of British Industry and the Trades Union

Congress are the leading examples, although there are many others. Only a small part of their effort is devoted to public advocacy of their positions. They are the new barons, and their influence on government is the modern equivalent of having the king's ear at court: tea and biscuits at the Department, or even beer and sandwiches at Number 10.

These consultations are, above all, confidential. This presents a dilemma for a pressure group on the edge of achieving such influence. After years of public campaigning, building up a membership, cultivating the press, lobbying M.P.s at least to put down Parliamentary Questions or raise something on an adjournment debate, they may finally be asked along to the Ministry. They go, almost always, and may get a hearing for one of their pet proposals and even be given some indication of what the government intends to do about it. If they are reasonable enough about it, they may have more of such meetings, and even achieve some real success. But the implicit price is confidentiality. The private negotiations and their publicity campaigns must be kept separate. They have been consulted; if they wish to talk too much about it they may not be consulted again.

These are, in the broadest sense, 'constitutional arrangements', and perhaps even partly 'political tradition', in the Franks terminology. The Committee also may have been thinking about the collective and individual responsibility of ministers when referring to 'constitutional arrangements'. Those are both dealt with in Chapter 4, because they are closely related to the barriers used to keep information about government from Parliament itself. But they deserve some mention here, if only because they represent a central fiction of British government. The fiction is that all members of the Cabinet agree on everything, and so are equally responsible. One result of this is the resolute refusal of governments to admit even the existence of Cabinet committees, let alone their number, responsibilities, or membership. It is a bit silly, since almost every government textbook describes them and names the more important ones. Occasionally an enterprising journalist will do some reading of memoirs, ask around a bit, and come up with a current list of committees and their members.

The candid arguments against admitting anything at all about them were made in a memorandum from James Callaghan when he was Prime Minister. It was leaked and printed in the *New Statesman* (10 November 1978). There were arguments of tradition and convenience, but the real justification for sticking to the rule was that 'any departure from it would be more likely to whet appetites than to satisfy them'.

The related convention of ministerial responsibility is also considered in Chapter 4. Simply put, it is that the minister in charge is responsible to Parliament for everything the department does, and will even resign if things go badly enough (and are found out). In practice the two conventions are closely related.

The effect of these constitutional arrangements and political traditions is that information flows upward through the civil service to the minister at the top (and controlling that flood or trickle of information into the minister's red boxes is an important part of a senior civil servant's skill). There information is properly disclosed as little as possible to the people's elected representatives (see Chapter 4), who may then criticize or applaud, but can do little else. Professor Finer's assessment of Parliament's law-making function is dismissive, but accurate. 'The Commons is not a true legislature but an extension of the executive.' Parliament first began to assert its strength against the Crown in the seventeenth century by refusing to supply money through taxes, but Finer's description of this basic fiscal power is just as abrupt. 'There is a fiction that the House "controls" taxation and expenditure. In fact it does neither.'

The Commons can criticize the way government is being carried out, but circumstances make the criticism as ill-informed as possible. Another effect of political tradition is that many of them can be effectively dissuaded from being too inquisitive. The opposition back-bench will be critical of almost anything the government does, in the nature of things. But the opposition front-bench can sometimes be diverted from criticism on 'sensitive matters' by invoking the Privy Councillors' oath. All ministers, and a few others, are made Privy Councillors and remain so (unless they disgrace themselves as John Profumo and

John Stonehouse did). Anything communicated to any of them on 'Privy Council terms' must go no further.

The government's own back-benchers also can often be persuaded to be less than insistent about demanding information. This is not just a simple matter of party loyalty. About a third hold some sort of office (including the unpaid Parliamentary Private Secretaries) from which they can be sacked. Of the others, only a few do not want to be ministers of some sort, someday; the rest realize keenly that nagging your own government too persistently will not help you to the front benches.

All of this is something of an introduction to the chapter on Parliament, but it fits here into the Franks listing of other 'factors' which make for openness in government. Constitutionally, what openness there is in British government exists through the medium of Parliament.

Another factor to be considered is 'national character'. This is dangerous ground for a writer who is a foreigner. 'National character' is usually less than quantifiable, and is used mostly in the aggressive humour of old jokes. Still, Lord Franks brought it up, and it is cited too often in articles and speeches (both attacking and defending secrecy) to be ignored. Also, there is some comparative sociological evidence on national attitudes to authority and government.

'Nanny Knows Best' was the title of a 1972 article by Jon Tinker in the *New Scientist*. He was criticizing secrecy on the part of authorities responsible for pollution control, and the title sums up a common attitude about authority (with an appropriate class tinge to it). The Alkali Inspectorate in particular has explained in interviews that the details of how it regulates air pollution from factories are best left to those in charge, if only because others might use them to criticize.

There is still something approaching deference to, or at least a trust in, authority in Britain. Hostility is likely to be directed towards the government of the day rather than being expressed as suspicion of (or even interest in) the machinery of government itself, and political action is directed mostly towards getting our people in charge of the machine in place of theirs. There is little of the near-reflex distrust of any government, approaching anarchism, which is found in some parts of America. In a 1963 survey, four-fifths of those questioned in Britain believed that civil servants would treat them fairly, and nine-tenths believed that the police also would. [5] It is possible that the responses might be rather different today, if only because of the cases of local government and police corruption that have become public. But defenders of secrecy ('confidentiality' is usually preferred) can, and do, turn this to their advantage. As Chief Justice Holt said in 1704, it is 'very necessary for all governments that the people should have a good opinion of it'. It is of course desirable for justice to be done in particular cases; but publicity about maladministration or corruption is often thought to cause a decline in public confidence.

The editor of the *New Statesman* criticized the secrecy surrounding the first commercial radio broadcasting licences in 1972 by remarking that much of British government seemed to be run on the lines of nursery maxims: not only 'nanny knows best', but also 'least said, soonest mended'. [6] 'Confidentiality is especially preferred in quasi-judicial administrative proceedings dealing with maladministration and the regulation of commercial activity. But the traditional reasons for keeping the courts open to the public should apply with even greater force. The first reason is what the criminologists call the effect of general deterrence (as opposed to the particular deterrence of the sanction applied to the culprit). Publishing the conclusions and sanctions applied for safety violations in cases like the one described on p. 14 can be a far clearer message to other companies to tighten up their safety precautions than hundreds of confidential words of caution from safety inspectors. They may also make justice subject to the check of public opinion. It is possible that the public may think a particular sanction to be too harsh or unjustly applied. It is also possible that they may think that a large company can, simply because of its financial resources, be able to negotiate a settlement that is hardly a sanction at all. It was Margaret Thatcher who introduced her private member's bill, mentioned in the previous chapter, to open local authority meetings by quoting the

1957 Franks Report comment that 'publicity is the greatest and most effective check against any arbitrary action'. Or inaction, she might have added.

The 1972 Franks Report also noted that 'habits and ways of thought' were important in determining openness in government. Quite apart from the general tendency of bureaucracies everywhere to keep their business to themselves, there are some expressions of this which seem almost peculiarly British. As one Member, Charles Pannell, put it in opposing the 1959 Thatcher bill on local government, 'reticence is a fine and decent quality, far more desirable than the garish desire for publicity which seems to oppress our civilization today'. It is something of a clubman's remark, and evokes the days, now assumed to be past, when important government decisions were effectively taken by quiet private talks in London clubs. Quite apart from raising questions of class and power, the 'habits and ways of thought' so expressed lead directly to the more functional argument over confidentiality and candour.

The argument comes up with monotonous familiarity in every discussion about information, whether it is over compulsory disclosure of documents to the public, 'privilege' against evidence being presented in court, or legal sanctions (both civil and criminal) for those who commit 'breaches of confidence' or make 'unauthorized disclosures'. It is invoked to justify all sorts of secrecy, from the eighteenth-century rule about House of Commons proceedings, to the inspectors' reports considered by the 1956 Franks Commission, to ministerial memoirs and civil service advice in the Crossman *Diaries* case, to archives, to credit reference reports and academic references . . . it seems applicable to everything, and is assumed to be self-evidently right.

It is not. The value of candour in a communication depends very much on its purposes, content, and circumstances. And the law has three alternatives in dealing with a confidential communication: it can compel disclosure, either limited or general; it can punish disclosure, either by criminal penalties or civil sanctions; or it can remain neutral, leaving the keeping or breaking of confidentiality to those involved.

There are circumstances when certain communications should be kept confidential for specific purposes, and when legal protection is justified. The secret ballot, which was introduced only in 1872, is a particular illustration. It is important in determining public preferences between candidates that voters should be able to express their opinions anonymously to avoid retribution from the powerful. It is also important for people to be able to be as candid as possible for the purposes of religious or psychiatric counselling.

But candour should not be the ultimate value when the communications are about the business of government which will affect the general public. It is a good thing for those who rule us to be honest in saying how they think we should be ruled. But it is also a good thing if those opinions can withstand criticism. Cabinet and departmental discussions are very different in purpose from the confessional and the psychiatrist's couch. If a senior civil servant calmly advises the minister that certain action is necessary because the day of judgment described in Revelation is at hand, then the soundness of his advice becomes at least as important as maintaining its confidentiality. Keeping his views confidential may still be important; but it is important for the purposes of psychiatric counselling rather than for government decision-taking.

The 'candour' argument is also something of a diversion from central issues in public records legislation. Much of the information sought by individuals, pressure groups, and the press is about facts rather than just opinions. Statistics, laboratory studies, and financial information often provide the bases on which opinions are formed, recommendations made, and decisions taken. Disclosure of such information would at least make possible other interpretations than the official ones.

Another 'habit or way of thought' affecting openness in government is the assumption that secret government is efficient government. To some extent this is simply a matter of appearances, or rather the non-appearance of information about inefficiency. We can only guess about the efficiency or safety of the national airlines of some eastern European countries, because information about accidents is only rarely made available about particular crashes, and few detailed statistics are given. Things are rather different in the West, but there are still areas where any argument about safety is hampered by refusal to disclose information. 'Details of near-miss inquiries' in aviation, for example, is one of the subjects on which M.P.s are not even allowed to table a Parliamentary Question.

Secrecy may also be a cover for gross financial inefficiency. Leslie Chapman, a former senior civil servant, has argued cogently in a best-selling book, *Your Disobedient Servant*, that much of the waste in government spending could be reduced by greater scrutiny. And if the 1972 report on the Crown Agents had been made public it might have alerted Parliament and the public to practices that would ultimately lose over £200 million.

Even when secrecy is justifiable in wartime, there is often a price to be paid in losing efficiency rather than gaining it. Histories of the Second World War describe in some detail how armies and intelligence services often worked at cross-purposes and with inadequate information precisely because they were secret. Far less dramatic cases occur in governments generally, with needless duplication of effort, lack of coordination, and the advancement of plans that were impractical from the start, simply because they were not more widely known and subjected to criticism at an earlier stage.

In terms of efficiency, the harm done by publicity is concrete and immediate. The word gets out, the minister is embarrassed, the plans must be changed or even dropped. The harm that can be done by secrecy, on the other hand, is both deferred and cumulative. The fault in the 'commercially confidential' design may not become apparent until the bridge collapses or the planes crash, and the cause may not always be clear even then.

The last 'habit or way of thought' to be considered is the effect of the two world wars on this country. In law, the effect has been direct. As explained in Chapter 3, the 1911 Official Secrets Act was passed hurriedly as an anti-espionage measure during a period of spy-scares before the First World War, and the 1920 Act was specifically passed to keep in force many of the Defence of the

Realm secrecy provisions which had lapsed with the war's end. In terms of national attitudes there has also been a pervasive effect. A generation that came of age under a barrage of slogans reminding them that 'loose lips sink ships' and that only those who 'need to know' should be told anything is unlikely to be open about government business generally. Besides, a 'secret' document is somehow more important than the same paper without the stamp, and one who is entrusted with it acquires at least some sense of importance.

All of this applies to government generally, but with greater force to information that has anything to do with national defence. British writers who do write about the sensitive topics of 'national security' argue that they are not disclosing national secrets to any potential enemies, but to the British people. Sophisticated intelligence services of potential enemies would long since have learned whatever a diligent researcher can find out from public sources. Such intelligence services have far more elaborate and sinister means to get their information, from satellite reconnaissance to bugging and blackmail.

Secrecy about matters of national defence involves a calculation of risks and gains, and the ultimate decision cannot, even in that area, be left to those in the secret world itself. They are psychologically still at war, and still assume that only those who need to know should be told, or allowed to learn, anything. Their arguments are even bolstered in a way described by Peter Laurie in *Beneath the City Streets*, [7] because there are some violent people with political objectives who do not have sophisticated intelligence systems. To a terrorist bent on assassination a street map of London and the name of the Prime Minister is 'information of value to an enemy'. Almost any secrecy at all can be justified if that is the sort of potential enemy to be considered, just as almost any sort of police-state repression can be justified to those in power. It is those who are subject to that power who suffer, even if they only suffer in, and from, ignorance.

Briefing and Leaking

'Confidentiality' is preferred to 'secrecy' by politicians and civil servants when refusing to answer difficult questions. It implies some sort of legal or moral obligation to keep silent, and it sounds better. While a minister can still speak of 'defence secrets' without attracting hoots of derision, it is not so easy to refer to 'social security secrets'. Since much of the concern about government secrecy is directed at the Official Secrets Act, one essential legal point must be made. Almost none of the examples of British government secrecy in this book are legally required to be kept secret. Section 2 of the Act only penalizes the 'unauthorized' disclosure of official information by a Crown servant. 'Authorized' disclosures of almost any government information are perfectly legal, subject to two qualifications. The disclosing official must be in a position to 'authorize' the disclosure. And in a few cases involving information obtained from persons or companies outside government the formal authorization to disclose must come from them.

Exactly, or even generally, who has authority to disclose what is one of the mysteries of British government. The Franks Committee tried very hard to find out how such authorization was distributed. The answer seemed to be that those who have it know, and those who are uncertain do not.

All of this bears directly on the question of what sort of law should replace the Official Secrets Acts.*

'Freedom of Information' has been accurately described by Baroness Sharp (a former permanent secretary to the late Richard Crossman) as a misnomer. Laws such as the U.S. Freedom of Information Act do not simply remove the restrictions on getting and spreading information. Instead they place a positive obligation on governments to make most records available to anyone who wishes to see them. It would be more accurate to describe such statutes with the equally hackneyed

---

*The details of various proposals such as the bills introduced by Clement Freud, Michael Meacher, and the Conservative Government elected in 1979 will be discussed in Chapter 11.

term of 'right to know' laws. They establish a right of people to inspect official records, with a corresponding obligation on governments to make the records available. If that obligation is to be a real one it must be enforceable by some authority other than the government itself. If the government is to be the judge in its own case it is far too easy to find persuasive reasons against disclosure.

Would such a law sweep away the elaborate systems of briefings (on the record, off the record, background only, deep background, and all the variations in between) and leaking? One of the most common arguments heard from journalists who are unenthusiastic about open government proposals is that they are unnecessary, and could possibly even be harmful to the 'free flow of information' (a term currently much used in international discussions). All that is needed to secure freedom of information, the argument runs, is the removal of legal barriers to the obtaining and publishing of information. A simple repeal of section 2 of the Official Secrets Act would accomplish much of this, followed by some changes in other legal rules such as defamation, copyright, and the law of confidence.

One part of this argument is that the law should concern itself as little as possible with the circulation of information. The whole subject, with some exceptions for national defence secrets, is best left to common sense and compromise. Another part is the assumption that such a law might firmly establish two clear categories of government information: first, those items which would be official matters of public record; second, those secrets which would be protected by criminal penalties unless they were released by specifically authorized persons. Such a distinction might, paradoxically, make it more difficult than at present to dig out and publish information which was not officially publicly available.

But none of the proposals, such as the bills introduced by Clement Freud and Michael Meacher, would do this. Under both of them, as under the U.S. Freedom of Information Act, there are three general categories of government information. The first would be the broad range of information contained in government documents, to be available to anyone on request as a legally enforceable right. The second would be information which would not be a matter of public record, but which could be disclosed by leaking or briefing without fear of legal penalties. The third would consist of those secrets, such as matters really vital to national defence, which should be protected by the criminal law against unauthorized disclosures.

The object of such a statute would not be to abolish leaking and briefing, but to reverse a fundamental assumption about government information generally: that it is to be made public when, and if, the government of the day so decides.

For those journalists who insist that the Official Secrets Act is no real barrier to freedom of information, there is a telling anecdote about the Callaghan memorandum on the secrecy of Cabinet committees. It came into the hands of *The Times* in the autumn of 1978. After a discussion of the Official Secrets Act the decision was taken not to publish it. The editorial decision was that it was not newsworthy enough, at least not enough to risk a prosecution. But the *New Statesman* felt differently, both about the news involved and about the Official Secrets Act, and published the entire memorandum some weeks later.

Whistle-blowing

Secrecy is a feature of nearly all organizations, if only because it is an important adjunct to the exercise of any power. It also serves important psychological and sociological functions. Sharing secrets is a bonding mechanism. To confide a secret to another person implies trust that it will go no further. The importance of the secret is not so much in its substance, but in its limited circulation. The sanction for breaking such a trust, quite apart from any legal consequences, is that one who breaks such a trust will not be trusted again, that he will no longer be a member of the club. The Radcliffe Committee on Ministerial Memoirs, which was set up after the decision in the 1975 Crossman *Diaries* case concluded that such informal penalties would enforce confidentiality between ministers better than any sort of legal restrictions. The Committee's conclusion was at least in part influenced by the particular result in the Crossman case: the Lord Chief Justice, Lord Widgery, had not, after all, stopped publication of the diaries.

'Leaking' is usually derided within any organization as 'sneaking'. It is, to be fair, a symptom of disloyalty, or at least of divided loyalties. Some Americans have coined, or rather revived, the term 'whistle-blowing' in an attempt to raise the status of such disloyalty. In its simplest form the term is applied to someone within an organization who tells the general public about some sort of wrongdoing, or at least about something which he feels the general public would regard as wrong. The organizational 'wrong' may amount to a crime itself, or it may simply be something which the 'whistle-blower' feels is a matter for legitimate public knowledge.

The motives of such 'whistle-blowers' may be mixed, at the very least, with reasons for going public including personal resentment or failure to gain promotion as often as any selfless dedication to the general public interest. If they are discovered, or proclaim themselves, they usually find themselves cut off from an organization that has often given them more psychological support than they may have realized. It is a rare whistle-blower who escapes at least some degree of isolation and obsession with his or her particular case.

Open government legislation does not remove the possibility of whistle-blowing or its desirability in many cases. But it does provide a legitimacy for openness which might otherwise be stifled by the pressures for secrecy in all organizations. If some kinds of information, the details of public expenditure for example, must be made public as a matter of law, it removes the burden on a would-be whistle-blower of choosing between organizational loyalties and an impulse to tell the outside world. Such legislation would also reduce the effect of bureaucratic penalties which serve to preserve secrecy as much as any possible criminal prosecution. When Merlyn Rees, then Home Secretary, announced his proposals to change the law on such criminal penalties, he emphasized that they would not mean that civil servants would be any more free to disclose information than before. They would, he commented, be treated just as the employees of any private business who disclosed information without authority. That remark in itself shows why a simple change in the criminal law would do little to bring about more open government.

Even under the most thoroughgoing open government systems, such as those in the United States and Sweden, leaking and whistle-blowing goes on. But whistle-blowing in those countries tends to be concentrated more on hard cases, where information has not been recorded, or where authorities attempt to conceal it in spite of their legal obligations. In both of those countries there have been statutory attempts to protect such whistle-blowers. In Sweden, an editor or journalist is usually under a legal obligation not to reveal the source of his information in any legal proceeding. In the United States an act has been passed to protect civil servants from administrative sanctions for disclosing some kinds of information without authorization.

In 1873, the Permanent Secretary to the British Treasury wrote: 'The unauthorized use of official information is the worst fault a civil servant can commit. It is on the same footing as cowardice by a soldier.' This was quoted by a modern permanent secretary in evidence to the Franks Committee, and repeated to a Ditchley Park conference on government information in 1978. A senior civil servant at the conference remarked that it 'still has a great deal of force today'.

That sums up one of the important 'habits and ways of thought' that the Franks Committee thought were at least as important as law in determining openness. It should be possible to think of unauthorized disclosures of official information about, say, 'mismanagement, a gross waste of funds, an abuse of authority, or a substantial and specific danger to public health or safety' that might be justifiable, and could even require bravery rather than cowardice. Those are the words of the 1978 U.S. 'Whistle-blower's Act' protecting civil servants who disclose such information from reprisals. An open government law would at least help to reverse the Permanent Secretary's fundamental assumption by giving disclosure of information a legal basis,

through establishing a public right of access to records.
perhaps some further consideration might then be given
protecting public servants who blow the whistle by unauthoriz
disclosures about maladministration.

Blunderbuss: the Official Secrets Act

There are actually several Official Secrets Acts, of 1911, 1920, and 1939, which were preceded by the Official Secrets Act 1889. But they are closely related, and 'Act' will be used to refer to all three laws.

Most of the attention given to the Act has been directed at its 'catch-all' provision, section 2 of the 1911 Act, which, when the 305-word sentence which is section 2(1) is unravelled, has a relatively simple and sweeping meaning. It is a crime for any Crown servant or contractor to disclose any information learned in the course of his job. It is also an offence, under section 2(2), to receive such an unauthorized disclosure. There is a possible defence if the recipient can, as the section somewhat quaintly puts it, prove that the communication 'was contrary to his desire'.

There is something about the Act which seems to inspire journalists and M.P.s to flights of metaphor. The Act has been variously described as a 'blunderbuss', a 'mangy old sheep', a 'punt gun', and a 'fishing net'; and that only includes the more recent and polite terms. The Franks Committee, which was set up in 1971 to review section 2, succinctly described it as 'a mess'. [1]

It is such a widely and badly drafted section that, as the Franks Committee explained: 'People are not sure what it means, or how it operates in practice, or what kinds of action involve real risk of prosecution under it.' Although the Franks Committee reported that over 2,000 differently worded charges could be brought under it, it is not even a prosecutor's delight. It is not clear, to take one of the most basic questions in criminal law, whether or not the section requires proof of 'guilty intent' (*mens rea*) for penalties to be imposed. The courts have not helped much, answering the question differently in different cases.

One popular misconception about the Act should be set aside. The ritual of 'signing the Official Secrets Act' has almost nothing to do with whether someone can be prosecuted under it. (The 'almost' is necessary because the ritual might be some proof of *mens rea*, if it did happen to be required.) The declarations themselves, as the Franks Committee noted, have no legal force, and many of them are positively misleading about the scope of the law.

The Act is not at all limited to cases of national security and spying. Section 2 covers any information which a Crown servant comes across on the job. Most M.P.s are a bit shy of criticizing section 1, if only because the description in the margin is 'penalties for spying', and few people want to appear to be soft on spying. But the marginal description has no legal effect, and a careful reading of the section makes it clear that it covers far more than what most people would consider as spying. The most recent illustration of this was the 'ABC' case in 1978. All three of the defendants were charged under both section 1 and section 2, although it was never even alleged in court that they had any connection with any foreign power.

The Act is, in the words of Franks, 'saved from absurdity' only because prosecutions must be approved by the Attorney-General, which still gives 'rise to considerable unease'. And so it should. A basic principle of the rule of law is that those subject to it should be able to determine with some degree of certainty what acts they can be punished for. The Official Secrets Act theoretically makes any disclosure of any official information, and its receipt, an offence, but leaves it to the Attorney-General of the day to decide who is to be prosecuted. It is, as a U.S. Senator once remarked in a different context, more power than a bad man should have or a good man should want.

It is easier to understand the Act by tracing its history than by attempting to untangle the sections and sub-sections. A review of the Act's development is particularly useful for one point which is relevant to the whole subject of government secrecy: Parliament may not have known what it was doing in passing such a sweeping criminal law, but the ministers and civil servants who prepared it certainly did.

As early as 1837 the Foreign Office tried without success to stop publication of some fairly well-known dispatches sent from Spain by Lord Wellesley in 1809. In 1847 the government tried unsuccessfully to stop *The Times* from publishing the correspondence of Lord Castlereagh at the 1815 Congress of Vienna. *The Times* justified publication as being in the 'rights of the public'.

The 1889 Official Secrets Act was specifically drawn to stop such leaks by civil servants and to punish others such as William Hudson Guernsey and Charles Marvin. Both were what today might be described as 'whistle-blowers' or even, in a small way, journalists.

Guernsey had a friend in the Colonial Office library, which he visited frequently in the late 1850s; he also apparently had a grudge against the Colonial Office for refusing him a job. In 1858 he got hold of two dispatches from the Lord High Commissioner of the Ionian Islands, the inhabitants of which wanted union with Greece. He sent them to the *Daily News*, which published them. The effect was to embarrass the government, which had just sent Gladstone on a mission to the Islands. An inquiry was set up, and Guernsey was charged with larceny. But, as the Younger Committee on Privacy was to point out over a century later, it is difficult to 'steal' information in the way that physical property can be stolen. Guernsey's counsel argued that there was no intent to deprive the owner permanently of possession of an article, and Guernsey was acquitted. The most that he could have stolen was the paper on which the dispatches were printed.

Even that technical theft did not exist in the case of Charles Marvin, twenty years later. Marvin was a civil servant in the Foreign Office, although only a temporary copying clerk. He had also been a contributor to the *Globe*, to which he turned when he came across details of a secret agreement between Britain and Russia made just before the Congress of Berlin in 1878. The £42 which he was paid may have helped to make up for his Foreign

Office pay of tenpence an hour; it also landed him in the Bow Street Magistrates' Court on a charge of larceny. But the charge was dismissed, for the same reason that Guernsey had been acquitted.

Marvin had not even taken any paper. By a remarkable feat of memory, he simply copied out what he had read. Also, the Bow Street magistrates found, he had assumed that details of the Anglo-Russian agreement were about to be disclosed anyway. As a civil servant, he was a leaker; as a journalist, he had a scoop.

The Foreign Office was cross, and said so in the House of Lords. *The Times*, which had not got the scoop, was severe, and said so in a leading article. The government machine began to work on the problem, and the first product was a rule that civil servants required permission to write anything about their departments.

The Franks Committee decided that the Marvin case was not, however, the cause of the first Official Secrets Act. There had been other leaks about the organization of the Exchequer and Audit Office, a possible pay rise for suburban letter carriers, and a copy of an 1884 proclamation by General Gordon before it was received by M.P.s.

These all have a somewhat familiar ring to them. Most of the leaks were of information which was about to be made public. The offences were not just that the disclosures were unauthorized, but that they were premature.

Only two of the nineteenth-century leaks which led to the 1889 Act actually had much to do with national defence (as opposed to diplomatic embarrassment) or spying. In 1887 the press published some instructions to the Intelligence Department of the Royal Navy, and in the same year a dockyard draughtsman was dismissed for allegedly selling warship designs, possibly to a foreign power.

The first draft of the 1889 Act was called the 'Breach of Official Trust Bill'. As the Franks Committee noted, it was not the damage caused by leaks which the bill was aimed at; it was the disobedience of instructions by civil servants. The draft was expanded to include a section on spying, and was renamed the

Official Secrets Act before it was passed by Parliament. One M.P. presciently remarked that the Act might impair Parliamentary control over government departments.

But the 1889 Act was not so wide as the section 2 that we now live under. The offence by a Crown servant or government contractor was communication 'corruptly or contrary to his official duty' to a person to whom it 'ought not, in the interest of the State or otherwise in the public interest, to be communicated at that time'. It is worth noting that this established, in a rough sense, a sort of 'public interest' defence for leakers or whistle-blowers. This was just the sort of defence which was urged upon (and rejected by) the Franks Committee in 1971 by Justice (the British section of the International Commission of Jurists). James Callaghan, who was then in opposition, presented the same argument in his testimony to the Franks Committee. And Shirley Williams, as shadow Home Affairs front-bencher, pressed the Conservative Government to consider such a defence during the June 1973 debate on the Franks Report.

But the 'public interest' provision of the 1889 Act apparently was never seriously tested in court. Most of the prosecutions under it dealt with military and naval secrets communicated to agents of other countries. One of these, in 1892, apparently led to the present section 1, which effectively shifts the burden of proving himself innocent onto someone who is accused of spying.

The only case under the 1889 Act which did not involve spying was a successful prosecution for what would properly be described as an attempt at official corruption. A clerk at the Woolwich Dockyards was convicted of offering to supply a firm of contractors with information about the prices asked by their competitors.

But leaks continued, including a press report in 1900 about the Home Secretary's decision to increase Metropolitan Police pay. Another report about undelivered old age pension books appeared in the press in 1909 before it was given to Parliament, and in 1910 there was a similarly premature leak of the Report of the Welsh Church Commission.

There were no prosecutions following these leaks, and the Franks Committee revealed the reason after reviewing the official files. The 1889 Act did not cover someone who had received an unauthorized disclosure. That, said the Director of Public Prosecutions, had to be changed. Attempts were made to amend the 1889 Act in 1896 and 1908, but they were abandoned after criticism in the press.

The growing spy fever in the years before the First World War gave the government its opportunity. Two Germans had been charged under the 1889 Act in 1910 and 1911, with one pleading guilty and the other sentenced to twenty-one months' imprisonment. It was during the second trial, in the hot and busy August of 1911, that the bill which became the Official Secrets Act was presented to Parliament. M.P.s and the press paid almost no attention to it. Their interests were directed to the constitutional crisis over the Parliament Bill and to the impending war with Germany. The bill was presented as a necessary measure to deal with spying, and no voices were raised against it in the House of Lords when it was introduced and debated during July. On 17 August it went through all of its stages in the House of Commons in under an hour.

The catch-all section 2 was the main difference between the new 1911 Act and the 1889 Act it replaced. But it was not mentioned once in Parliament. The provision may have been passed in ignorance and haste, but it had been prepared carefully and at leisure. It was designed to cover all those who communicated or received any kind of official information without authorization. The unsuccessful 1908 bill had attempted to include publication of unauthorized disclosures. The 1911 Act went even further.

The Franks Committee concluded that the government 'clearly intended it to operate as a general check against civil service leaks of all kinds'. The first draft of the bill was dated a year before it was introduced, and many of the provisions were derived from the 1896 and 1908 bills.

The new Act was applied frequently and vigorously during the war, mostly against real German spies. But some of the cases gave an indication of how far the law could be stretched. In 1915 a young Belgian was convicted under section 2 and sentenced to twelve months' hard labour. He had been employed in the Censor of Neutral Countries' Mails, and he had told a London schoolmistress that her mail was under observation after she had indirectly received a letter from a friend in Germany. The next year two men pleaded guilty to charges of communicating and receiving War Office information critical of senior officials for publication in a paper called the *Military Mail*. And in 1919 a War Office clerk was convicted under section 2 after he revealed information to a tailoring firm about contracts for officers' uniforms.

There was also one important ruling by the Court of Criminal Appeal about the scope of section 1. An ex-sailor named Parrott was charged with communicating naval information which could be useful to an enemy. His defence was that most of the case against him was only based on suspicion, and that there was no clear evidence about what he had communicated. The appeal court held that the jury was entitled to infer the communication from general circumstances, and that the burden was on the defendant to show that such communication was not for a purpose prejudicial to the State. 'Enemy', the court concluded, could cover 'a potential enemy with whom we might some day be at war'.

The Act was supplemented by broad Defence of the Realm Regulations, but these lapsed with the end of the war. An inter-departmental committee from the War Office, the Admiralty, and the Home Office prepared a bill to re-establish some of them as a part of the Official Secrets Act 1911. In June 1920 the bill was, like the earlier one, introduced in the House of Lords.

Parliament was more sceptical than it had been in 1911, and awkward questions were asked in both Houses before the bill became the Official Secrets Act 1920 in December. The assurances given in reply to some of the objections were, through negligence or intent, misleading. In the House of Commons the Attorney-General, Sir Gordon Hewart (later to become Lord Chief Justice), said: 'We are dealing only with offences or suspected offences under the principal [1911] Act or this Act. In other words, to put it shortly, we are dealing with spying and attempts at spying.' As Franks commented, it was not clear how he came to make this 'obviously erroneous statement', particularly in view of the conviction for a leak about tailoring contracts the year before.

Most of the provisions of the 1920 Act extended both sections 1 and 2 of the 1911 Act. Their use in celebrated cases since illustrates how far both sections went beyond spying. Section 6, which was added in 1920 (and which was under discussion when Sir Gordon Hewart gave his explanation about spying), made it an offence to withhold information about any offence under the Act. This was to result in the only significant later amendment to the Act after a Member of Parliament, Mr Duncan Sandys (now Lord Duncan-Sandys), was threatened in 1938 with prosecution under section 6. His alleged offence was to ask the Secretary of State for War about the adequacy of anti-aircraft defences, probably based on information which he had as an officer in the Territorial Army. The matter was raised in the House as a possible breach of Parliamentary privilege, and a Select Committee was set up. Before the Committee reported, the Government introduced a bill, which quickly became the Official Secrets Act 1939, limiting section 6 to withholding information about offences under section 1.

The 1911 Act had made it an offence under section 1 to approach or enter a 'prohibited place' for 'any purpose prejudicial to the safety or interests of the State'. Section 1 had also effectively thrown the burden on the accused to show that such conduct was not for such a prejudicial purpose. It made it possible for a jury to infer that such action was done for a prejudicial purpose from the circumstances of the case, or from the conduct or known character of the accused. The 1911 Act also gave powers for the government to designate such 'prohibited places'. This was to be applied in the early 1960s case of *Chandler v. Director of Public Prosecutions* in which nuclear disarmament campaigners were convicted for attempting to enter an airbase. The decision was upheld by the House of Lords which also ruled that it was for the government to decide what was or was not 'prejudicial . . . to the interests of the State'. [2]

The Act, after it was amended in 1920, created a broad range of offences related to sections 1 and 2, some with a maximum sentence of fourteen years and others with a two-year maximum. Minor offences included (and still include) improperly using any military or police uniform, falsely pretending to be a person holding office under the Crown, and retaining any official document. These all require that the acts be done for a purpose prejudicial to the State, with the burden effectively on the accused to show that there was no such purpose. Section 7 makes it an offence to do any act preparatory to the commission of any offence under the Act.

The burden of proof under section 1 was shifted even more firmly onto the accused by the 1920 amendments. Any proof of communication with or an attempt to communicate with a 'foreign agent' would be taken as evidence that the accused had 'for a purpose prejudicial to the safety or interests of the State, obtained or attempted to obtain information which is calculated to be or might or is intended to be directly or indirectly useful to an enemy'.

The effect of the 1920 Act was twofold. The 'spying' offences, with a maximum sentence of fourteen years, included a whole range of acts which the accused would have to show were not done for some purpose prejudicial to the interests of the State. The lesser offences, with a maximum sentence of two years, included not only the unauthorized communication or receipt of any official information, but also embraced preparatory acts and specific acts and omissions, such as failure to comply with regulations regarding the business of receiving letters at an accommodation address.

It did not go through without protests. A Law Lord, Lord Parmoor, regretted that the bill would 'seriously interfere with ordinary freedom in various directions'. One Member of the House of Commons found it 'difficult to confine my language in regard to this Bill within the range of Parliamentary propriety'. It was, by coincidence, Sir Donald Maclean. His son, who was later to demonstrate that even such a sweeping law could not catch a really determined spy, was then seven years old.

The bill became law, despite the criticism, and perhaps because of the misleading assurances given by the Government that it was only to catch spies. Apart from the relatively minor amendment in 1939, which would almost certainly not have been made if the law had not been invoked in an attempt to intimidate an M.P., it is the law we still live under.

How has it been used in the sixty years since it took its present form? It has certainly been used in real cases of espionage to convict those who were communicating information harmful to national defence to enemies and potential enemies. In such cases the fourteen-year maximum sentence under section 1 was extended somewhat. George Blake was sentenced to forty-two years when the Lord Chief Justice ruled that he should serve three fourteen-year sentences consecutively. (Blake somehow escaped from Wormwood Scrubs in 1966.) Vassall, the blackmailed Admiralty clerk, was sentenced to eighteen years in 1962 by the same technique of consecutive sentences. Gordon Lonsdale and his associates were given sentences far longer than fourteen years in the 1961 Naval Secrets case by being charged with conspiracy to breach section 1, for which the maximum sentence is life imprisonment.

The Act is broad enough to make convictions of real spies easy enough, with sentences as long as the courts choose. There is little dispute that Britain needs a law to cope with espionage, and the scope of such a law is considered in Chapter 11. It would, so far as one can tell from reports of the spy cases held largely *in camera*, have been adequate to convict any of the spies who have been convicted under the existing Act.

But the Act has also been used in many cases far removed from espionage, with nearly all of its various provisions being invoked. These are the cases which demonstrate how successive Attorneys-General have actually applied their discretion to prosecute. And some of them may point the way for appropriate changes in the law on government information.

With two exceptions, most of the prosecutions under section 1 have been limited to cases that seem to involve genuine espionage. In 1972 the Franks Committee reported that there had been twenty successful prosecutions since 1946, and there have been another four (in nine cases) since then. Nineteen of the cases involved passing information to a foreign power (usually the Soviet Union, but also including Czechoslovakia, Poland, and Iraq) or a conspiracy to commit such an act. There was one unsuccessful prosecution. A Member of Parliament was accused of passing information to Czechoslovakia in 1968, but was acquitted. The sentences for those convicted ranged from three to forty-two years.

Until the ABC case in 1978, the most controversial application of section 1 was in *Chandler v. D.P.P.*, already mentioned. The six defendants were sentenced to eighteen and twelve months' imprisonment. In the ABC case the charges under section 1 were withdrawn during the trial.

The Franks Committee reported that there was no comprehensive record of prosecutions under section 2 from 1911 to 1945. The 1972 report summarized thirty known cases between 1916 and 1972, and there have been another eight prosecutions (four of them successful) under the section since then.

It is difficult to decide how justifiable many of the prosecutions were, if only because it is often impossible to determine what sort of 'confidential' or 'secret' information was involved. Some of the cases may have involved real espionage, but with a decision taken to prosecute under section 2 for some reason. Others would more properly be described as corruption or invasions of privacy.

It is clear that many of the prosecutions were for disclosures very far from spying. For example, in 1926 a retired governor of Pentonville Prison was fined for writing an article about what a murderer had said on the morning of execution. In 1932 a clerk and a journalist were both gaoled after the clerk had given out information about wills. The journalist's paper printed the information on the morning of the day when it was officially released.

The next year, 1933, Compton Mackenzie pleaded guilty to disclosing confidential information which he had dealt with as a Royal Marines officer during the First World War. The disclosure was in a manuscript he had sent to his publisher.

In 1934 the Attorney-General, Sir Thomas Inskip, personally

prosecuted Edgar Lansbury, son of the leader of the Labour Party, for quoting from Cabinet documents about unemployment in a book about his father. Despite the defence argument that the information had already become public knowledge before the book, a fine of £20 was imposed. The case illustrates how the Attorney's discretion can be exercised, because there was no prosecution of George Lansbury, who had provided his son with the documents.

The threats made in 1938 to Duncan Sandys, M.P., have already been described. But a successful prosecution had been brought two years earlier under the same section 6 of the Act, which makes it a crime to refuse to provide information required in connection with an offence. The *Manchester Express* had published an article about a man wanted by the police for fraud. It was based on a circular (not marked 'confidential') which had been sent by a chief constable to other police forces. The journalist refused to reveal the source of his information, and he was fined.

He appealed, arguing that a police officer was not a 'Crown servant' under the Act, but the conviction was upheld. Lord Chief Justice Hewart, who as Attorney-General had assured the House of Commons in 1920 that the Act was directed against spying, ruled that a police officer was a Crown servant. Therefore, an unauthorized communication was an offence, and refusal to give information about such an offence was also a crime.

The case, *Lewis v. Cattle*,[3] led to a conference called by the National Union of Journalists and the National Council for Civil Liberties. Dingle Foot, M.P., spoke at the conference, and later introduced a bill to limit the scope of section 6.

It is curious that the Act, which was passed to deal with German spies during the First World War, apparently was not used at all against spies from the same country during the Second World War. But a civil servant was fined in 1945 for giving a shipping broker information about shipments by allied governments during the war, and in 1946 two men were fined after a publication said that one of them had been employed by Military Intelligence.

Section 6 had been amended in 1939 so that it would only be a crime to refuse to give information about offences under section 1. But *Lewis v. Cattle* had extended the definition of 'Crown servant' to police employees, and in 1948 a police telephone operator and a Yorkshire journalist were fined. Their offence was that the telephone operator had told the journalist about an accident report. The police had faked this report in order to trap the operator and the journalist in an unauthorized disclosure.

In 1951 three young men, two of whom worked at the Royal Aircraft Establishment, were fined for telling each other about aircraft being produced. The same year charges were brought against a writer who included 'copies of official documents' in a book. The charges were withdrawn when the documents were returned and the book not published.

A photographer was imprisoned for six months in 1956 for passing on a sketch used in a 'prohibited place', an aircraft factory. In 1958 two Oxford undergraduates were sentenced to three months after writing about their National Service in the Navy for the university publication *Isis*. There was a long *in camera* trial at the Old Bailey, but the harshness of the law was mitigated slightly: their sentences were to be served in 'most favourable circumstances' and away from criminals.

Although the Attorney-General's consent is required for an Official Secrets Act prosecution, any citizen can make an arrest without a warrant. In 1959 a young man who had just left the Royal Navy was subject to such a citizen's arrest for showing official documents to a friend. He was fined, and gaoled for one day.

During the 1960s section 1 of the Act was used in major espionage trials, as well as in the still controversial *Chandler* case. Section 2 was used in some near-espionage cases, and cases of criminal corruption. But there were at least two cases, in 1961 and 1966, in which an Admiralty clerk and an ex-R.A.F. officer were fined for retaining official documents. It was at the end of the decade that section 2 was used unsuccessfully in the major case against the *Sunday Telegraph* and others.

The full story is told in *Officially Secret* by one of the defendants, Jonathan Aitken (now Conservative M.P. for East Thanet). It involved a report by the Defence Adviser to the British High Commission in Nigeria about the extent of British aid to the federal government there during the civil war. The major damage of the leak was that it varied distinctly from the accounts which were being given by the Government to Parliament. Once again the Attorney-General's discretion was used selectively, and one of the links in the chain of unauthorized disclosure, Hugh Fraser, M.P., wrote to *The Times* demanding to be prosecuted as well. In his summing-up to the jury, Mr Justice Caulfield was critical of the Act, remarking that the jury might feel that it was time for the Act to be 'pensioned off'. All the defendants were acquitted in February 1971, and a Departmental Committee under Lord Franks was set up by the Home Secretary in April to review section 2 of the Act. (The 1972 Franks Report was adamant that the *Sunday Telegraph* case had not been the reason for the Committee's appointment. The Government apparently had such a committee in mind, and had only deferred the announcement until the case was over.)

The report was thorough, and included a mine of information about the Act which is still valuable. Among other things, their research disclosed that there are many other statutes making it a crime to disclose various kinds of official information. They found sixty-one of these, which they listed in Appendix V as 'protecting the confidences of the citizens'. The description is only accurate if one considers a company to be a 'citizen'. Most of the statutes made it an offence to disclose various kinds of information obtained from companies, although a few clearly apply to personal information. Many of these laws are subject to the same objections made against section 2 of the Official Secrets Act. In particular, civil servants such as the factory inspector described on p. 12 would not only be inhibited by the Official Secrets Act from disclosing hazards to the workers; they would also be subject to penalties under laws such as the Factories Act 1961 (s. 154).*
Even if section 2 of the Official Secrets Act were to be repealed

---

*This has been only slightly modified by disclosure provisions later provided in some areas such as the Health and Safety at Work Act 1974 and the Control of Pollution Act 1974.

there would still be many smaller versions which cover particular types of information nearly as thoroughly. And the Committee did not find, or perhaps did not look for, laws which penalize unnecessary secrecy rather than unauthorized disclosures.

During the 1970s section 1 of the Official Secrets Act was used in some genuine cases of espionage. The editor of the *Sunday Times* was warned under section 2 after his paper published a report of possible rail cuts (first leaked to the *Railway Gazette*). A young journalist was charged under section 2 and held for ten days after police found a 'Restricted' Ministry of Defence manual (the classification used for cadet manuals on how to march) in his flat, but charges were eventually dropped. Criticism of the Act grew, and various private members' bills were introduced to reform its criminal provisions and establish an open government system. The Labour Government promised in 1974 to introduce such a reform, but with varying degrees of success tried to suppress the Crossman *Diaries* and information about thalidomide. Then, in 1977, arrests were made in what came to be known as the ABC case.

On the night of 18 February 1977 two young journalists went to a flat in North London to interview an ex-soldier. Afterwards all three were arrested by waiting police and charged under the Official Secrets Act. A year and a half later they walked out of the Old Bailey as free men. They had been convicted of charges under section 2 of the Act, but had been given conditional discharges and a suspended sentence. A lot had happened in between, but the full story may not even be known when records about the case reach the Public Record Office in thirty years' time.

The Attorney-General who authorized the prosecution, Sam Silkin, once told an American audience that a part of his job was occasionally to place the 'blunderbuss' of the Official Secrets Act against his brittle shoulder and pull the trigger. The results of that particular prosecution included revelations of jury-vetting and a long legal battle over the naming of a Colonel Johnstone, one of the government witnesses. After the end of the case Mr Silkin explained that sometimes evidence did not prove to be as persuasive in court as it had seemed when the prosecution case was being prepared.

Together with the *Sunday Telegraph* prosecution at the beginning of the decade, the ABC case (so called because the defendants' surnames – Aubrey, Berry, and Campbell – were in convenient alphabetical order) was a dramatic illustration of the wide scope of the Official Secrets Acts, and how they could be misapplied.

Even a summary of the ABC case must begin, not with the arrest of the three, but with earlier orders to deport two American writers, Philip Agee and Mark Hosenball. The deportation orders under the 1971 Immigration Act were served on the two in November 1976, and they were finally deported in May 1977. The deportation of Philip Agee was at least understandable. He had been an officer of the American Central Intelligence Agency, serving mostly in Latin America, who became disenchanted with his work and 'went public', in the American phrase, with his book, *C.I.A. Diary*, which was published in Britain in 1975. Ironically, he had come to Britain in order to get information for the book. The British Museum had the most complete file of Latin American newspapers he could find, and he used them to refresh his memory about dates and incidents. He stayed on, first in Cornwall and then in Cambridge, continuing his new work of exposing the C.I.A.

The American authorities were predictably furious, and attempted to blame Agee for the murder of a C.I.A. officer in Athens in 1975. Although undertakings were later given that he would not be prosecuted if he returned to the United States, there were clearly other possible civil legal proceedings that might be brought against him if he returned to American soil.

Mark Hosenball was a far less obvious target. When he received his deportation order he had just moved from a job with *Time Out* to the London *Evening Standard*. Apparently he had attracted the attention of the security services by an article he wrote for *Time Out* in May 1976 on the communications interception centre in Cheltenham. 'Apparently' must be used because of the peculiar character of the deportation hearing. His deportation order had only said that his continued presence in the United Kingdom would not be conducive to the public good for reasons of national security, and that he had 'communicated information harmful to the security of the United Kingdom'.

The hearing for both Agee and Hosenball was before 'three wise men', chosen by the Home Office. They merely heard representations from the two men, without providing any more information about what they were supposed to have done which made them so dangerous to Britain's national security. (This informal procedure was substituted in 1971 for a quasi-judicial hearing which had been successfully used to deport Rudi Dutschke, the German left-wing activist.)

The job of the three-man panel was to hear what the two had to say for themselves and advise the Home Secretary on whether to carry out the deportations. The significance of the *Time Out* article could only be guessed at then. The panel seemed to be quite interested in Hosenball's explanation of how it came to be written. In his defence he explained that the information about the communication centre came from sources already available to the public. He also explained that much of the research had been done by Duncan Campbell, a freelance journalist with an Oxford degree in physics who wrote mostly on electronic surveillance for journals such as the *New Scientist*.

Although the two men chose different methods to defend themselves, a vigorous Agee–Hosenball Defence Committee was formed. At times it seemed as though their opponent was more the American C.I.A. than the British Home Secretary or British security services. Much was made of the arrival of a new C.I.A. head of station at the London embassy shortly before the deportation orders were issued. There was an implicit assumption that a British Home Secretary, and a Labour one at that, would only do such a thing under American duress.

Despite petitions, meetings, and questions in Parliament, the deportations were duly carried out. Hosenball appealed to the British courts, getting as far as the Court of Appeal, where Lord Denning commented that in national security cases 'even the rules of natural justice had to take second place'. Agee appealed without success to the European Commission of Human Rights in Strasbourg.

That Agee's deportation was at the request of the C.I.A. seems a plausible explanation. He knew and wrote very little about the British security services. And the American authorities might even have thought that the British would be cooperative enough to 'deport' him (which simply means to order him out of the country to somewhere, anywhere, else) by putting him on a plane direct to the U.S. This would amount to 'extradition', that is, returning a fugitive to another state to face trial there. A proper extradition proceeding would clearly have been unsuccessful. Agee had not even been charged with espionage, which is not an extraditable offence in any case. But the British authorities had been obliging in 'deporting' a convicted Russian spy named Soblen to the U.S. in 1962.

There are still questions about why Hosenball was also chosen. At the time there was a widely circulated theory that his deportation order was produced at least partly to give the Home Secretary room to compromise. If public and Parliamentary pressure became too great, it might have seemed statesmanlike to withdraw the Hosenball order and still get Agee out of the country. But, for whatever reasons, both were expelled. Hosenball returned to America, while Agee bounced from one European country to another.

One effect of the proceedings was to draw out Britons who might be inclined to imitate Agee and start writing books similar to his about the British security services. One British journalist had already begun, although he lacked Agee's inside knowledge. Tony Bunyan, who had also worked for *Time Out*, had written a book in 1976 called *The Political Police in Britain*. [4]

It seems clear that various telephones used by the Agee–Hosenball Defence Committee were tapped, and that mail was also opened. There was no other way, short of an inside informer or intensive personal surveillance, that the police could have known about the meeting between Crispin Aubrey, John Berry, and Duncan Campbell. John Berry had served as a lance-corporal in a signals unit stationed in Cyprus. After he left the Army in 1970 he had various jobs as a lorry driver and social worker. His political attitudes changed, and he was so aroused by the Agee–Hosenball deportations that he wrote to the Defence

Committee offering to tell them about his military experiences.
The meeting was arranged by a telephone conversation between Aubrey and Berry. Duncan Campbell was asked to come
along because of his electronics expertise, which had been used
before by *Time Out* in the story under Hosenball's by-line. After a
two-hour conversation, which Aubrey recorded on a cassette, they
opened the door to Berry's flat to find the police waiting.

There was an element of comedy as the police drove round and
round searching for the Muswell Hill police station where the
three could be locked up. When the Home Secretary was
informed of the arrests his reaction was understandable in view of
the political criticism he was already getting over the Agee–
Hosenball deportations. 'My God,' he exclaimed (according to
someone who was with him when he was told), 'what are they
trying to do to me *now*!'

But the real burden was on other ministerial shoulders this
time. Or rather, as Sam Silkin insisted, it was on his shoulders
in his capacity as an independent law officer of the Crown.
Prosecutions under the Official Secrets Act require the consent of
the Attorney-General, and it has long been argued that the wide
coverage of the Act is mitigated by this requirement that he must
be convinced that the severity of an offence merits prosecution
(and that he is answerable to Parliament for his decisions).

The original 'holding charges' against the three were under the
catch-all section 2 of the Act. Eventually they were released on
bail, but it was several months before Mr Silkin issued his *fiat*
approving prosecutions under both section 2 and section 1 of the
Act.

The first of many legal problems with the case lay in a statement which the Home Secretary had made to the House of
Commons in November 1976. He was explaining the Government's plans to amend section 2 of the Act, more or less in
accordance with the Franks recommendations. 'Mere receipt' of
an unauthorized disclosure, he said, was no longer to be an
offence when the law was changed. And while the old law
remained on the books, it was 'open' to the Attorney-General to
consider this in deciding whether to prosecute or not.

The essence of the charges against Campbell and Aubrey was just such 'mere receipt'. But both the Home Secretary and the Attorney-General weathered the storm of political criticism, and the case continued on its bumpy way to the Old Bailey. The first major bump came during the committal proceedings at the Tottenham Magistrates' Court. One of the witnesses declined to give his name, and was identified in court only as Colonel 'B'. But a combination of his testimony and a quick perusal of *The Wire*, a publicly available service journal, was enough to determine that his name was Colonel H. A. Johnstone.

Two left-wing journals learned this quickly enough, and published the name. They were charged with contempt of court, only to be eventually exonerated by the House of Lords. A near-constitutional crisis then developed when several M.P.s shouted out the colonel's name in the House of Commons. The 'free speech' (for M.P.s) provision of the Bill of Rights 1688 was cited, and for a few weeks the papers were full of letters and articles about the relative rights of M.P.s to say what they wished and the courts to compel secrecy in the interests of justice or national security. The House of Lords finally ended the debate, without really resolving the fundamental issue, by deciding that the magistrates' court had not actually forbidden the witness's name to be disclosed. Therefore, it was not a contempt of court to figure out the name and print it.

The Agee–Hosenball Defence Committee more or less resolved itself into the ABC Committee, and the round of protest meetings continued. On the government side there was mounted what can only be described as a whispering campaign. At the time of the case this was difficult to document, but some written evidence of it later emerged in the form of an 'internal' London Weekend Television memo. The campaign usually took the form of off-the-record briefings by ministers and civil servants to M.P.s and journalists who were inclined to criticize the prosecution. The gist of it was that the case was far more sinister than it appeared to be. Sometimes it was hinted that the K.G.B. was involved (following earlier stories that Agee was a 'turned' agent working for the Soviet Union); sometimes the hints were about the I.R.A.

It was not limited to allegations about the three defendants. The London Weekend memo, published in the *New Statesman* on 15 February 1980, mostly contained misinformation about Phil Kelly, a London journalist who was active in both the Agee–Hosenball and ABC defence committees. The campaign was at least partly effective, although many, including Conservatives such as columnist Peregrine Worsthorne and Jonathan Aitken (now a Conservative M.P.), continued their criticism.

The trial finally began at the Old Bailey in September 1978, only to be halted after another of the curious twists in the case. The jury had been vetted to ensure that jurors with 'strong political motives' would not hinder a fair trial. Despite this precaution, the foreman of the first jury was a former member of the Special Air Services, and was loudly in favour of convictions from the first day. Although the vetting had been disclosed in court, the judge had ordered that it go no further. But Christopher Hitchens, covering the trial for the *New Statesman*, let it out on a Saturday night television programme.

The trial was stopped, the judge fell ill, and a new trial was begun, with a new judge and jury. The whole question of jury-vetting turned into a running debate. The trial continued, although the charges that the three were serious threats to national security began to fade when measured against the evidence. An essential part of the defence was that the information involved, especially that collected by Duncan Campbell, was from public sources. Prosecution witnesses were discomfited when they insisted that information (such as the term 'SigInt' for Signals Intelligence) was secret, only to be presented with newspaper articles and photographs of signs outside SigInt stations with the names of units written on them. The judge, Mr Justice Mars-Jones, made it clear that he thought the section 1 charges were 'oppressive' and pointedly remarked that the Attorney-General had the power to withdraw, as well as initiate, them.

Mr Silkin took the hint, and the section 1 charges were dropped. The judge had also said that he did not intend to impose any custodial sentences, but he did not want this to be reported lest it prejudice the jury. This time journalists and others kept relatively quiet, and the judge's remark was not printed or broadcast (although it spread by word of mouth through London within days).

The jury retired, and duly delivered their verdicts of conviction under section 2. The two journalists received conditional discharges, and John Berry received a suspended sentence of six months. In suspending Berry's sentence the judge indicated that he thought it a more serious offence for one who had been privy to secrets to tell than for others to hear. 'Whistle-blowers' from the services would not be tolerated.

One effect of the ABC case was to stiffen Conservative resolve to get a respectable and effective substitute for section 2 of the Official Secrets Act through Parliament as quickly as possible, with no nonsense about an accompanying law to require public disclosures of anything. So the Protection of Official Information Bill 1979 was put together from the Franks proposals, the Labour modifications, and Conservative refinements.

The bill was having a hard time of it in the House of Lords when Andrew Boyle's book, *The Climate of Treason*, appeared. That led to the naming of Sir Anthony Blunt, former Keeper of the Queen's Pictures, as a one-time Soviet agent. This was confirmed by the Prime Minister in the Commons, and Blunt was stripped of his title. It was widely remarked that Andrew Boyle would have been committing an offence under the terms of the bill by writing his book at all, and the bill was withdrawn. Blunt gave a press conference to *The Times* (and one *Guardian* reporter) during which he turned away many questions by replying that he was, after all, bound by the Official Secrets Act.

The 'old blunderbuss' is still in the armoury of the Attorney-General, who may consider the experiences of his predecessor before taking it down again and pointing it in anyone's direction. The more complicated legal questions of what, if anything, should replace that law are considered in Chapter 11. But nagging questions persist about how and why the whole ABC affair began, going back to the related decision to deport Agee and Hosenball.

Part of the answer may be that Sam Silkin defied convention only once, when he refused the knighthood that usually goes with the job of Attorney-General. He could or would not refuse to take legal action when it was advised by the Director of Public Prosecutions, other civil servants, or his ministerial colleagues (even accepting the standard explanation that the Attorney-General may seek the advice of ministers, but is not proffered it). However, he could and did refuse to bring (or rather to consent to) a legal action brought by an interfering outsider such as John Gouriet, a decision in which he was vindicated by the House of Lords, if not by Lord Denning. In both the Crossman *Diaries* case and the ABC prosecution he went to law to uphold rather different kinds of government secrecy, and he effectively lost both times.

But Mr Silkin's suggestibility does not account for the Agee–Hosenball deportations, which were decided by the then Home Secretary, Merlyn Rees. The explanation, apart from the constitutional ministerial responsibility, is in the persuasiveness of advice given by senior civil servants, including those in the security services. Advice from the security services would have carried even more weight in the Agee–Hosenball and ABC cases. This most likely would have been communicated through Sir Leonard Hooper, who was then the Cabinet's coordinator and liaison with both M.I.5 and 6. A hard look across the Atlantic, where the F.B.I. and C.I.A. were being relentlessly scrutinized, could have been enough to convince their British counterparts that such things were not going to happen here. The British security services, M.I.6 in particular, had endured enough from the Americans in the years after Burgess, Maclean, and Philby. Now they could again set an example, as they had done when the C.I.A. was formed in the image of M.I.6 after the Second World War, of how a real secret service keeps itself, above all, secret.

The American security services had allowed themselves to be drawn into Nixon's Watergate mess, however tangentially, and they were caught up in the waves of recrimination and revelation afterwards. After Ellsberg came Agee, then Victor Marchetti and John Marks, then Frank Snepp, John Stockwell, and the whole spectacle of the C.I.A.'s director, William Colby, telling nearly everything to the Church Committee in the Senate, with most of it ending up in the press.

As stories of C.I.A. plans to poison Castro's beard came into print, there probably were recollections of awkward British incidents like the disappearance of a diver under a Russian ship during Khrushchev's and Bulganin's 1956 visit. That should have been as much of a lesson for the security services as the Suez crisis was to the nation a few months later. But the lesson was that the political masters could not always be relied upon if word of an incident like that got out. A glance at an old Hansard would have shown the Prime Minister of the day, Sir Anthony Eden, firmly shifting the onus onto unnamed subordinates.

The line against any disclosures had to be drawn hard and fast, and held. The deportation machinery was newly made and effective enough for dealing with foreigners. And it had the unanticipated benefit of leading them from Hosenball to Campbell as the one who had really put the pieces together about SigInt. When John Berry wrote his letter (which was almost certainly opened) the temptation would have been irresistible to make an example of a small-time 'whistle-blower', and possibly to pick up others as well.

The only machinery to hand was the slightly battered Official Secrets Act, but the section which was supposed to deal with espionage had escaped criticism. Using that, together with some well-placed briefings, would place the case on a different footing from the abortive *Sunday Telegraph* case. With so much at stake, it must have seemed a good idea, in that enclosed atmosphere, at that time. It just turned out rather differently.

Chapter Four

Secrets Kept from Parliament

During the June 1973 debate on the Franks Report in the House of Commons the Attorney-General of the day, Sir Peter Rawlinson, explained why there could be no British Watergate. Ministers in this country, he explained, had to stand at the dispatch box and answer questions.

That is the essence of the constitutional argument against open government legislation: the government of the day is accountable to the representatives of the people in Parliament. Ministers are collectively responsible for government policies, and are individually responsible for their own departments. They are answerable on the floor of the House of Commons and the House of Lords, and they can (sometimes) also be questioned by Parliamentary committees.

'Answerable' is not quite accurate to describe the frequently uncomfortable position of a government minister faced with Parliamentary Questions. Faced with an inconvenient Question, a minister has the right, firmly established by an 1893 ruling of the Speaker, to refuse to reply. There may be a price to pay in facing waving order papers and shouted supplementary questions, but such stonewalling can be and is done.

There are less embarrassing ways of achieving the same effect. It is difficult in examining answers to Parliamentary Questions to determine whether a minister cannot or will not give the information requested. The pages of Hansard are littered with replies like 'that information is not available'. The essential ambiguity of such an answer is in whether it means that the information is not available to Parliament, or not even available to the minister. Another version of the reply is that 'the information is not available without a disproportionate expenditure of time and effort'.[1]

It is a Parliamentary version of the more general argument against disclosure of information on grounds of cost and efficiency, and it conveys a comforting message of governmental thrift: civil servants shouldn't always go rooting through files just because an M.P. wants to know something. It can also involve a careful assessment of what the information would cost in terms of political repercussions if it were disclosed.

There are even more subtle ways of avoiding real answers to Parliamentary Questions. A partial disclosure of the more convenient bits of information is possible. This is particularly useful in dealing with written questions, because there is no opportunity for the M.P. to follow up the answer with supplementary questions, to probe for inconsistencies and ask for more specific replies. Even if the Question is an oral one, and assuming that the minister does get to it (and only about one-third of questions put down for oral replies are actually answered that way), there is not much Parliamentary time for such intensive follow-up questioning.

The basic constraint of limited time on the floor of Parliament has led to another restriction on the right of M.P.s to know, imposed at the beginning of a typical Parliamentary Question. The House of Commons has decided, through a combination of rulings by successive Speakers and their application by the Table Office of the House, that no further questions on a subject may be asked during a session if a minister has refused to answer. This has the supposedly laudable aim of not wasting the time of the House on Questions that are demonstrably non-starters. It also has the effect of protecting ministers from the possible awkwardness of refusing to answer questions on a subject more than once a session.

The result of this practice is what amounts to a blacklist of taboo subjects. These fall into two general categories. If a

minister has refused to answer a Question the subject can be
revived during the next session (if only to get a similarly dusty
reply). But if 'successive governments' have refused to answer
Questions on a subject it goes on a more or less permanent list of
taboo subjects on which the Table Office will not accept
questions. There have been some minor changes in the application of this rule, and there are also devious Parliamentary tactics
for getting half-way round it, but the principle remains.

The existence of this blacklist was hardly known until 1972. It
emerged, significantly enough, during an inquiry by a House of
Commons Select Committee into what was called 'Question-
packing'. The practice came to public and Parliamentary attention only when a memo was leaked. The procedure, which
presumably has not been followed since, was simple. Civil
servants were instructed to prepare banks of easy questions, ones
which the appropriate ministers were happy to answer. These
were then furnished to cooperative back-benchers of the Conservative Government of the day, who demonstrated their loyalty
by putting them down for the ministers to answer.

When the incriminating memorandum got out to the *Sunday
Times*[2] the House of Commons set up a Select Committee to
inquire into the matter. The Committee questioned civil servants,
including the head of the Home Civil Service and the Clerk of the
Table Office. The report was published in July 1972 and included
a transcript of the proceedings.[3]

The Clerk of the Table Office had explained the rules on
Parliamentary Questions and furnished the Committee with a list
of the 'matters about which successive administrations have
refused to answer Questions'. There were then ninety-five of
these forbidden subjects, published as Appendix 9 to the Report.
They ranged from some national security matters to less understandable subjects such as the White Fish Authority.

The testimony revealed, however, that an ingenious M.P.
might at least put a Question on one of the subjects to a minister,
with luck and timing. The trick lay in the inconsistency with
which the same rule was applied by the Table Office, which
accepts Questions to be put to ministers, and the Speaker. The

Table Office strictly applied the rule about subjects on which successive governments had refused to answer Questions: the subjects went on the list, and no Questions about them were accepted. But Speakers tended to be considerably less strict about it.

So there was, and is, a way for an M.P. to ask a question about such a forbidden subject as, say, telephone-tapping. The wily M.P. simply puts down an acceptably innocuous Question to the minister for an oral reply. If the Question is high enough on the list to be reached, the M.P. has a chance after the minister replies to the Question on the order paper. M.P.s are more or less entitled to at least one 'supplementary' question after a reply to an oral Question, and Speakers do not follow their own rulings as strictly as the Table Office. So M.P.s can at least leap in with another question on the real subject, which usually receives the predictable refusal.

It was just such manipulation of the rules which prompted Peter Mills, M.P., to describe the rules on Questions as 'mumbo-jumbo' during the proceedings of the Select Committee. Of course the gambit can only be taken to the point of putting the Question to the minister, who can still refuse to reply.

The list of forbidden subjects was used by Clement Freud during the second reading debate on his Official Information Bill on 29 January 1979. During the same debate a Labour M.P., Jeff Rooker, described his strenuous efforts to find out just what was on the list in 1979. It was a longish story, involving approaches to the Table Office, to the Speaker, and to various government departments. Finally he got his revised list, and a concession from the Speaker that once in each session M.P.s would be allowed to ask ministers if they had changed their minds about answering any Questions on those subjects. The conclusion was a mild reprimand to Mr Rooker from the Speaker for revealing all of this to the press. Communications between Members and the Speaker, the Speaker reminded Mr Rooker sternly, were supposed to be confidential.

The list of forbidden subjects now includes
* agricultural workers' wages
* forecasts of changes in food prices

* details of foreign arms sales and the numbers of foreign forces training in Britain
* accident rates for aircraft
* numbers of abortions for areas smaller than regional health authorities
* financial assistance to companies (beyond what is published in *Trade and Industry*)
* reasons for investigation or non-investigation of aircraft accidents

Occasionally former ministers will draw aside the curtain of confidentiality and reveal how their departments went about preparing replies to Parliamentary Questions. Michael Meacher was a junior minister at the Department of Trade in the 1974–9 Labour Government, and he described a typical example.[4] A Conservative M.P. had asked how many applications there had been to export works of art following the sale of the Mentmore collection. The information was readily available, but Meacher's civil servants advised him not to answer. Mr Meacher was also a minister at the Department of Health and Social Security, where he fought a long battle with his civil servants to answer a Question on the estimated number of deaths of old people from hypothermia in 1970. The story was told in the *Sunday Times*, and illustrates how answers to Parliamentary Questions can be slanted to avoid political embarrassment.[5]

Briefly, Meacher thought that the figures which were supplied to him were too low, and did not take into account four independent research studies which had been drawn to his attention by pressure groups. The battle by memoranda between Meacher and his civil servants went on for a month, and finally forced some of the candid advice which is conventionally so important to British government. In a memo from a deputy secretary to Meacher on 6 February 1976, the effects of including information from the other studies was explained. The information 'in this politically sensitive area . . . may be misleading and . . . could certainly be used against the government. It is almost certain that any reply which suggested that large numbers of old people might be suffering from hypothermia would be used to bring pressure on the government to improve heating provision for old people in some way.'

The limits of time, the ability of ministers to avoid complete and candid replies, and the fundamental advantage of a minister in having access to the files and a small army of civil servants to draft replies have all combined to alter the nature of most oral Parliamentary Questions. They have increasingly become vehicles for general policy debates rather than serious attempts at getting information. More and more oral Questions are of a very general nature. The real question, which follows in the supplementary, is often a general attack on government policy.

Such clashes, whether praised as the real 'cut and thrust' of Parliamentary debate or derided as merely scoring party political points, have a place in Parliament's job of keeping the government accountable. But Parliamentary Questions are increasingly unsuited for actually finding out how the government is doing its job. Questions, particularly written ones, can still serve to focus attention on particular subjects. And oral Questions can also serve to highlight policy conflicts, sometimes after the information which is necessary for a real argument has been obtained by other means. But Parliamentary Questions in their present form are not enough to provide Parliament with the answers required.

An increasingly important method of getting information is through Parliamentary committees. Since the mid-1960s the establishment of such committees has been a subject of occasional debates in Parliament, the press, and among academics. During his time as Leader of the House Richard Crossman began to establish specialized select committees to scrutinize government. The opponents of such innovations are not at all united on the basis of party politics. Two of the most vehement critics have been what has been described as representatives of the romantic right and the romantic left, Enoch Powell and Michael Foot. Their basic common argument is that committees would only detract from the essential business of Parliament, which they see as debating issues on the floor.

They are right in contrasting the skills and functions of

committees with those required for Parliamentary debates. The
patient questioning of ministers and civil servants is not the stuff
of oratory. But it is this accumulation of information that can
raise the level of resulting debates beyond arguments from
principle, however stirring these may be.

Specialized committees to 'shadow' government departments
were established on recommendations of the Select Committee on
Procedure in 1978. But there are still fierce arguments about how
the committees should go about their business, and some of these
go to the heart of Parliamentary government in Britain.

There had been crises of authority between governments and
Parliamentary select committees before the present system was
established in 1979. In 1973 Airey Neave, then chairman of the
Select Committee on Science and Technology, defied the government by publishing a report on government research. The report
itself was of no great substance. It had been commissioned by
the government, which then disagreed with its proposals and did
not want it made public. But the Committee had a copy, and
released it.

There were other skirmishes between select committees and
governments during the 1970s, such as the unsuccessful attempt
to question Harold Lever about the subsidy to Chrysler U.K.
Harold Wilson insisted that the Prime Minister would decide
who would or would not appear. His successor, James Callaghan,
went further in disciplining a Labour M.P. who used a leaked
document to criticize the Chancellor of the Exchequer in committee hearings. The M.P., Brian Sedgemore, was Parliamentary
Private Secretary to Tony Benn, and the Prime Minister dismissed him for his impertinence.

The most effective scrutiny is carried out by the Public
Accounts Committee, assisted by the Comptroller and Auditor
General and his staff of auditors. But the P.A.C. has been
hampered by its retrospective and slightly legalistic function. Its
job, simply stated, is to see that government money has been
lawfully spent. It has only gone beyond that a few times, as when
it criticized the Department of Industry under Mr Benn for
subsidies provided to cooperatives. And it has sometimes been

reticent about sharing its information with the rest of Parliament and the public. The most glaring example of this was in its 1973 report on Concorde, which had pages studded with asterisks about the costs of Concorde, which had been deleted 'for reasons of commercial confidentiality'. Despite this concern, the Committee gave a rather fuller account when it reported again in 1977. Then it concluded, as it might have done earlier, that Concorde was costing vastly more than had been estimated, and that the project would never break even.

When the new system of Select Committees was established during the summer of 1979, the Leader of the House, Norman St John-Stevas, was slightly vague about the crucial question of their powers to require information from ministers and civil servants. In effect, he gave a Parliamentary version of an assurance that it would be all right on the day, that the government would treat requests for appearances and information with sympathy. Restrictive guidelines for civil servants appearing before committees were published later.

The committees did get some sort of supporting staff, although nothing like the Comptroller and Auditor General. Most of them have at least one expert outside consultant. But one of the first crises came over the sacking of one such staff member who had been critical of refusals by ministers and civil servants to answer questions.

The new committees have already had considerable difficulty in getting information from ministers and civil servants. One victory was won by the Select Committee on Employment in January 1980. The Committee asked the chairman of the Manpower Services Commission to appear and provide details of the M.S.C.'s 'corporate plan'. At first, the M.S.C. chairman, Sir Richard O'Brien, refused on the ground that the plan was 'confidential'. But the Committee threatened to raise the dispute in the House and test its power to compel disclosure of information. The M.S.C. then retreated and provided the Committee with a copy. [6]

Other committees were not so fortunate. The Foreign Affairs sub-committee on overseas development met a nearly solid stone wall when they attempted to find out about the effects of raising overseas students' fees. They were particularly interested in whether there had been inter-departmental discussions of such effects. At first the Overseas Development Administration agreed to provide a paper on such assessments. But when Dr Rhodes Boyson, Under-Secretary for Higher Education, and six senior civil servants appeared before the committee in March 1980 they refused to answer any questions at all about inter-departmental consultations. Lord Gordon-Lennox, Assistant Under-Secretary at the Foreign Office, refused to say whether there had been any consideration of political consequences within the Foreign Office. Dr Boyson said that he was under instructions not to comment on such matters.

The instructions were explained in a letter from the Secretary of State for Education, Mark Carlisle, to the chairman of the sub-committee, Kevin McNamara. The decision to raise fees for overseas students, he explained, was a collective one which was part of the Government's plans to cut public expenditure. Because of this the committee could not expect to get information about the advice given by officials or the process by which the decision was arrived at. [7]

There are at least two fundamental problems that the committees will face if they continue to press for disclosure of information to them by ministers and civil servants: one is the Parliamentary problem of how far they can take their demands; the other is the question of how confidential should be ministerial exchanges and advice given ministers by civil servants.

The first problem is a limitation inherent in Westminster-style parliamentary government. A committee of the House of Commons established with the usual powers to call for 'persons and papers' can only compel disclosure of information by referring refusals to the House itself. The ultimate sanction is to find someone who refuses such an order in contempt of Parliament (or in violation of Parliamentary privilege – the two terms are used almost interchangeably).

Faced with a refusal to attend or to give evidence, a committee could vote to refer the matter to the House. Party discipline on committees is usually not enforced so strictly as it is on the floor of the House. But membership of such committees reflects the balance of party strength in the House itself, and a government with an overall majority would have a majority on any committee. Party loyalty could be decisive in a committee vote on whether to refer a refusal to the House as a possible contempt, and the whole matter could easily end there.

But even if the committee voted to refer the question to the House the matter would go through several more steps. The usual procedure in cases of contempt or breach of Parliamentary privilege is for a member to raise it with the Speaker, who then decides whether to refer it to another committee, the Select Committee on Parliamentary Privilege. That committee then considers the matter and makes a recommendation to the House.

The House of Commons then decides whether there has been a contempt or breach of privilege, and also decides on the punishment. The procedure is slightly rusty, and rests on the constitutional powers of Parliament to regulate its own affairs and to impose penalties which can include imprisonment of an offender (or even expulsion of an elected M.P.). It has been nearly a hundred years since anyone was actually put in custody for a contempt of Parliament, and that was only for one night. But the procedure has rarely been used to compel disclosure of information, and never to its full extent. The most extreme exercise was when an Assistant Serjeant at Arms of the House was sent with a formal order for Sir Charles Villiers to appear before the Select Committee on Nationalized Industries to answer questions about the British Steel Corporation.

The reason why the House of Commons has not used its power in this way is fairly obvious. The government of the day has a majority in the House, and it would be highly unlikely for that same majority to vote in favour of penalties against ministers of the government or their civil servants for refusals to disclose information. If it came to that, the matter would be close to a vote of confidence in the government as a whole.

The same political constraints do not apply when the House is applying contempt penalties against persons other than ministers or civil servants. That is why most breach of Parliamentary privilege cases have involved penalties against the press. When the procedure is used against such outsiders, it shows its defects. These essentially amount to what administrative lawyers would call violations of the rules of 'natural justice'. The House is acting as a judge in its own cause, and the procedure lacks the safeguards that those accused would expect before a court or administrative tribunal. The offence itself is vague, and amounts to whatever the House of Commons says is a breach of privilege.

In 1958 the editor of the *Sunday Express* was summoned before the Bar of the House and formally censured for publishing a cartoon implying that some M.P.s were unfairly avoiding petrol rationing. More recently, the *Economist* was charged with publishing the contents of a Parliamentary Committee's report before it was formally presented to the House. The Select Committee on Parliamentary Privilege recommended that the editor and his Parliamentary correspondent be barred from the precincts of the House of Commons, but the House refused to impose the penalty.

The contempt powers of Parliament require some careful consideration if they are to be used to compel disclosure of information. One danger is that they could be abused if they were applied to outsiders such as journalists and their sources. Critics of Parliamentary committees in general have long pointed to the real abuse of legislative inquiries by committees of the U.S. Senate and House of Representatives in the 1950s. Ordinary citizens and some civil servants were imprisoned for contempt of Congress when they refused to answer questions about alleged subversion. One safeguard against such abuse would be to require judicial review before such penalties were applied. Such review was required in the United States, but it was not always sufficient to protect recalcitrant witnesses.

The danger that the powers of legislative committees could be so misused may be remote, but it should be anticipated. A solution might be to require judicial review before any criminal penalties could be applied. Such a limit on Parliamentary power would be a justifiable one. Parliament is sovereign, but that sovereignty is confined to the making of laws. Constitutionally, it should not include the power to act as a court of law, imposing penalties for acts that were not violations of any law when they were committed.

Such a safeguard would prevent the unlikely possibility that the new Parliamentary committees would direct their powers of inquiry against those outside government who would be least able to defend themselves. It would be a measure to safeguard the liberties of the subject, but it would not deal with the real problems which the committees are much more likely to en-counter, and which they are already meeting: the refusals of ministers and civil servants to provide information to Parliament.

The government of the day, particularly if it has a comfortable majority, is more than able to defend itself against such pressure from Parliament to provide information. The resolution of the dilemma lies in Parliament itself, and more particularly in the House of Commons. One solution would be a clear decision by the House of Commons that refusals by ministers and their civil servants to provide information or appear before committees should not be treated as party political matters, but as matters affecting the authority of the House to be decided on a free vote without party discipline. It should only be in rare cases of a government's refusal to provide information in defiance of a decision by the House that the government's continuance in office would depend on a vote of confidence.

Such secrecy in the face of a carefully considered decision by the House of Commons would be a proper issue to be decided on political grounds, with the ultimate sanction being the political one of losing office. It would also have the virtue of imposing responsibility squarely on the government of the day rather than imposing quasi-criminal penalties on individual ministers or civil servants.

The second major problem, that disclosure of information would threaten the confidentiality of advice and discussion, is really two separate problems, usually labelled the collective responsibility of ministers and the individual responsibility of ministers. The authority of a British government rests on its support by a majority in the House of Commons, but that support should be as informed as possible. One of the lessons of the leak to *New Society* in 1976 of Cabinet discussions about child benefits was that back-bench Labour M.P.s had been misled in order to get their support for a Cabinet decision.

The convention that members of a government agree on all political issues is a fiction, and not always such a polite one in its application, which ultimately derives from the very basis of the government's authority in having the support of a majority in the House of Commons. In realistic terms, this means that the government of the day has the support of a majority for its overall conduct of the public business of government. In modern times it does not mean that the continued exercise of executive authority depends on a government's ability to get specific legislation passed. It does mean that a government will be obliged to resign if a majority in the House say that they no longer have confidence in the government. This can follow defeat on a particular legislative issue, but it is quite possible (as the Callaghan government demonstrated for some time) for legislation to be defeated or discarded by a government which continues to survive no-confidence motions.

During the 1970s there was an increasing tendency for political realities to modify the convention of ministerial agreement. It was formally abandoned during the months before the 1975 referendum on the issue of continued membership of the European Economic Community. Ministers were given dispensation to intervene publicly on either side of the debate and they did so (although the convention was preserved on the floor of the House itself). After James Callaghan became Prime Minister it was reimposed with something like a vengeance. For instance, on the occasion of the European Assembly Elections Bill in 1977 Callaghan declared: 'I certainly think that doctrine [collective responsibility] should apply except in cases where I announce that it does not.'

Callaghan gave notice that he expected the support of (or at least that he would not tolerate opposition from) not only Cabinet members and ministers not in the Cabinet, but also of those on the lowest rungs of the ladder to ministerial power, Parliamen-

tary Private Secretaries to Ministers. (There was in this insistence an element of the old boy insisting that new members go
through the same stringent initiation imposed on him: when
Callaghan himself was a P.P.S. he resigned because he disagreed
with the Attlee government's policy on American loans.)

Such stringent party discipline should be tempered by a
realistic assessment of how reasonable ministers and ordinary
M.P.s can agree on basic governmental policy while disagreeing
over particular issues. Leaks and hints of such disagreements are,
after all, the very stuff of much political journalism. The disclosure of such disagreements should not be considered, as it still
is by many, as the worst of political sins.

At the very least, it should be acknowledged to Parliament and
the public that the Cabinet is not a monolith in its organization
or functioning. Specifically, the existence, responsibilities, and
membership of Cabinet committees should be announced as
routinely as the appointment of ministers. The conventional
arguments against such disclosure, as presented in a letter to
ministers from James Callaghan in 1978, are not particularly
convincing. Some of the objections must have seemed hollow to
Callaghan himself, such as the statement that if membership of
the committees were known it would be difficult to make changes
in them. The same argument could be made just as easily to the
regular reshuffles of departmental responsibilities. If such members would be subject to political pressure once their duties
became known, that would seem to be essential to government in a
democracy. The argument which was probably most convincing
to the Prime Minister himself, that disclosure would 'be more
likely to whet appetites than to satisfy them', is not more
persuasive by being true. The legislative process should include
Parliamentary and public discussion of proposed laws before they
are presented to Parliament. This has already happened to a
limited extent through the 1960s innovation of 'Green Papers'
outlining legislative alternatives, and the new select committees
are pressing for even more thorough and earlier examination of
legislation.

The one issue about the conduct of government which has not

been the subject of a Parliamentary vote of confidence has been the very secrecy of the process itself. The possibility, suggested earlier, that a government might lose office for a determined refusal to provide Parliament with relevant information might have a salutary effect in preventing the sort of arbitrary government which can too easily accompany secrecy.

There is also a fundamental historical fallacy in the origins of the convention of Cabinet confidentiality. The supposed unanimity of Cabinet ministers itself originated as a device for protecting the then limited democratic functions of ministers from arbitrary royal power. It was, in effect, a decision by ministers that they would present a united front to the sovereign who appointed them in order to make it more difficult for an arbitrary king or queen to thwart the will of Parliament by dismissing ministers individually. That threat has disappeared through the evolution of the constitution. The threat now is not so much from arbitrary royal power as the threat of arbitrary power in the hands of what Lord Hailsham has called 'elective dictatorship'.

Individual ministerial responsibility, and its relationship to the role of civil servants, presents different problems. The possibility of losing office if a department is guilty of serious maladministration should be a powerful incentive for a minister to guard against just such actions. Instead, it has become an effective incentive to keep the process of administration as secret as possible. Successive governments have recognized the relative harshness of the rule, and it has rarely been carried to its ultimate requirement of resignation in the 1960s and 1970s. The last clear case of a minister resigning because of the actions of his civil servants (as opposed to resigning because of his own indiscretions, as in the Profumo, Lambton, and Jellicoe cases, or because of a personal decision, as when James Callaghan resigned as Chancellor of the Exchequer in 1967 after devaluation) was when Sir Thomas Dugdale resigned over the Crichel Down affair in 1954.

There has been an increasing recognition that a minister cannot personally supervise all the work of a huge department, and not just in Parliament. The report of the Inquiry into the

Vehicle and General collapse in 1972 carried this almost to an extreme.[8] The Inquiry report assigned blame for the failure to supervise the company properly almost in inverse order to the level of office. Successive ministers who had nominally been in charge were absolved because they knew nothing about the matter. Civil servants who were more directly involved were more heavily criticized the more closely they were connected with the affair, and the lower they were down the executive ladder. But the greatest blame of all, in the Inquiry's opinion, was reserved for the lowest possible civil servant, and the offence had nothing to do with the company's collapse. Rose Norgan, a photocopy clerk, was dismissed in disgrace for leaking a copy of a report on the company to her son, who was also in the insurance business. The Inquiry concluded that the leak had nothing to do with the fate of the company and the losses to its policy-holders. But she and her son only escaped prosecution (probably under section 2 of the Official Secrets Act) because they were granted immunity in exchange for testifying.

The fiction that civil servants right up to the highest level are apolitical servants of the elected government of the day was developed to avoid the evils of political patronage. The aim was laudable, and it is still a good thing that the job of those who carry out routine administration does not depend on party allegiance. But it is a fiction that civil servants at higher levels do not have a political role, and that they do not have strong opinions about policy questions. Perhaps its most extreme application is in the still little-known rule that ministers do not have access to most of the papers of their predecessors in office under a previous government. One of the first public acknowledgements of this 'self-denying ordinance', as he described it, was in the testimony given by Sir William Armstrong to the Select Committee on Parliamentary Questions in 1972.[9]

The rule effectively admits that senior civil servants do give candid political advice to their ministers, and its purpose is to ensure that incoming ministers do not find out what was written to their predecessors. It places new ministers, with perhaps one or two advisers of their own choosing, at a distinct disadvantage in directing their departments. It is not enough to invoke a sort of political virility and say that this only happens to 'weak' ministers. The advice given by Shirley Williams, in a lecture to the Royal Institute of Public Administration on 11 February 1980, is good, but not sufficient: '. . . it's a question of remembering to keep asking for the same information and when you've asked for it three times and had nothing, hitting the roof in a structured sort of way.' [10]

If Parliament should have more information about how government is carried out from ministers, the ministers themselves should have the tools to require more information from their own departments. This means that they should have more, not less, independent advice as an alternative and a possible addition to hitting the roof, whether in Shirley Williams's 'structured' way or the less structured reactions of Richard Crossman revealed in his *Diaries*. An expansion of the political adviser system, even to the extent of the French *cabinet* system, would help them in this.

But what political, parliamentary, and legal responsibility should civil servants have? Most civil servants are not, as is commonly thought in various quarters, devoted to particular political persuasions and given to devious thwarting of the popular will as expressed in the most recent general election. Just as there should be a realistic acceptance that the continuance of a government in office does not depend on unanimity on every issue, there should be an acceptance of the fact that senior civil servants have views and that they express them to ministers. If this means that Parliament will be aware of the alternatives considered, together with the background information that is weighed in choosing between them, then it is likely to make Parliamentary decisions better informed. If ministers then have a harder time in persuading Parliament, there should be some compensation for them in having some help of their own choosing in running their departments.

The arguments often advanced against disclosure of government information to Parliament through Questions and select committees, and to the public through open government legislation, give the impression that such records consist almost entirely of opinion and advice. If this is true, then it is an indictment of the existing system and an admission that policy decisions are taken more on opinion and unsubstantiated argument. Most relevant information sought by M.P.s and the public is more likely to be concerned with facts and their interpretations, such as the studies of hypothermia or the number of export licences for works of art, than with whether the Permanent Secretary told the Minister that a particular course of action would be politically unwise.

But many government records are a combination of fact and argument. These can, and should be, separated as much as possible, as the 1977 directive from the Head of the Home Civil Service attempted to provide for. There can, and should be, a limited degree of confidentiality attached to pure advice and consultation between ministers and between civil servants and their ministers. But this should not be protected by the criminal law. In the metaphor used by *New Society* [11] such advice would be in the middle basket of information not available to the public as a legal right, but not protected by the threat of prison sentences either. In a word, it would be 'leakable'. The continuation of confidential discussion would be left where it properly belongs, to political forces. An appropriate forum for the balancing of such political forces would be in the House of Commons. As already suggested, it should be for the House to decide whether keeping particular information from Parliament was unjustifiable. If so, the sanction should be a political one applied by Parliament.

And some consideration should be given to the commonly held view that advice which becomes public is necessarily worse. A memorandum on implications of open government legislation prepared for the First Division Association, the union for senior civil servants, repeats this argument. One of the possible consequences of disclosure of information, the report concludes, is that officials 'would offer balanced but totally anodyne advice, reserving their personal views for unrecorded interviews with ministers or their colleagues'.*

* *The Times*, 13 March 1980. It is worth noting that the report itself was leaked after the F.D.A. decided against releasing it.

But a rather different view was expressed by a former Treasury civil servant, in a series of radio talks in 1977, who commented that much of what he wrote at the Treasury would have been of higher quality if he had known that it would be made public.

Chapter Five

'Muzzled Sheep'?: Secrecy and the Press

Reform of the Official Secrets Act and its replacement by some sort of open government law are often considered to be primarily for the benefit of the press. Most information about government reaches the public through the media of newspapers, journals, and broadcasting, and it is only natural that they would resent legal restrictions.

But before considering how restricted or free the press should be, it is important to consider how it functions now. A standard definition is that the job of the press is to 'inform, entertain, and educate'. But the way in which much of the British press goes about its work makes Nye Bevan's gibe that 'you can't muzzle a sheep' relevant even today.

A variation is that the press is simply another industry in the mixed-economy system. Whether it is publicly owned, like the B.B.C., or in the private sector, it is essentially no different from British Steel or I.C.I. Those who work in it do so to produce a product which is not much different from packets of cornflakes or automobiles, except in being more perishable. Its employees see their role as being similar to that of other workers. They simply get on with the business of securing the best possible terms of pay and working conditions for themselves.

Much of the management see the job as producing a product that will compete successfully with those of their rivals. The measure of success is profit and circulation. The profitability of newspapers depends largely on the advertising they are able to attract, and advertisers pay more to be read by people with more money to spend. The advertisers do not often attempt directly to dictate what goes in the space between the adverts, but their existence is important in determining what is 'news' for a particular paper and what is not. To take a simple example, only the 'quality' papers attempt any sort of comprehensive reporting of Parliament because only their readers, determined by the combination of education and income, are assumed to be at all interested in reading such reports, and perhaps glancing at the accompanying advertisements.

This is not an argument for abolition of advertising, or for a Swedish-style system of subsidies to encourage diversity in the press. The point is that the Official Secrets Act and other legal restraints are not the only, and probably not the most important, limits on what is printed and broadcast or not. Just as important is what may be called the sub-culture of journalism, its values and methods of work. And this begins with how journalists see themselves.

The Journalist as Reporter

Until very recently, the job of a British journalist was generally considered to be that of a skilled worker, and not a particularly reputable one at that. University education was very nearly a disqualification, and training was by apprenticeship. The apprenticeship is still served on a local newspaper, where the would-be reporter serves out what are called 'indentures' learning the basic skills and values of the trade.

'Reporting' is the essence of the job. Broadcasting and publishing executives often reminisce about the days of their basic training, going to fêtes and magistrates' courts, getting the names spelt right, learning to bash out a few clear paragraphs against a tight deadline . . . The essential skills were, and still are, shorthand and typing, and the ability to use them to write in a simple and dramatic way.

A more subtle, but no less important, part of such training is in learning 'news values'. The most basic of these is the 'local angle' to any story. There are countless variations on the theme of 'local man injured in Latin American coup'. If there was no local man, it is simply not a story, and the rule of thumb is that readers are not particularly interested in things that do not immediately involve themselves or their neighbours. It is, journalists argue, only a reflection of society. People are parochial and nationalistic, and do not much want to know about things that do not directly concern them.

Another element of such news values is that news is bad news. Violent death, natural disaster, and strife are what people like to read about, and so must be reported. They are unusual, and meet the test of William Randolph Hearst that dog bites man is not news; man bites dog is. They are also immediate, and violent.

This is the sort of 'breaking news' that sends packs of journalists racing to a plane crash. It is a newsworthy event which deserves reporting, at least if there is a local or national angle to it. If there is not, then it becomes a 'Latin American bus plunge' story, worth perhaps a paragraph on the inside pages.

There is also another kind of 'news' that fills the pages and television screens, which is patently 'managed'. These are the events that someone, almost always someone of influence, wants to have reported. They violate Hearst's other dictum that 'news is what someone, somewhere, does not want reported; all the rest is advertisement'. But they serve to fill up the pages, and they fill them rather easily. Any press or public information officer of any organization is a journalist of sorts, with the basic ability to write a news story. That, essentially, is what a press release or news release is, and the press officer is most successful if the release is reprinted exactly as it was written, and given a prominent place in the paper.

Most newspapers would be lost without this kind of daily fodder. It is, of course, not printed automatically. The journalist, the sub-editor and the editor all apply their training in deciding if, and how, the story is to be presented. The source is considered, the story rewritten slightly or extensively, and a telephone call or two (telephone numbers and names 'for further information' are always included) will be made to get a quote or two, if only to make the paper's story different from those of competitors.

Some attempt may also be made to get a suitable reaction quote or two from the other side of the story, if there is one. There usually is if the 'story' is worth pursuing, because conflict of any sort is an essential element of news values. The reaction is also necessary because 'balance' is, at least in theory, drilled into the apprentice reporter.

The 'news' of such stories is quite openly and carefully timed. Almost any news release will carry an 'embargo' on the story saying that it is not to be used before a certain day and time. This is usually chosen with care to get maximum exposure. Any time in August is good for getting coverage because everyone is assumed to be on holiday and not creating any 'news' (but not reading it either). Observing or breaking an embargo involves a calculation of possibilities by an editor. If the story is newsworthy he naturally is tempted to publish a day or two early. On the other hand, the sanction for such a breach is that the source of the release may not send any more to that particular newspaper, and may even spread the word to other press officers.

There is a peculiar form of embargo for most government reports known as the 'Command: Final Revise'. This has an extra twist to it, and a rather more serious possible sanction than that of not sending any more reports to offenders. The constitutional theory is that government reports are published by 'command' of the Sovereign, and are presented to Parliament before anyone else. Thus, the fiction is maintained that copies of such reports which are circulated to the press are not the report itself, but only the 'final revise' of it. The terms of the embargo are also a little stiffer than usual. Not only is nothing to be published about the report before the set date and time, but 'no approach is to be made to any organization or person about the contents before the time of publication'.

This can have fairly serious consequences if it is observed. A government report is likely to be long, and often on a controversial subject. Any sort of reasoned criticism requires time for reading and analysis, or, at the very least, some explanation of what the report contains. But this is just what is forbidden. The sanction, which has been applied in some cases (see Chapter 3), is whatever Parliament decides is appropriate for such a breach of Parliamentary privilege.

The effect is that government reports are often presented uncritically, or at least without the informed criticism that can come from those who have studied the subject reported on. Critical analysis which comes two days later is no longer particularly newsworthy. If reactions from pressure groups to government reports sometimes seem superficial, it is likely to be for a very practical reason. The pressure group representative has had a few minutes to glance at several hundred pages; the journalist writing the story has had several days to look through the report and supplement the accompanying release.

A Pack of Journalists

Not all managed news is conducted by releases or 'final revises'. Many events, such as conferences, negotiations, major trials and such, are considered newsworthy by consensus, and are attended by reporters from nearly all the major newspapers and broadcasting organizations. A curious mixture of competition and co-operation often results. All of them are competing for some bit of news, some angle, that the others might miss out on, but informal rules of reciprocity also develop. The competition will normally be for an exclusive word on the side with one of the news-makers. But they also have a common interest in not being caught out missing an important announcement that comes while one (or several) of them are napping, having a drink, or otherwise occupied. So informal rotas develop, with notes being compared before stories are filed. A more formal arrangement is a 'pool' of reporters who are granted limited access to the news-makers on the understanding that they will share their stories with the others.

The best-established British pack are the Westminster Lobby correspondents. These are journalists covering Parliament who are allowed entry to the Members' Lobby of the House of Commons. Over the years they developed into a formal club, complete with written rules. The rules themselves were confidential, until a sociologist published them. [1] Some of the rules have a slightly antique flavour, such as the injunction against actually writing anything down in the Lobby itself, and not report-ing 'incidents, pleasant or otherwise' that they see in the Lobby.

Similar, but less formal, lobbies develop among correspondents who cover a particular department, or who attend Prime Ministerial briefings. Informal rules always develop, usually about what statements can or cannot be attributed. The most important characteristic of such systems is that they exist on the sufferance of the officials involved, and may be terminated if they go too far in their reporting (just as Harold Wilson's Press Secretary terminated briefings for a while in June 1975).

The Journalist as Confidant

The most important characteristic considered so far of the journalists' sub-culture is the relative passivity. Despite the rushing about, alone or in packs, reporters are writing down what people, usually officials of one sort or another, choose to tell them. Their skills combine those of a good secretary and a last-minute cramming student: the ability to transcribe accurately, type quickly, to absorb and simplify complex subjects quickly and under pressure.

The good journalist, verging on the investigative, also develops contacts. These vary greatly in number, type, and degree of intimacy. At their simplest they may be a fairly formal acquaint-ance with various press or public information officers, used for little more than getting a telephone call returned quickly with an explanation of what the story is about. An automatic response for many journalists when faced with any document longer than a press release is to ring someone and say, 'Why don't you just tell me about it?' It is sensible enough, under the pressures of most journalism. The story will probably be well under a thousand words, and it is faster to make a few notes on an explanation, take a quote or two from the text, and get on with the next story than it would be to read, understand, and explain a long and com-plicated document.

But contacts often involve far more delicate relationships. The journalist who is hunting for stories that are not routinely available to every other paper will try to get to know the people beyond the public information officer in an organization, whether it is a government department, a corporation, or even a pressure group. The exchanges between journalists and those whose job it is to deal with the press may not always be cordial, but at least the parties are more or less agreed on the rules. The interests of a press officer may coincide or conflict with those of journalists, but the people involved more or less understand each other.

Officials who do not deal regularly with the press are in a rather different position. The more cautious will simply refer any question from a journalist to the public information office, and government departments frequently make this a rule (or rather draw civil servants' attention to an old rule). Others may be more ready to talk about their work, frequently without having any clear understanding of how the journalist will use the information. Such openness is often laudable, and certainly understandable, even if it is likely to be at least a technical breach of the Official Secrets Act. After all, a civil servant who has been working long hours on a complicated subject may welcome someone who is willing to listen, and might be pleased if the important work got a little attention in the press.

The conscientious journalist will find and cultivate such contacts carefully. Lunches and dinners will be had, often producing no immediate stories at all. The object, for the journalist, is to gain the confidence of someone who knows what is going on before it is officially announced. How the information will be used, or not used, is not understood clearly, if at all. Often a tacit basis of trust will be arrived at. After a few weeks of informal conversations, the journalist writes a generally favourable piece based on what the contact has told him. The contact may be slightly surprised, perhaps pleased, at the attention, and decide that the journalist is someone who can generally be trusted to get it right. Their next meeting may include an explanation of a minor slip here or there, and perhaps a few more bits of information to be filed away for future use.

Such relationships can blossom over the years, and those who read newspapers regularly may learn to identify journalists who depend on them. They can also turn sour overnight. The essence of the relationship is the source's control over information. Journalist and source may think each other fine fellows, but the basic transaction is trading information for its favourable presentation, or sometimes for its suppression.

So far, the description has sounded almost like espionage, because 'information' has been left neutral. But the information usually is very far removed from anything like national defence. It may be how things are looking on proposals for a compulsory seat-belt law, who the leading contenders for Permanent Secretary are, whether there really is a draft cost analysis of a change to driving on the right . . any of the routine business of government. The value of the information lies in what an Israeli academic has called the 'added value of scarcity'.

This added value is illustrated by Parliamentary debates, which were secret before 1771. The reason was the ancient argument, expressed by William Pulteney in 1738, that 'no man can be so guarded in his expressions, as to wish to see everything he says in the House in print'. Once the debates became published as a matter of routine the excitement of clandestine reports was dropped.

All of this is common knowledge to journalists, politicians, and civil servants. But it serves to explain why many journalists are indifferent or even hostile to any sort of formal open government law. Bluntly, many of them have a vested interest in the existing system. The basic rules of secrecy give the discretionary leaks or briefings that they manage to get an artificial value. A different system might make their jobs rather different, and perhaps harder.

D Notices

In the demonology of the left, the Defence, Press and Broadcasting Committee, better known as the D-Notice Committee, is an instrument of censorship. Almost any article which touches on the military or security services will, it is often said, have a D Notice 'slapped' on it.

Its defenders, on the other hand, describe it as being positively helpful. As one member explained, 'We are there to advise on how to write as much as possible on sensitive subjects without endangering national security.' It is possible to agree, as Duncan Campbell wrote on 4 April 1980, that 'neither the *New Statesman* nor any other responsible publication would wittingly publish information which endangers life or serious national interests'. But while responsible editors may occasionally want advice on whether a proposed article might unwittingly endanger a serious national interest, they are at least equally concerned to get advice on the danger to themselves. They will want to know whether publication can land them in the dock on an Official Secrets Act charge.

The D-Notice Committee won't help them much. A paper as responsible as the *Sunday Telegraph* discovered that in 1970 when they sought the advice of the Committee on their articles about the Nigerian civil war. Clearance did not save them from prosecution under the Act in one of the more celebrated cases (see Chapter 3).

The Committee has no legal status, and its notices have no legal effect. The only thing official about it is that several of its members are senior civil servants (the others are from the press), and that its full-time Secretary is paid £15,000 a year by the Ministry of Defence. The Secretary is the key to the system. The notices themselves, of which there are twelve that have been issued since August 1971, are mostly phrased in general terms.

The notices are supposed to be kept by 'responsible' editors, and to function as preliminary cautions. If news turns up on one of the subjects, such as war precautions and civil defence or British intelligence services, the editor or journalist gives the Secretary (now Rear-Admiral W. N. Ash) a ring to ask how far they should go with the story, if at all.

The system has been around in more or less its present form since 1945, although it was shaken up a bit after the 'cable-vetting' story published by the *Daily Express* in 1967. This began when an employee of a commercial cable company approached Chapman Pincher at the *Daily Express*. In the terms already used Robert Lawson was a leaker or perhaps a 'whistle-blower'. Pincher did not particularly take to him, but thought that the story deserved publishing as an illustration of whole-scale government invasion of privacy. As he explained later, he took what he thought was the precaution of determining that his informant had not 'signed the Official Secrets Act'.[2] (Whether he had or not would have made almost no legal difference if there had been a prosecution under the Act.)

The D-Notice system was familiar to Pincher, who was the paper's defence correspondent, and he rang the Secretary of the Committee, then Colonel 'Sammy' Lohan. They agreed to meet for a gentlemanly lunch. Lohan had two D Notices in his pocket which he thought covered the story, and he left with the impression that Pincher had agreed that it should not be published. Pincher, on the other hand, left thinking that the story did not come under the Notices, and that he was free to publish.

The story was published, the Prime Minister was outraged, and a Committee of Privy Councillors was established. There were other developments while the Committee sat. The *Spectator* dug out its D Notices and published one of them. The Committee of Privy Councillors published a report which was critical of Lohan, who resigned, but concluded that the Notices in fact did not seem to cover the cable-vetting story. The Government followed with a White Paper.[3]

A new Secretary to the Committee was appointed, and the Notices were reorganized and reissued in more general terms. The Committee kept more or less out of the public eye for the next few years, under the Secretaryships of Admirals Denning (brother of the Master of the Rolls) and Farnhill. Admiral Farnhill's advice about the revised edition of *Beneath the City Streets* illustrates how the D-Notice system works. The first edition of the book by Peter Laurie, which describes government preparation for national emergency, was published by Penguin Books without objection in 1970. When the revised second edition was ready to be printed, the ABC prosecution (see Chapter 3) had begun. To avoid endangering national security and to get informal advice on whether the author and publishers might be liable to similar prosecution the manuscript was sent twice to the Secretary of the D-Notice Committee.

At first there was no indication that the book contravened any D Notices, but four months later it was pointed out that it did. Some twenty-eight pages were objectionable. Laurie felt this was a bit wide, and wrote again to various officials, including the Attorney-General. The most specific advice he was able to get was a letter from the Ministry of Defence, later endorsed by the Attorney-General, that there was 'no doubt' that information about defence communication 'would be of great assistance to any enemy'. Apart from the general objection to twenty-eight pages, that was as specific as the advice became.

Peter Laurie has not been charged with anything, perhaps because the abortive ABC prosecution left Duncan Campbell in the *New Statesman*'s Great Turnstile offices instead of in prison. Campbell's articles on telephone interception in the autumn of 1979, and the appointment of a new Secretary at the beginning of 1980, prompted a memorandum to editors. Admiral Ash reminded everyone that 'the need to protect the information on the intelligence services . . . is unchanged and remains of the first importance in the interests of national security'. The Secretary would remain available 'at all times for consultation and advice on any aspect of the D-Notice system'. The *New Statesman* published the correspondence, including its reply, along with an article suggesting that the Committee should be wound up, 'ideally to be replaced by a more genuinely representative interface between Fleet Street and Whitehall which sought to open up the government and not to close down press investigations'. The result was an inquiry by the House of Commons Select Committee on Defence during the summer of 1980. After hearing witnesses the Committee, by a close vote, concluded that the system should be continued.

The D-Notice system is the most explicit example of what is either self-censorship or responsible journalism, depending on who is speaking. An essential element is that it is an agreement between competitors about certain areas where they will not compete. As the introduction to the D Notices explains (quoting the 1962 Report of the Committee on Security Procedures in the Public Service to add a bit of authority): 'Its success depends on

goodwill, and in effect, upon very little else.' Relationships
between editors are characterized as much by bitter competition
as by goodwill, but even they, like journalists in a pack who
recognize at least some common interests, can occasionally agree
on what is, or is not, to be written about.

There is an almost ritual breakdown in this agreement every
few years when a new chief is appointed for the Security Service
or the Secret Intelligence Service. The usual interpretation of D
Notice number 10 is that his name, or that of anyone else connected with security, should not be published. Newspapers usually
observe the rule for a while until someone breaks it. The system of
collective censorship expressed in the D-Notice system is remarkable only for two distinctive features: the rules are written down,
rather than simply understood; and there is a particular person
available for advice and interpretation.

Secrecy is Nothing New

The essential point which has been belaboured thus far is that
journalists are usually reporting what someone, somewhere,
wants reported. Whether it is rewriting a press release, simplify-
ing a technical article, or summing up hours of drinking and
talking with a shadow minister, the journalist is more of a
translator than a speaker. Of course the original speaker or writer
may not like the truncated and simplified version, and will (along
with many others) often say, 'If it's anything you know anything
about, they always get it wrong.'

Secrecy itself is not news to a reporter. To take an illustration
from the world beyond Britain, there are many countries which
simply do not exist in the newspapers. This is not just because of
the parochialism of newspapers and their readers described
earlier, but because many countries do not allow foreign
journalists within their borders, and some hardly allow foreigners
at all.

There is not enough space in a book about government secrecy
in Britain to consider the wider subject of 'free flow of infor-

mation' internationally. The frequent complaint by developing countries that they are considered newsworthy in the West only when there is famine or war has some justification. But the accompanying proposal for some sort of licensing of responsible international journalists could make the control of international information even easier.

There is a combination of professional machismo and common sense in the assumption that secrecy is not news. In the first sense, secrecy is an affront to the journalist's professional skill: if there were a story worth writing about, the reporter would be able to get it. The common sense is that there is not much one can do about secrecy except to object, and the objection must by definition be in the most general of terms. A leading article, perhaps, but no story.

The Journalist as Performer

The world of journalism is like that of the theatre and cinema in many ways. Some conservatives complain that it is all a modern trend, and that the rot set in when *The Times* started naming reporters. Others blame it on television, and long for the Reithian days of the B.B.C. when newsreaders were anonymous.

Whether it is a modern corruption or a recognition of the proper role of the press in modern society, journalists are often public figures today, in much the same way that performers are. This can easily lead to a narcissism that is not always consistent with writing about the complicated business of how society is run. There is a common power struggle between some writers and their editors that has almost exact parallels in theatre and cinema. Just as some film stars can contractually command the right to final approval of how their performances are edited, so some journalists have agreements that whatever they write will not be cut, and may even have guarantees about how many words they are entitled to and where they will be placed.

There is nothing intrinsically objectionable in this, particularly in that part of journalism that is obviously written to entertain. Columns of opinion which are primarily to educate (or at least to comment) may be enhanced by being clearly identified as one writer's personal view. And such columns can also provide a much-needed perspective on news. This is particularly true when news is presented as short items, selected, pushed out, and forgotten. At its best, the more personal sort of journalism can explain current history, giving some sort of coherence to what would otherwise be a jumbled blur of falling governments, rising prices, plane crashes, and random violence.

But there are dangers of both self- and public deception that have more serious consequences in journalism than in theatre and cinema. Association with those who wield real political power can lead to a sort of fellow-feeling which obscures what journalists and politicians can and should do. This is, essentially, the same dilemma presented to the journalist and his contact, but on a grander scale. The most extreme illustration in a Western democracy was probably Washington in the days of the Kennedy administration. Many journalists and editors were so entranced by John Kennedy that they nearly forgot the essentially ad-versarial roles of government and the press under the U.S. constitution. The sense of identification with the President was as potent as arguments about national security in deterring most newspapers from publishing what they knew about prep-arations for the abortive Bay of Pigs invasion of Cuba. They learned a bitter lesson, and stubbornly stuck to it when Lyndon Johnson asked whose side they were on in reporting the Vietnam war.

There is also a danger that the public may not realize that, however favourable the contractual terms of their favourite writer or broadcaster, he does not have anything approaching control over the medium. Behind every journalist and broadcaster is the editor, the producer, the controller, the chairman, and all the other men who do not mistake the illusion of exposure for the reality of control. If anything, such men in the newspaper world have become less public figures than they were in the days of the blatant press lords. There also seems to be a new reality in the division between ownership and control. It was, for example, Lord Thomson's policy not to interfere in the editorial decisions of *The Times* and the *Sunday Times*. Advertising revenue and editorial content are separate matters.

At the beginning of 1978 there was a clear demonstration of this. Trafalgar House, a conglomerate which had acquired the Cunard line, was offended by two stories in Thomson publications. One, in *The Times*, reported on difficulties in refitting the *Queen Elizabeth II* in Southampton. As mentioned in a previous chapter, the other, in the *Sunday Times*, was based on reports by U.S. public health inspectors about the *QE II* and other Cunard ships. The reports had been obtained in America under the U.S. Freedom of Information Act. In January Cunard informed Thomson that £18,000 of advertising was being cancelled because of the stories. This information was passed on to the editors of the two papers. The communication was both an illustration of the policy of editorial independence, and an open communication of what it could cost. Victor Matthews, who had not been in control of Trafalgar House very long, reacted to the stories rather like a press lord of the old style (he had also acquired the *Express*). Nothing like that would appear in *his* paper, and he considered buying others to ensure that nothing like that appeared in them.

The Journalist as Accuser: Investigative Journalism

'Investigative journalism' is sometimes thought to be a recent import from America, but British examples can be found at least as far back as 1885. W. T. Stead was making news for the *Pall Mall Gazette* when he exposed child prostitution by going out and buying a twelve-year-old girl. It led to a good story, a change in the law, and some time in gaol for Stead, whose purchase was taken seriously by the court.

An 'investigative journalist' is going about as far as possible from the role of the reporter who goes along to the public event, takes down the details in shorthand, and turns in a quick factual account. It is more than just thorough research, because it almost always concludes with an allocation of blame.

Of course, an 'investigation' can range from a few minutes looking through newspaper cuttings to months or even years of research. Investigative journalism of the second sort is expensive. Journalists are paid to write, not to research. Even if the editor ultimately decides to spike the story or the controller decides not to broadcast the programme, that does not change the print or broadcasting journalist's basic obligation to come up with material for such decisions. Few news organizations are willing to pay journalists to spend months digging around for something that just might turn out to be newsworthy.

Because of this, much 'investigative' journalism is actually the use by journalists of investigations carried out by someone else. The real investigator may be a pressure group, an academic, or just an obsessive individual. The relationship between the journalist and such freelance investigators is almost the reverse of the relationship with an inside informant. The investigator wants to get everything he has found into the newspaper, and usually wants to be acknowledged as the source. Sometimes he may even want to have a hand in writing the story, and sometimes may even get it.

The journalist must be careful in using such sources to avoid being used too much himself. Part of the problem is that the journalist is, in theory at least, dedicated to balance and fairness in writing; the 'private investigator' is partisan by definition. A much more practical part of the problem is not so much the journalist's training in balance as his training in what is 'news' and what is not. One dramatic illustration is worth pages of statistics. A few bodies will always help a story along. What is 'news' is not just the journalist's personal opinion, but also his prediction of how the editor will react.

Some subjects and some sources will be rejected out of hand. One of the initial barriers for an individual or a group approaching the press is simply to establish their sanity. Many journalists develop a working assumption that anyone who approaches them with a 'really good story' is likely as not to be a loon. The shambling figure with the gleam of conviction in his eye and the carrier bag full of photocopies is usually to be avoided. The fifteen-page single-spaced typed letter, filled with block capitals, underlined sentences, and exclamation points, is probably a crank. Exciting new evidence about UFOs or conspiracy theories about fluoridation will usually not get much of a hearing.

But freelance investigators, and pressure groups in particular, are still extremely useful to investigative journalists. Much of Ralph Nader's success in the United States was due to his ability to supply journalists with a stream of stories that they did not have the time, energy, or teams of assistants to get themselves. Many of Britain's new breed of investigative journalists get much of their information directly from particular pressure groups, usually with some acknowledgement of the ultimate source.

There is still considerable uneasiness in Britain about investigative journalism. It is usually devoted to exposing something that is thought to be wrong and demanding that it be put right. Sometimes only the sanction of publicity is relied on, and sometimes there is a call for legal action. The *Sunday Times* series of articles on thalidomide was primarily an argument that the manufacturers had a moral obligation to pay greater compensation to the victims of the drug, even if their legal obligation was not clear.

But the House of Lords ruled that it was for the courts, not the newspapers, to decide on whether compensation should be paid and how much it should be. The articles were suppressed because they were an interference in the judicial process, an attempt to 'pressurize' the defendant in the legal action to pay more than might be legally required. That was in 1974. The articles were finally published some years later, but only because the editor of the *Sunday Times* had taken the trouble to complain to the European Commission of Human Rights and the Court of Human Rights, which ruled that the restriction was an unjustifiable limitation on the freedom of communication guaranteed by the European Convention on Human Rights. The suppression was a somewhat novel use of 'contempt of court' to stop publication of articles critical of a large corporation involved in a civil action which had been dormant for nearly ten years. When the injunction against the articles was finally lifted after the complaint to the Human Rights Commission, substantial settlements had made with the families of nearly all the thalidomide

t of court' is far more commonly used to stop publ... / of information which might prevent a defendant from getting a fair trial in a criminal prosecution. In short, it is to prevent what is usually called 'trial by newspaper'. It has also been used, or at least attempts have been made to use it, to protect the anonymity of witnesses because of national security or other reasons.

Another doctrine, the judge-made 'law of confidence', is potentially the broadest of the legal restrictions on the press. It was successfully applied, in a second case, to keep the *Sunday Times* from using documents about Distillers' testing of thalidomide before it was marketed. A less successful attempt was made under the doctrine to stop publication of the Crossman *Diaries*.

As for investigative journalism and the law of defamation, there is almost no possibility that Britain will adopt anything like the U.S. 'public figure' doctrine. Under this rule[4] publication of something which is false and defamatory about a 'public figure' will only require payment of damages if it was done maliciously or with a reckless disregard for truth. The Faulks Committee on defamation specifically rejected such a proposal in their 1975 report.[5]

But changes do need to be made, and one of the more important ones would be to reverse the present system which effectively limits the protection of the laws of libel to public figures, or at least to those with enough money to finance a libel action, because legal aid is not available in defamation actions. One of the less attractive parts of journalism is the calculation of power and the possibility of retaliation in deciding what to print. It is enough of a problem that the powerful can retaliate simply by refusing further cooperation. It is crude (and remediable) that the poor can be libelled with greater impunity than the rich. The relative ease of such libels, and the callous treatment often given by the press to those who stumble into the limelight, as in the aftermath of disasters, justifies caustic comments about some

British journalism. Far too often the press lives down to such evaluations and forfeits the case for protection. As Roy Jenkins commented in his 1975 Guildhall lecture, if Britain had a written constitution it is very unlikely that its first amendment would be to protect freedom of the press.

)e Done: Secrecy and the Courts

Supporters and critics of the Official Secrets Act usually agree that it is not the most important influence for secrecy in Britain. Government would not become noticeably more open if the Act were repealed, because other forces for secrecy would continue. One of those is the law decided by judges when there is no rule laid down by Parliament. A look at how they decide between secrecy and publicity when left to their own devices is useful in considering what Parliament might do to bring government into the open.

Some of the cases in which questions of secrecy are decided by the courts are close to classical censorship, or what the U.S. courts would call 'prior restraint'. In such cases the question is whether or not the courts will stop someone from printing something. If there has already been publication the courts may also become involved in deciding if it violated a legal rule so that criminal penalties or civil damages must result.

The British press has been accurately described by Harold Evans, now editor of *The Times*, as only 'half-free', especially when compared with journalism in the United States. The laws of defamation, obscenity, confidence, copyright, and contempt of court place the British press under a variety of limits, some more justifiable than others.

The distinction between judicial censorship, or 'prior restraint', and punishment or damages after publication is not one with which the British courts are much concerned. The definition in Blackstone's *Commentaries* of press freedom as the absence of prior restraint is taken more seriously in America. If publication would violate a law, courts in this country apply essentially the same rules in deciding whether to stop it before it happens as in punishing it afterwards. The only general exception is in the law of defamation. If I feel that an article to appear in next week's paper will defame me, I can ask for an injunction to stop publication. If the publisher's defence is that the article is true, then the courts will not stop publication. The legal battle over the truth of the article can take place afterwards, with damages if the publisher's defence fails.

Otherwise, there is no British legal rule comparable to the U.S. constitutional doctrine against 'prior restraint', as opposed to subsequent penalties. The leading American illustration of this was the Pentagon Papers case in which the U.S. Supreme Court refused to stop *The New York Times* from printing a government report on the origins of the Vietnam war. But several of the justices clearly felt that criminal penalties might still be applied if any law had been violated.

During the 1970s the British courts were involved in several important attempts to suppress information. The particularly interesting ones are those in which secrecy was said to be justified 'in the public interest'.

One of these cases, *Beloff v. Pressdram*, [1] was a dispute between journalists, although the information involved had come from a conversation with a government minister. A memorandum written by the *Observer*'s political correspondent about Edward Heath's possible successor had come into the hands of *Private Eye*. The legal question was whether the *Eye*'s publication of the memo was an infringement of copyright or a breach of confidence. The short answer given by Mr Justice Ungoed-Thomas was that the action was brought by the wrong person. The *Observer*, rather than its employee, should have sued *Private Eye*, because the copyright belonged to the employer.

So *Private Eye* was in the clear. But the judge went on to make further remarks about the defence that publication was justified 'in the public interest'. It would only justify a breach of confidence, he said, to disclose matters 'in breach of the country's security, or in breach of law . . . including matters medically dangerous to the public; and doubtless other misdeeds of similar gravity . . .' The mention of 'matters medically dangerous' was probably an allusion to an earlier decision that publication of a book about Scientology was justified in the public interest even if it involved a breach of confidence. [2]

This balancing of the public interest against the legal obligation of confidence was a relatively minor judicial exercise, and not really necessary to decide the case at all. But the 'law of confidence' and 'the public interest' reappeared in the High Court three years later in a case that went to the centre of British government: Cabinet secrecy. [3]

The question in the Crossman *Diaries* case was whether the court would stop publication of the *Diaries* of Richard Crossman, who had written them while a minister in the 1964–70 Labour Government. Although he was an outspoken advocate of open government, Crossman had also sacked a lowly social security officer who had written without authorization about alleged dole frauds. Still, his tape-recorded diaries contained a wealth of 'blow-by-blow' (as it was later described in court) information about how the Labour Government had gone about its business.

The manuscript was delivered to his publisher shortly before Crossman's death, and parts of it were published in the *Sunday Times* in 1975. In June the Attorney-General took action against both the newspaper and Crossman's publisher to stop further publication.

The full story of the battle is told in a book, *The Crossman Affair*, by Hugo Young. [4] The case itself made public previously secret government information, including the Cabinet Office's guidelines for the writing of ex-ministers' memoirs. It also emerged that these 'guidelines' had not even been written down until the affair began. There was a slightly ridiculous legal misunderstanding between the parties that did not come out until after the case was decided. The publishers' counsel argued repeatedly that publication did not violate the Official Secrets Act, while the Attorney-General replied that he was only mentioning the Act because it was a general indication of the policy of keeping such things secret. After the trial it was learned that the Attorney-General had assumed that the Act did not cover the *Diaries* because Crossman was dead, a possibility which had not even occurred to the defence counsel.

Instead of relying on the Act, the Attorney-General based his claim for suppression on the law of confidence and a more generalized argument that it was against the public interest for discussions between ministers and between them and their civil servants to become public knowledge, at least before these became available in the Public Record Office after thirty years.

Lord Widgery did not give his decision at the end of the trial in the summer of 1975, but waited until the end of the long judicial vacation in October. Then, in a paradoxical judgment, he agreed with nearly all of the Attorney-General's legal arguments, but allowed publication. He had read the first volume, which was the immediate subject of the case, and decided that publication ten years after most of the events described would not do sufficient harm to justify an injunction. In theory the later volumes, which dealt with later events, might have been stopped. But the Attorney-General decided not to try.

There was a neat bit of legal footwork at the end of the case, however, concerning the delicate subject of advice given by civil servants to ministers. Lord Widgery had not quite agreed with the Attorney-General on this point. The Lord Chief Justice could 'find no ground for saying that either the Crown or the individual civil servant has an enforceable right to have the advice which he gives treated as confidential for all time'. Or even for so short a time as ten years, he might have added.

Putting a brave face on things, the Attorney-General announced that he would not appeal against the result in the case. After all, since the court had agreed with the Crown on so much of the law, it hardly seemed worth bothering the Court of Appeal and possibly the House of Lords just because the object of the action had not quite been achieved. But something had to be done about those words concerning civil servants, and something was. When counsel for the Attorney-General appeared in court to announce the decision not to appeal, he added an innocuous-sounding little question. Were these remarks, he asked, just about the Crossman case, or did they amount 'to a general ruling . . . that the courts had no power in any circumstances to restrain publication of confidential advice by civil servants to ministers'. Lord Widgery replied that the former was intended.

Having carved out that particularly distasteful bit of the judgment, counsel for the Crown retired, announcing that 'the major issue of principle' had 'been determined in his favour'. No one, except perhaps Lord Widgery, was entirely pleased with the decision. The *Sunday Times* called it 'Widgery's Fork'. Although the decision allowed publication, it had also created quite a lot of law that could cause problems for future editors in publishing Cabinet leaks.

As might have been anticipated, the Government then appointed a Committee of Privy Councillors under Lord Radcliffe to consider the whole subject of ministerial memoirs. They were equally unenthusiastic about Widgery's work when they reported in January 1976.[5] In a guarded expression of disapproval they complained that 'no fixed principles of legal enforcement' had emerged, and concluded that perhaps it would be better not to involve the courts in such matters again. They did not think 'that a judge is likely to be so equipped as to make him the best arbiter of the issues . . .'

Instead they recommended a system of what 'rightly or wrongly have come to be known as gentlemen's agreements', in which 'everyone . . . knows what is expected of him and that . . . there is no condonation of the transgression by the others'. For a period of fifteen years memoirs would be subject to vetting by the Cabinet Secretary, and on matters of advice by civil servants the period should be extended until the civil servant's retirement. In short, they were not pleased with Widgery for letting the side down, and their attitude was not improved by his agreement with the Attorney-General on matters of legal principle. The only clear result in law was the assertion of judicial power to decide whether such memoirs could be published or not.

Since the Crossman affair, there has been a significant amendment, or at least a clarification, of the 'guidelines' for ex-ministers seeking information. As they emerged in the Crossman trial, these apparently involved a kind of bargain: ex-ministers would be allowed access to the records of their term in office, and they would submit any memoirs to the Cabinet Secretary for vetting. But such 'access' to records turned out not to be a right to inspect and copy such records. When Alfred Morris, who had been Labour Minister for the Disabled, asked to see his departmental records, he was told that it meant only his personal right to have a look. It did not mean that he could photocopy anything, and it certainly did not include the right to have a research assistant examine them.

Cabinet secrets appeared in the news, if not in the courts, in spring 1976, when *New Society* carried an article about legislation for child benefits which was far too well informed for the Government's pleasure. The author was Frank Field, head of Child Poverty Action Group and now M.P. for Birkenhead. From the article it was clear that he had either seen Cabinet minutes or had had them quoted extensively to him. There was a thorough leak inquiry and an emergency debate in the Commons, but no legal proceedings. The Attorney-General did not prosecute under section 2 of the Official Secrets Act. A civil action for breach of confidence might have been embarrassing, even if the Government had won. There could not have been an injunction, since the article had already been published, and it might have been difficult to convert political embarrassment into pounds and pence in damages.

But the courts were relatively busy during the 1970s in balancing the public interest in secrecy against the public interest in disclosure, even if only in regard to limited disclosure of information to someone needing it to bring a lawsuit. This involved what used to be called 'Crown privilege', and is now increasingly known as 'public interest privilege'. Until 1968 the rule was clear: if the Attorney-General objected to the production of any evidence, his certificate was final. The leading case until then was one in which the courts refused to order disclosure of information about submarine construction in an action brought by relatives of those who had died when the *Thetis* sank just before the Second World War. [6]

In *Conway v. Rimmer* [7] the House of Lords reversed their earlier decision (in keeping with a 1966 'practice direction' that they might change their minds on an issue). The information sought was official, the reports on a probationary constable. It was relevant to his case, brought against a superior who had accused him of stealing a torch. And the House of Lords ordered that it be disclosed, in face of a claim of Crown privilege. The case was notable for one of those revealing judicial comments on hypothetical cases far removed from the facts before them. Lord Reid said that even limited disclosure of Cabinet records in litigation would be against the public interest because 'disclosure would create or fan ill-informed or captious public or political criticism'.

The courts were presented with several similar cases after that, many of them involving disclosure of information from government departments. The courts, frequently the House of Lords, were cautious. In *Lewes Justices* the Law Lords refused to order disclosure of reports made to the police and Gaming Board regarding 'dubious characters', even though the private prosecutor in the case had actually received the document from another source. [8] In *Crompton Amusement Machines* they refused to order disclosure of customs records to the plaintiff to use in his action against competitors. [9] In *D. v. N.S.P.C.C.* they refused to disclose the name of the person who had reported the plaintiff to the N.S.P.C.C. as a child-batterer. [10] But in *Norwich Pharmacal* the Lords did order disclosure of records to a manufacturer to use in his action against an importer who he thought was infringing his patent. [11]

So the Crown, or 'public interest', privilege not to disclose information, even for the limited purposes of a court case, seemed relatively secure. In a decision which was not appealed, Mr Justice Templeman refused even to examine, let alone order disclosure of documents from ministeries and the Monopolies Commission, because 'the threat that they might have to answer to an alleged monopolist for all their thought processes would be bound to hamper their efficiency'. [12]

But in the autumn of 1979, the courts began to reflect changing public opinion and to examine claims for secrecy a bit more sceptically. An important case was one brought by *Burmah Oil*, alleging that it had been unfairly pressurized by the Bank of England and the government to hand over British Petroleum shares at a bargain price as part of a government bail-out of the company. [13] Burmah wanted to see all sorts of departmental records which it thought would help the case. Burmah lost the claim to see the records, although by an accident some of the files had already been handed over. But there were some significant differences from the earlier cases. Four of the five Law Lords (excepting Lord Wilberforce) actually examined the documents before concluding that they were not sufficiently relevant to order disclosure. Lord Keith commented on the 'trend towards more open government than in the past . . .' saying that 'in a limited number of cases . . . the inner workings of government should be exposed to public gaze . . . [which] might lead to criticism calculated to improve the nature of that working as affecting the individual citizen'. Lord Scarman, who in a speech the year before had praised the United States for 'grasping the nettle' by passing the Freedom of Information Act, also examined the documents before concluding that they need not be produced. But he went on to ask what, apart from documents concerning national safety, diplomatic relations, or 'some state secret of high importance . . . was so important about secret government that it must be protected even at the price of injustice in our courts?'

In another decision given the same day the Lords went halfway to ordering disclosure of employment records in cases alleging discrimination on the basis of race, sex, and trade union activity. [14] Although they did not actually order disclosure, the Lords sent the cases back to the appropriate tribunals with 'guidelines' to follow in deciding whether disclosure was necessary and how to go about it. These included, in the words of Lord Wilberforce, the possibility of 'substituting anonymous references for specific names or . . . hearing *in camera*'.

An equally important, although less noted, decision was in the case of *Waugh v. British Railways Board*, in which the widow of a train driver wanted to see the British Rail report on the crash in which her husband was killed. [15] The argument against disclosure here was not actually based on 'public interest' privilege. Instead, British Rail argued that the report was covered by the lawyer−client privilege, because it was prepared at least in part for use in possible litigation. That was not good enough for the Law Lords (or for Lord Denning in the Court of Appeal). That was not the only, or the dominant, purpose of the report, and it was made available in order for justice to be done in the case.

These are all cases which show developing judicial attitudes towards secrecy, some of which involved only semi-governmental information (as in the cases of the N.S.P.C.C., the Science Research Council, British Rail, and British Leyland). Lower courts began to follow the trend. The High Court ordered disclosure of documents on prison special control units [16] and the Liverpool County Court ordered production of a police report on a man allegedly beaten up while in custody.

But it should not be thought that these are anything like the balancing of interests by American courts under the U.S. Freedom of Information Act. It is not the public right to know generally which is being slowly developed, but rather the right of someone bringing a legal action to see relevant evidence. The judges may first examine the documents to see if they really are relevant, the documents may be handed over to lawyers for the party bringing the action, but they must go no further. Judges were not pleased when the *Guardian* published the information about prison control units.[17] The legal principle applied in 1974 to stop the *Sunday Times* from publishing similar documents still stands. (This was a different legal case from the paper's ultimately successful battle to publish articles about thalidomide.)

The documents were about the testing of thalidomide by its makers, and they had been handed over to an expert witness for the children's parents as a part of pre-trial 'discovery' to prepare their case. The witness took them to the *Sunday Times*. Mr Justice Talbot ordered the paper not to print anything about the documents. There was, he said, 'no crime or fraud or misdeed on the part of [Distillers] and . . . negligence, even if it could be so proved . . .' could not justify publication. [18]

The cases are, in a way, like the cases in the U.S. under the

Administrative Procedure Act of 1946, in which someone who wanted to see government records had to show some legal 'interest', like a pending lawsuit, in order to get disclosure. But the courts in America began to take a different view after Congress passed the Freedom of Information Act in 1966 and amended it in 1974 to make it stronger. British courts might follow a similar path in interpreting a similar act of Parliament. As Lord Keith said in *Burmah Oil*, there is a trend towards more open government, although 'no doubt it was for Parliament and not courts of law to say how far that trend should go'.

One case illustrates how the courts might enforce an open government law if Parliament decided to go that far. The Local Government Act 1972 contains some of the few 'right to know' provisions to be found in British statutes. Margaret Thatcher's private member's bill, which she successfully introduced very shortly after being elected to Parliament, required local authority meetings to be open to the press and public (see Chapter 1). In 1972 this was extended to local authority committee meetings as well, to combat the tendency of authorities to exclude the public by resolving themselves into a committee.

Sections 159 and 228 also require local authorities to make certain financial documents available to local electors, and there is a penalty for violations. In 1976 a group of ratepayers in Hillingdon brought a private prosecution after that authority refused to let them see records about construction expenses. The authority was fined £10 (and ordered to pay £1,000 towards the prosecution costs) at Uxbridge Magistrates' Court. This was upheld in April 1977 on appeal to the Middlesex Guildhall Crown Court. Apart from the judge's concluding comment that he thought the appeal 'an absurd waste of the ratepayers' money', it is noteworthy for his decision on the conflict between commercial confidentiality and a statutory obligation to be open. Rejecting the argument that the documents were commercially confidential, he said: 'A question of whether or not the parties to a contract have provided that certain information is to be treated as confidential is quite irrelevant to any consideration as to whether a local authority is obliged to disclose that information by permitting inspection of a document from which it can be ascertained'.

British courts do not inevitably side with established governmental authority. Although they are quite capable of deferring to broad executive discretion and secrecy, as in the Agee–Hosenball case, they are also capable of resisting government over-reaching, as Mr Justice Caulfield did in his summing-up to the jury in the 1971 *Sunday Telegraph* case (which ended in acquittal under section 2 of the Official Secrets Act), and as Mr Justice Mars-Jones did in the ABC case, when he as much as directed the section 1 espionage charges to be withdrawn and indicated that no one would go to gaol, even if the defendants were convicted under section 2. Both the *Sunday Telegraph* and ABC cases, furthermore, involved a sweeping law passed by Parliament, said to be in the interest of national security. In all of these cases the courts dealt with governmental and quasi-governmental claims for secrecy. But how open are the courts themselves?

Institutions and individuals usually are more in favour of secrecy the closer it comes to their own interests. In passing the Freedom of Information Act in 1966 the U.S. Congress was imposing openness on the executive branch rather than on itself. Congress continued until very recently to have many of their 'marking-up' committee sessions (in which they determine the final form of bills to be returned to the House or Senate) in private. In Sweden, with its ancient open government provision in the constitution, committees of the Riksdag often meet in private. And newspapers frequently rediscover the high value of personal and corporate privacy when roles are reversed and they are being scrutinized.

Even the U.S. Supreme Court is not particularly pleased by a recent book which purports to tell the inside story of how the court has reached some of its better-known recent decisions.[19] Journalists such as Anthony Lewis criticized it for damaging the confidential relationship between the justices and their law clerks,[20] an argument almost identical to the familiar one in Britain that secrecy is essential to maintain the necessary candour between ministers and their civil servants.

Seen to be Done . . . Public or Private Justice?

A large part of the business of government is judicial, that is, deciding disputes between people and applying the law of the general community to punish those who have broken it. When this is done by the courts these two kinds of proceedings, civil or criminal, are usually open to the public. Openness is the general rule, subject to the important qualification that once a dispute is referred to the courts (or even before) the press is limited to publishing only what takes place in open court.

It is generally felt that Britain has the balance between publicity and privacy in legal proceedings about right, avoiding the extremes of secret tribunals and trial by newspaper. But there are two trends that call for a more serious look at the issues involved in public trials. One is the tendency of the courts and Parliament to carve out more exceptions to the general rule of open courts; the other is the development of quasi-judicial functions carried out by more secretive administrative bodies.

It is not clear whether courts are open to the public to ensure a fair trial for the parties or for the benefit of the public more generally, and the real reason is probably a mixture of the two. Secret trials are thought to be particularly dangerous in criminal cases, and Jeremy Bentham thought that public trials would keep 'judicial injustice' subject to the check of public opinion.

But criminal proceedings are not kept public solely or even primarily in the interests of the accused. If they were the defendant would surely have the option of a public or private trial, just as he has under the Criminal Justice Act 1967 the right to have reporting restrictions lifted if he thinks publicity at the preliminary stage would be in his interests.*

The major danger to an accused if he chose a secret trial would seem to be that he might be unfairly coerced into asking for it by authorities who would also prefer to avoid publicity. But that does not seem to be an adequate explanation for the rule that

*The possibility of a conflict of interests between co-defendants was dramatically illustrated in the committal stage of the trial of Jeremy Thorpe and others in 1978.

nearly all criminal trials are open to the public. A better reason is that the judicial system relies fairly heavily on the sanction of public opinion for a variety of purposes.

One of these is to provide a check on both the decision to prosecute and on the veracity of witnesses. As Lord Salmon said to the Royal Commission on Tribunals of Inquiry, 'secrecy increases the quantity of evidence but tends to debase its quality'.[21] The prospect of making an accusation in a formal public proceeding and being questioned on it should deter petty or unsubstantiated prosecutions. In other words, publicity can ensure that criminal charges are acceptable to the public as well as being technically correct, and can also reinforce the law of perjury to encourage honest witnesses.

Another reason is the fairly obvious one that the public humiliation of a conviction reported in the press is often far more of a punishment than the imposition of a fine. Local journalists who regularly cover magistrates' courts are quite aware of this, and not uncommonly are approached by those who have been convicted of minor offences with pleas that their names be kept out of the paper. In minor cases like these, the imposition of a fine or even a short sentence is the least serious of the consequences for many offenders. Publicity in the local paper, or even a national, if they happen to report the case, is usually far more damaging.

Even if the local reporter happens not to be in court that morning, the entry of the conviction in the Criminal Records Office files may be more damaging in the long term than a fine. The convicted person is not likely to know where the record of the conviction is kept, how long it is kept, or to whom it is disclosed. According to the Report of the Lindop Committee on Data Protection in 1978, not all convictions are recorded in the national Criminal Records Office. Only convictions in 'certain categories' are kept in a manual file (now about 3.8 million). The manual file is linked to an index in the Police National Computer. Many more records not in the national file are kept in regional criminal records offices, but the index to these is 'not currently' held on the P.N.C. For aliens convicted of any offence, even speeding, there is a special system of reports to the Home Office. [22]

The Rehabilitation of Offenders Act 1974 provides, by a rather complicated timetable based on the seriousness of the conviction, that certain offences will be considered 'spent' after a period of years. Mostly, this is a restriction on the press, because it would be a libel to publish anything about a 'spent' conviction, and it would be no defence to argue that it was true. However, there is a broad range of occupations for which a conviction will never be considered 'spent', and there is no provision for the police to remove the record of a conviction from their files.

The government will always be able to remember a conviction, and anything else they choose to put in their files (see Chapter 7). But for the public to notice it at all, let alone remember, is largely a matter of chance. The courts are mostly 'public' to acquaintances of someone involved in a case that day, perhaps a few pensioners who make a habit of going to watch, and frequently a local reporter, who may or may not write down what goes on, depending on whether there is something about the case that is 'news'.

It is paradoxical that in Sweden, where so much of the executive side of government is open to public inspection, there is a self-imposed rule of the press not to report the names of people accused of offences, and usually not to report them even if they are convicted. This is not legally binding, however, and names are sometimes printed, particularly when the person convicted is very roughly what would be a 'public figure' under U.S. libel law (see p. 96).

England has made modifications to the principle of open trials in recent years, although it started with the judge-made power to protect the anonymity of witnesses. This was considered to be appropriate for sparing use, as in blackmail cases, and was tested and upheld fairly recently. [23] Then it was extended by statute in the Sexual Offences (Amendment) Act 1976. The reason was that rape victims were often unwilling to testify because they found the publicity humiliating. So a provision for anonymity for witnesses in such cases was provided, and an amendment to the bill as it went through Parliament extended the same anonymity to the accused, at least until he was convicted.

A few similar statutory provisions had already been made for limited reporting of matrimonial cases and those involving children. Most of these restrictions are because almost anything sexual is 'news' and also because a published report of evidence is protected by absolute privilege in the law of libel.

In 1967 restrictions were also placed on reporting of committal proceedings, for rather different reasons. Briefly, the committal proceeding is only a presentation of the prosecution case for the magistrates to decide whether it should proceed to a full trial. It was felt that publication of only one side of the case might prejudice the right of the accused to a fair trial, and so the accused was, and is, allowed to decide whether reporting restrictions will be lifted or not. The equivalent in the United States is a hearing before a grand jury (abandoned in England in 1933), and such proceedings are entirely secret. Even the intrepid Woodstein team who uncovered Watergate only timidly attempted to find out what went on in the grand jury room, and quickly abandoned the attempt.

In this country it is probably best to be sceptical about proposals to restrict reporting of certain kinds of cases and allow anonymity for various witnesses, especially when it is claimed to be necessary for reasons of state security (as was unsuccessfully done in the *Leveller* and *Peace News* spin-off cases from the ABC affair). It was only because of the open bankruptcy proceedings in the Poulson case that a whole string of local government corruption cases began to emerge.

The courts in this country are, compared to the executive, relatively open. Evidence is taken in public and reasons for decisions are usually given. But there are some aspects of the judicial process that are kept secret, and they deserve at least some inquiry. Until the ABC case it was assumed that jury lists were taken at random from the electoral register. It was only by accident during that trial that the public learned that jurors were 'vetted' in certain kinds of cases, and that the process had been going on for some time. Similarly, jurors had been instructed solemnly for years that whatever went on in the jury room was to be kept secret, although there was no legal basis for the rule. It was tested by the *New Statesman* in the summer of 1979, and the resulting contempt of court action led to a slight liberalization of the rule. The *New Statesman* was not in contempt of court by reporting what one juror said, but that was largely because of the circumstances of the particular case. Another juror, and another sort of article, could well be in contempt of court for telling too much.

If potential jurors are vetted, and have been in some cases for quite a while, this should raise the question of whether judges, and magistrates in particular, are subject to vetting, and for what. The process by which ordinary people are selected to be magistrates particularly needs questioning. We know that there is a form for nomination, and that it includes a section for political affiliation, which is said to be to ensure balance rather than the opposite. There are local advisory panels which consider such nominations and advise the Lord Chancellor's Office, which makes the appointment. The membership of such panels is difficult, but not always impossible, to learn. But the process by which nominations are approved or rejected is largely unknown.

This is not an argument for election of judges, as in some U.S. states under various systems, or for any of the other variations such as the elected Swedish 'juries'. But if the apparently long-standing process of jury-vetting deserves inquiry and explanation, then the process by which magistrates are chosen or not chosen deserves to be paid at least as much attention, and at least as much information should be provided, if justice is not only to be done, but also seen to be done.

Chapter Seven

Race to 1984: 'Data Privacy'

Secrecy and personal privacy are often confused, sometimes as a debating ploy. There are important differences between them, both in the basic values they represent and the appropriate legal measures to protect those values. There are some areas in which the secrecy or publicity of government information affects personal privacy.

The most important of these is what has come to be called 'data privacy'. It is easier to illustrate the concept than to define it precisely, and many writers simply refer to George Orwell's *1984* to show what they are afraid of. In this horrific anti-utopia, everything about everyone is known to the State. Big Brother watches everyone all the time.

What, in the abstract, is so bad about that? It can be argued that the real evil in *1984* was that Big Brother was malevolent. A change of regime to a benevolent Brother could mean that such constant scrutiny would only be exercised in the best interests of those scrutinized. Or, in the common argument, only those with something to hide are exercised about their privacy.

It is true that notions of personal privacy vary greatly from time to time and place to place. Those who grow up in villages of almost any country are usually aware that the sense of community in such places means that there is very little about them that is not known to all of the inhabitants. There is a theory of American history which places great emphasis on the existence of a frontier in moulding American attitudes. Apart from economic opportunity, the chance to escape the past and start again is still an important part of American mobility.

To some extent such attitudes may just be the results of a

hiccup in history. The Reformation led to a much greater emphasis on individual conscience, on good works, and the constant promise of a new beginning. The extended family, the hierarchy of agrarian communities, the sense of stability and belonging, gave way to more private strivings.

Whatever the causes, and however transient, most people in Western countries feel that there are some kinds of information about themselves that they would rather not have generally known; to be more exact, there are some kinds of personal information that most people would like to be able to control.

These are not necessarily shameful things. A survey commissioned by the Younger Committee on Privacy in 1972 found that 35 per cent of those asked felt that it was an invasion of their privacy for a public electoral register to contain their names and addresses.[1] Seventy-eight per cent of them would object to publication of their income.

The Younger Committee decided against recommending a general legal 'right of privacy', largely because it could come to no useful definition of something variously affected by peeping toms, private detectives, reporters, and dossiers. It was further inhibited by the terms of reference: both Labour and Conservative governments refused to allow the committee to consider possible invasions of privacy by government bodies.

The Lindop Committee, which reported in December 1978, was concerned with the more limited notion of data protection, and was allowed to inquire into actions by both public and private bodies. The Lindop recommendations deal directly with the point at which government secrecy and personal privacy overlap: the collection and dissemination of personal information by governments.[2]

Much of the concern about privacy and data protection is directed at computers. But storage of personal information electronically is only different in degree from storage of the same information by hand in files. And, as the Lindop Committee pointed out, advances in technology may soon make the distinction between computer and manual systems disappear altogether for practical purposes.

The degree is important, though. One of the more effective data protection measures in the past was the practical difficulty of collecting, storing, and retrieving information. Computer technology has changed that, and it is likely to change even faster in the immediate future. For example, it is now possible for any police officer to learn the name and address of the registered keeper of an automobile within seconds.

The example is a useful one for several reasons. We have some information, from the survey by the Younger Committee, that many people would object to having their names and addresses available to the general public. We do not know how many people would object to the same information being readily available to any police officer who saw them driving by and felt like checking on them by radio. Under the present law, however, the police officer commits an offence if he discloses such names and addresses without authorization. In 1979 an officer of the Metropolitan Police was charged with providing such information to a gambling casino which wanted to attract the customers of a competitor, but was subsequently acquitted.

It is also a simple illustration of an American definition of data privacy, which was used by the Lindop Committee. That is 'the individual's ability to control the circulation of information relating to him'. The information is the name and address. Drivers and keepers of motor vehicles are required by law to provide the government with this, which removes the individual's ability to control the circulation in the first place by not telling anyone.

The simple illustration becomes more complex when we consider the next questions. What limits should there be on how a government department, the Driver and Vehicle Licensing Centre, circulates the information? To whom, and when, should they be free (or required) to provide the information? Perhaps equally important, once the rules on such circulation are decided, is who will enforce the rules and how.

Attitudes about the rules themselves vary very widely, not only from person to person, but also depending on an individual's circumstances. Someone who grumbles at the requirement to supply the D.V.L.C. at Swansea with his name and address as the owner of a white 1974 Cortina, registration XYZ 000Z, may change his mind if the car is stolen. Then he might be more than happy to have the information readily available to every police officer in the country, and perhaps even to any alert citizen. But he might object strenuously to the circulation of such information after the car had been recovered.

Even if rules about circulation of information were established, it would not determine how they would be enforced. Should the hypothetical Cortina owner be able to take legal action against the D.V.L.C. if his name and address is provided to someone in breach of the rules? So far, the illustration is fairly simple in one respect. The information is personal, in providing certain facts about the car owner, but not terribly sensitive, and not particularly detailed. The information is presumably accurate, and not linked with any other information about the car owner.

The Lindop Committee proposed seven statutory principles for the regulation of automatic handling of personal data in the United Kingdom. These were intended to cover all automatic data handling by both government and non-government data 'users', and so are fairly general. But they provide a rough checklist for considering the relationship between a 'data subject' and 'data users'.

The first principle, one of five 'in the interests of data subjects', is that 'data subjects should know what personal data relating to them are handled, why those data are needed, how they will be used, who will use them, for what purpose, and for how long'. The Cortina owner knows that his name and address are in the computer. He is not told, but probably guesses, some of the reasons why they are needed. Depending on the reasons, he may guess (but do no more than that under the present law) how they will be used, who will use them, for what purpose, and for how long. If one of the reasons he is required to supply the information is to assist in recovering stolen automobiles, he will not be surprised to learn that any police officer has access to the name and address of the car's registered keeper. The D.V.L.C. magnetic tape is physically transported to the Police National

Computer every day. He may know roughly, then, how they will be used, who will use them, and for what purpose. He probably has no idea how long the information is used. According to the Lindop Report, the record in the Police National Computer usually contains only the details of the vehicle, name and address of the owner, and (where appropriate) a marker indicating that the vehicle has been stolen. The Cortina owner might hope that the computer would forget part of this if, for example, he has reported the car stolen and then remembered that a friend had borrowed it.

Lindop's second principle is that 'personal data should be handled only to the extent and for the purposes made known when they are obtained, or subsequently authorized'. Under existing law, the subject is not told when he reports his name and address to Swansea that these data are transferred to the Police National Computer.

Lindop's third and fourth principles are that 'personal data handled should be accurate and complete, and relevant and timely for the purpose for which they are used; no more personal data should be handled than are necessary for the purposes made known or authorized'.

If the car owner is conscientious he will have reported his change of address when he moved house. This is relevant and timely for recovering the car if it is stolen, and it is necessary to 'handle' the name and address in order to recover a stolen car. But if the owner happened to read the Lindop Report he might have some questions. He could guess that the police have access to his name and address, but he probably would not think of the Investigation Branch of the Board of Customs and Excise, who have the same access. And he might be slightly uneasy to learn that the record also has 'free text space' in which any police force can record 'additional comments'. He is, let us say, a confirmed vegetarian, but he does not think that it is 'relevant' or 'necessary' for any purpose he knows of to have this recorded along with the description of his car, his name, and his address. He would not be persuaded if it were explained to him that the entry was made because his car was seen parked near a slaughterhouse that mysteriously burned down. He knows from his reading that the Home Office has said that 'occasional information about association with an organization has been held for a limited period on the index when an officer judged it relevant when reporting a vehicle suspected of being used in a crime'.

If he knew, he could explain that he was out of the country at the time of the fire, and is not in sympathy with the radical action faction in his vegetarians' society. But he does not know, and at present has no way, in the words of Lindop's fifth principle, to 'be able to verify compliance' with these principles.

What if our car owner does find out about the entry? Suppose his brother-in-law, a police constable, learns about the entry by asking the Police National Computer one day as a way of learning how the system works. Breaching the Official Secrets Act, the police officer tells his brother-in-law about it. He defends the entry to the angry vegetarian by reciting Lindop's sixth principle: 'Users should be able to handle personal data in the pursuit of their lawful interests or duties to the extent and for the purposes known or authorized without undue cost in money or other resources.' Surely, says the constable, the police should be able to handle such data in pursuit of their duties. All information is accurate, and it is relevant for the purpose of detecting criminals. If the brother-in-law didn't know about this purpose when he sent in his new address, he certainly knew after he read that bit of Lindop. He hasn't been arrested or charged or harmed. Would he want his taxes spent on posting him a copy of the entry?

Besides, says the policeman, Lindop's seventh principle is that 'the community at large should enjoy any benefits, and be protected from any prejudice, which may flow from the handling of personal data'. If the police had to tell registered 'keepers' of vehicles what was entered with their names, the London bombers would never have been traced and caught. Surely that was a benefit to the community at large. Two men died in the slaughterhouse fire, and the vegetarian's car and affiliation were noted in the continuing inquiries to determine who, if anyone, started it. No harm was done by the entry, and the owner wouldn't even have known about it if it had not been for the now-regretted breach of the Official Secrets Act.

The car owner is not happy. But he calms down, and makes some decisions. He will resign from the society, and leave his car in the garage. And he hopes that none of this will affect his chances for that civil service job, even if it does require positive-vetting for the security clearance. Before putting away his copy of Lindop, he glances at the section on another police computer, the Metropolitan Police system for criminal intelligence. He is relieved to learn that it 'will not be connected to any other system'. In any case, it is only concerned with 'crime, criminals, and their associates'. He is not a criminal, and has never associated with any that he knows of. He respects the police, and is rather proud of his brother-in-law. They were quite right not to tell Lindop more about this system, and the Committee was perhaps going a bit far to say that they did not have enough evidence to give a firm assurance to the public (actually, had 'no reason to believe that the public need be unduly alarmed') about all aspects of the use of computers for police purposes. It is only slightly interesting to learn that this system can answer the question 'Which red-haired Irishmen on record drive a white Cortina with MR and 6 in the registration?' He is neither red-haired nor Irish, and his white Cortina's registration has neither M nor R nor 6 in its registration.

Lindop proposed a Data Protection Authority, with broad powers to establish and enforce codes of practice for various kinds of personal data handling. They did not recommend any general right of 'subject access' – for the 'data subject' to see his record – and specifically ruled it out for records kept by the police and security services. They felt that it would cause 'extreme difficulties in the prevention and detection of crime'.

The Committee did not want the comments on the police and security services to be over-emphasized in relation to the whole report. It did propose that a Data Protection Authority should have a senior official with a security clearance who would help the Home Office and the security services to work out rules and safeguards for their systems. And the report noted that the

Swedish Data Inspection Board can inspect all police files to check on their accuracy, and that the Swedish Board had found some convictions which had been wrongly recorded.

The Lindop Committee found some areas in which 'subject access' was the practice, and sometimes even the rule. Civil servants regularly receive the part of their record which is kept in the Personnel Record Information System, although this does not include the 'assessments of ability, performance, and potential'. Although credit reference reports are made by commercial companies rather than a government department, it is worth noting that the Consumer Credit Act 1974 has a provision giving individuals the right to inspect and correct a copy of the file held on them. Students also have the right to a copy of their entry on the Further Education Statistical Record.

The Lindop Committee considered that such subject access was a means to an end rather than an end in itself. The end would be to see that the statutory principles were being complied with. Under some codes of practice such subject access might be appropriate, as in the case of most automated social work records. For that sort of information the Committee dealt rather briskly with the familiar argument that disclosure would inhibit candour. 'If, as B.A.S.W. [the British Association of Social Workers] suggests, it causes a social worker to think twice before placing information on computer, so much the better.'

Much of data protection is not directly related to secrecy or openness in government. The laws in many countries are primarily directed at databanks in the private sector. Also, many of such laws cover only automated records, although some also regulate manual records, and the distinction may soon become practically irrelevant.

But the two do overlap on the question of how open government information about individuals should be. To some extent the values of open government and those of 'data protection' or 'data privacy' conflict. 'Data privacy' is about the individual's right to control the circulation of information about himself or herself, including the information held in government files or computer memories. Usually, this will mean the individual's right to have such information kept secret, at least from the general public.

Attitudes, and the legal rules resulting from them, vary sharply from country to country about the publicity given to information held on individuals by governments. There are even what appear to be paradoxes within particular countries, at least to foreign observers. An overwhelming majority of Britons would object to public disclosure of their income. Yet in Sweden the income taxes paid by nearly everyone are a matter of public record. It is also in Sweden, though, that newspapers have a self-imposed rule (through the Press Council and Press Ombudsman) that the names of accused persons in criminal cases are not usually published, even after they have been convicted.

So the essence of data protection can be, and often is in law, an exception to the principle of open government. Information held by government about a particular person can be kept secret from the general public. In the United States this takes the form of an exemption under the Freedom of Information Act for personal records 'where disclosure would constitute a clearly unwarranted invasion of privacy'.

The two principles coincide, however, on the specific question of 'subject access'. An individual may object strongly to allowing anyone to see what is in his government dossier, but also assert the right to see for himself what is there. This is usually to see if the values represented by Lindop's proposed principles, such as accuracy and relevance, are being observed.

The question of subject access to government dossiers also throws some of the arguments over disclosure generally into sharp relief. The 'candour' issue is made particularly sharp. If disclosure to the public would inhibit an official's 'full and frank discussion' on matters of public policy, what effect would disclosure to the particular subject discussed have? It is quite possible for the same people to take very different stands on such subject access, as in the case of the British National Union of Teachers. They are strongly in favour of teachers having the right to see the files kept on them by their employers, but equally opposed to allowing students and their parents to see school records on the students. The same person is often, to use the terminology of Lindop, both a 'data subject' and 'data user', with the appropriate values for each.

The subject access side of open government is also important because it arouses more intense personal interest. It is understandable that most people will be more interested in the information in a government file about themselves than they are in, say, statistics on air pollution. Interest in disclosure (and in preventing further disclosure) increases with its proximity to one's own interests.

The hypothetical Cortina owner probably would take little interest in statistics on automobiles. But he might be quite curious about what the file on him contains. The Police National Computer holds the information used by government officials, and the Home Office has admitted that information about the affiliations of a registered keeper may be kept if they are considered relevant to a suspected offence. And in two reported instances this has included association with groups such as the Hunt Saboteurs Association and the National Council for Civil Liberties.

Open government laws must deal with the question of personal records kept by governments. They usually do this by exempting from general public disclosure personal information that would constitute an invasion of personal privacy if disclosed. But that cannot be a reason for refusing individuals access to their own files. Such refusal must be justified on other grounds. Exemption of police investigative files can be justified on grounds of efficiency, but this does not preclude some other method of regulation to ensure that principles such as those advocated by Lindop are observed. Exemption of personal files generally on the ground that disclosure would inhibit candour is far more difficult to justify. Candour is not, after all, the supreme value, especially when weighed against the value an individual may place on having his record accurate, and the consequences of inaccuracy. Inhibition of erroneous opinions recorded as facts would not be such a high price to pay.

Personal and Corporate Privacy

The Lindop Committee did not seem to have much trouble in understanding that its terms of reference were limited to information on 'persons' in the usual sense of human beings. But many other committees and many other laws, both here and in other countries, treat information about people and information about companies as being essentially the same. In the comparative literature on data protection it is known as the 'natural person/ legal person' distinction.

There are reasons for protecting some information about companies just as there are reasons for protecting some information about individuals. But the reasons are different, and the rules should be different, simply because companies and people are different. Even though they may be treated the same in law for certain purposes, like making contracts, they are, fundamentally and obviously, not the same.

This difference is particularly important in considering corporate and personal 'privacy'. A brief attempt has already been made to consider why individuals want to keep certain information about themselves more or less to themselves. But almost none of those reasons applies to information about companies. Although companies may have an interest in maintaining a reputation, they are not subject to the sort of mental distress that can be caused to real people by invasions of privacy, breaches of confidence, or unjustified libels. A company's reputation is something which is commercially valuable, of course. Millions of pounds are spent on institutional advertising designed not so much to persuade consumers of a product's merits, but rather to think well of the manufacturer generally.

A company is created under legal rules for the purposes of making goods, providing services, and, of course, making a profit. The law on corporate information should be related to those purposes instead of to the simple assumption that because a company is a 'legal person' information about it should be treated in the same way as information about a real person.

It is surprising how casually this assumption is often made. The Franks Committee made no distinction at all in discussing 'a citizen or firm suffering damage as a result of an unauthorized disclosure of confidential information entrusted to the Government . . .' and its proposals are the same for 'information given to the Government by private individuals or concerns . . .'

The Scottish Law Commission, unlike the Law Commission for England, also considered that 'privacy' included both personal information and 'the expectation of commercial or industrial interests that their information and affairs should be protected from intrusion and disclosure'.

Data protection laws in most countries recognize that the privacy of a natural person is fundamentally different from that of a legal person, and make different provisions for protecting them. The privacy of a corporation is essentially composed of two elements. The first is the desire to plan and decide in private before announcing a decision. Much of this is justified by the same arguments about the need for candour that supposedly justify government secrecy generally, and often the effects of such decisions by a large corporation are very similar to decisions taken by government.

The second is to protect what are commonly known as 'trade secrets'. It should be remembered that patent law already provides considerable protection for many commercial processes. If the processes are sufficiently novel, and if the originators are willing to comply with the statutory procedures, the law effectively protects a monopoly on their use. Other 'trade secrets' are information which either does not qualify for such statutory protection, or which the originators are not willing to submit to the necessary procedures. The law concerning such trade secrets is nothing more than a specific application of the general law of confidence.

The law on exemption of trade secrets in government hands from compulsory disclosure under open government laws is discussed in Chapter 11. Generally, it should aim to avoid giving one company an unfair commercial advantage over another. It should not, as was pointed out by the court in the Hillingdon case (p. 107), amount to handing over the government's 'secret' stamp to a company.

The law on trade secrets generally should recognize that there is commercial information deserving of some legal protection, even if it does not come under patent law. But that law should consider, as the Law Commission has begun to do, that there is a public interest in disclosure to be balanced against commercial secrecy. As large companies behave more and more like the governments with which they are often closely linked, the law should give far greater protection to disclosures, both by requiring them in some instances and by not automatically punishing them when they are made without authorization. It is not just 'iniquity' in commercially confidential dealing which deserves public discussion.

The law at present seems all too ready to treat the management of a large company which affects the lives of thousands directly as if it were a private exchange between two gentlemen about the state of their health. It seems even more stringent when the corporate information is disclosed by a 'servant'. There are, of course, individuals who run businesses themselves, and one can distinguish between information about them in their personal and in their commercial lives. The Consumer Credit Act 1974 makes just such a distinction, between the rights of 'consumers' to see credit reference files on them (section 159) and the more limited rights of 'business consumers' (section 160). But that is about the only part of English law which recognizes the basic difference between personal and commercial privacy in any way at all.

Chapter Eight

Opening Government: the American Way

It took the United States nearly two centuries to enact an open government law. Before then it was generally felt that the best way of achieving what has come to be called freedom of information was to keep the press as free from legal restrictions as possible. This was in keeping with the libertarian notions of the eighteenth and nineteenth centuries, which assumed that government was at best a necessary evil and saw minimal government as an ideal. If legal limits on the press were kept to a minimum the market-place of ideas could be depended upon to provide the information necessary in a democracy. Thomas Jefferson said both 'that government is best which governs least' and that he 'would rather live without government than without newspapers'.

The First Amendment to the U.S. Constitution provides that 'Congress shall make no law abridging the freedom of . . . speech, or of the press', and the Supreme Court has generally interpreted this in ways which seem excessively liberal, if not literal, to most British observers. The American press is not, and never has been, absolutely free. But it is far less subject to legal restrictions than the press in this country. In particular, the law has rarely been able to impose what the Supreme Court calls 'prior restraint'. Whatever constitutionally permissible legal penalties may be imposed for publishing offending information must nearly always come after publication, and are almost never used to stop publication.

The Pentagon Papers case is the furthest the American courts have gone in applying the libertarian philosophy of the First Amendment to unauthorized disclosures of government information. But as a legal method of securing public knowledge of government generally it still has shortcomings. The relative absence of penalties for disclosing information means that 'whistle-blowers' such as Daniel Ellsberg may go public without necessarily going to jail. But this still leaves such disclosures to the conscience or pique of civil servants or government contractors who are sufficiently outraged by what they have been involved in to risk the personal and professional consequences of betraying confidences, although they now have some protection under the 1978 'Whistle-blowers' Act.

A few years earlier Congress had attempted to place disclosure of government information on a more routine basis than just relying on the encouragement of leaks provided by an absence of legal restraints. The 1966 Freedom of Information Act imposed a legal obligation on the federal government to allow public access to most documents in their possession. Although this was the first such federal law, there had been similar attempts in various states. Many of these were also what we would now call 'sunshine' or public-meeting laws, requiring government councils to admit the press and public to most of their meetings.

'Freedom of information' and 'the right to know' are now common catch-phrases, and deserve some consideration of their implications. As Justice (the British section of the International Commission of Jurists) pointed out in their 1978 report, 'freedom of information' is not really an accurate title for the U.S. Act of the same name. 'Freedom' simply requires the absence of restraint, and particularly of legal penalties. A citizen is 'free' to 'receive and impart information' (in the words of the European Convention on Human Rights) if he can do so without fear of punishment. But it does not mean that there is any obligation on government to provide any information to the citizen. A 'right to know', on the other hand, implies that there is a corresponding obligation. If there is a right to know about government, then government has a duty to inform. The Justice committee may perhaps have been engaged in a bit of English sniffiness at American misuse of the language, but the distinction leads to one of the more important arguments on the subject (discussed further in

Chapter 11): if there is a government duty to inform it will cost taxpayers' money. Filing, retrieving, and photocopying documents all require public expenditure, and it is not surprising that governments would rather spend the money on hospitals or aircraft carriers or providing information on how well they are doing than on handing out information that is likely to be used against them.

Despite the imprecision of the title, the U.S. Congress passed the Freedom of Information Act in 1966. It was not the product of massive political pressure or even influence by special interest groups, but the result of a long campaign by Representative Carl Moss of California, who chaired the influential House Committee on Government Operation. Federal law before then had suffered from two basic flaws. The 1946 Administrative Procedure Act made some federal records available, but only to those 'persons properly and directly concerned', and even for them there was no provision for a remedy if they were denied information. The Freedom of Information Act expressly overruled the requirement that those who wanted to see government records should demonstrate their 'need to know'. The right of access to public records was to be a general right of all 'persons' (U.S. citizens, at the very least) rather than the right of someone with a grievance to information that would help his case. The final arbiter of whether documents could be withheld under the exceptions to the Act was to be the judiciary rather than the executive.

The Act contained nine general exceptions. Some of them, such as the provision for withholding records relating to defence or foreign policy or files involving personal privacy are understandable in principle, although subject to considerable argument in application. Others, such as the exception for geological data about wells, are less obvious. The political explanation for the geological exception now seems clear: President Lyndon Johnson, from the oil-rich state of Texas, let the bill's sponsors know that he would use his veto if the exception was not added.

So the exception went through, although the unanimous support in both Houses would have overcome a veto. On 4 July 1966, Johnson signed the Act with a characteristic rhetorical flourish. It went into effect one year later.

It took a while for the Act to have much impact, and for its limitations to be made clear. This was partly because it was enforced and interpreted through appeals in the federal courts. The agencies of the federal government had opposed the legislation, and resisted compliance. They were assisted by a memorandum from the Attorney-General advising them that most of the exemptions from the obligation to make records public could be interpreted fairly broadly.

The agencies quickly developed ways of using the exemptions to frustrate requests for access to records. These included refusals to say whether they had the information requested, and inflating the costs of searching for and copying the records. Clearly exempt records were filed with others to justify refusals to disclose any of them. And delaying tactics were used so that many cases took months or years to reach the courts.

The early cases, like most of those being decided now, would sound strange to those who automatically think that laws such as the Freedom of Information Act are primarily for the benefit of the press. Almost everyone except journalists seemed to be using the Act in attempts to force out records. Historians, companies, individuals, and pressure groups all started to file their lawsuits. They had their successes and their failures in court, and pressure began to build in Congress to strengthen the Act. The political climate in the early 1970s was increasingly favourable to such changes. As the story of Watergate began to emerge public opinion became increasingly suspicious of arguments for secrecy based on the President's need for candid advice and even against claims based on national security. There was a near-constitutional crisis in 1974, when the Supreme Court ruled that the President must hand over the celebrated tapes to the Watergate Special Prosecutor. It was not a Freedom of Information Act case, but a claim of 'executive privilege' (roughly the equivalent of British Crown privilege) to withhold evidence relevant to a legal proceeding, and a criminal prosecution at that.

One effect was that when the 1974 amendments to the Freedom of Information Act reached the President's desk for signature, it was Gerald Ford rather than Richard Nixon who refused to sign, saying that they were 'unconstitutional'. But the amendments became law when two-thirds of both Houses of Congress approved them and overrode the President's veto. The law now in effect is the Act as amended in 1974 and 1976, and as interpreted by the courts. But it is not the only U.S. federal law on government information, and is closely related to other statutes. These are also fairly recent laws, commonly known as the 1974 Privacy Act, the 1972 Federal Advisory Committee Act, the 1976 Government in the Sunshine Act, and the 'Whistle-blowers' (Civil Service Reform) Act of 1978.

These will be described in more detail later, but their essential purposes should be kept in mind when considering the Freedom of Information Act. The Privacy Act regulates the collection and transfer of personal information by federal government agencies. It overlaps the Freedom of Information Act in providing individuals with the right to see most records held on them by federal agencies. The Advisory Committee Act requires government meetings with industry groups to be open. The Government in the Sunshine Act takes its name from a much-quoted observation, by Supreme Court Justice Brandeis, that 'sunshine is the best disinfectant'. It generally says that the governing bodies at the head of many federal agencies must deliberate in public. The Whistle-blowers' Act is designed to protect from administrative retaliation civil servants who disclose 'wrongdoing, waste, or inefficiency'. The Freedom of Information Act has been the basis for hundreds of law suits, particularly since 1974. There is a near-industry devoted to books, newsletters, and conferences monitoring the Act. The principle is simple enough, but the details are complex.

Essentially, the Act says that federal government records must be made public, and that they can only be withheld for reasons provided in the nine exemptions. Equally important as this general rule of disclosure is the provision that the federal courts can order agencies to disclose records if the exemption claimed is not considered to justify secrecy.

The law actually requires three types of disclosure. Rules

followed by agencies (very roughly equivalent to the British A-Codes on supplementary benefits) are to be published in the *Federal Register*. Other records are to be made available in reading rooms and indexed, or to be disclosed on request. Most of the cases have concerned refusals to make requested information public.

The 'agencies' subject to the Act are those in the executive branch of the federal government, including the semi-autonomous regulatory commissions. The law does not cover the judiciary, Congress, or the state governments (although most states now have equivalent laws). The exemptions from the rule of disclosure are in general terms, unlike the much more specific (and more numerous) provisions in the Swedish equivalent. Because of this they cannot really be understood without looking at the court cases interpreting them.

The first exemption is for information which can be kept secret in the interest of defence or foreign relations. But in order to be kept secret the records must have been 'properly classified' in such interests, and the courts have the final word in deciding if classification is proper. This was established by the 1974 amendments to reverse the interpretation made by the Supreme Court in 1973.[1] The case was important for reasons other than the interpretation of the exemption under the 1966 Act. Patsy Mink was a member of the House of Representatives from Hawaii, and she had brought the action with other members of Congress to force disclosure of records on the environmental effects of a proposed nuclear test in the Pacific.

The records were classified, and the Supreme Court held that under the original exemption the classification could not be questioned in court, 'however cynical, myopic, or even corrupt' the classification may have been, in the words of Justice Stewart. The 1974 version of the exemption clearly gives the courts the right to inspect classified records and see if the classification was proper under the law and the current Presidential Executive Order on classification.

The courts themselves have the power to examine the documents privately *in camera* to determine if the classification is still justified, and they can also require considerable preliminary disclosure to attorneys for the person seeking access in order to argue whether the classification is in fact 'proper'. President Carter established a new system for classification (Executive Order 12065) in 1978. This requires classifying officials to consider 'whether the public interest in disclosure outweighs the damage to the national security that might reasonably be expected from disclosure'.

The second exemption is for internal personnel rules and practices of an agency. This has been fairly narrowly interpreted, and the Supreme Court has said that 'exemption 2 is not applicable to matters subject to genuine and significant public interest'.[2] It only protects minor 'housekeeping matters' such as parking facilities and sick leave, and Civil Service Commission reports on inspections of agencies must be made available on request.[3] Instructions to agency staff that would affect a member of the public must be available to the public generally, and the Supreme Court has rejected claims that they are exempt as 'internal' if they have this effect. 'Secret law', said the court, 'is an abomination.'[4] Investigative manuals for tax authorities can be withheld only if 'the sole effect of disclosure would be to enable law violators to escape detection'.[5] The third exemption is for information which has been exempted from disclosure by another statute. Until 1975 it was generally thought that the original Act had implicitly repealed all earlier laws which authorized secrecy. But the Supreme Court decided that year that Congress had intended to delegate authority to withhold information under the other existing statutes, of which there are about a hundred.[6] If that was the original intention, Congress changed it in 1976.

Other secrecy laws can now be used to justify secrecy if they 'leave no discretion' as to whether the records are to be kept secret, or 'establish particular criteria' for such secrecy. This means that individual tax returns are not generally available because of provisions in the tax laws.[7] But a secrecy provision in the Consumer Product Safety Act was no justification for the

Consumer Product Safety Commission to withhold information obtained from the manufacturer when it was requested by an injured consumer. [8]

Some records of the Central Intelligence Agency can be kept secret under this exemption because the National Security Act of 1947 allows the C.I.A. to keep secret information that would reasonably be expected to lead to unauthorized disclosure of intelligence sources and methods. [9]

The fourth exemption is usually described as protection for 'trade secrets'. It exempts information if it qualifies as 'trade secrets and commercial or financial information obtained from a person and privileged or confidential'. It was a vague mess when it was originally passed, and it still is. The courts have begun to sort it out, and they have had the assistance of companies that can afford expensive lawyers' time to argue all possible interpretations, because 'persons' includes such companies.

It has also been the subject of protracted litigation because commercial interests frequently appear on both sides. Companies use the Act to get information in government hands about their competitors. Just about as often, companies have gone to court in attempts to stop disclosure about themselves, in what have come to be called 'reverse Freedom of Information Act' cases.

The law worked out by the American courts under the 'trade secrets' exemption is worth careful consideration, and not just because Congress handed them a sentence that is difficult to parse. The connection between government and commerce is closer than many realize in the modern world, and it does not matter much whether the system in a given country is described as a socialist one or a mixed economy. Professor Finer has commented on the 'closed' relationship between producers, described as more powerful than consumers, and the civil service. [10]

Appropriately, one of the first cases under the Act involved this section, and it was brought by Consumers' Union to get information on comparative tests of hearing aids by the Veterans' Administration. [11] And the latest interpretation by the Supreme Court concerned somewhat similar issues, although it was in a 'reverse F.O.I.A.' action brought by Chrysler to stop disclosure of reports they had submitted on employment of minorities.

First of all, it is clear that this exemption only applies to information obtained from a 'person' outside government. But the information is not protected just because there is a government promise of confidentiality or an expectation of confidentiality. Instead, according to the federal Court of Appeals in the District of Columbia, the test involves two possible questions. Commercial or financial information is protected if disclosure would be likely to (1) impair the ability of the government to obtain similar information in future, or (2) cause substantial harm to the competitive position of the person from whom it was obtained. [12]

Chrysler lost, finally, and the information which the company was required as a contractor to furnish the Department of Defense under civil rights legislation was released. [13] The Supreme Court said again that the Freedom of Information Act exemptions were not mandatory. In other words, they might justify secrecy, but they did not require it. They also decided that the U.S. 'trade secrets' statute, which makes it a crime for federal employees to leak trade secrets, did not give Chrysler any right to stop disclosure of the information in a civil law suit. After the decision it was announced by the Department of Justice that federal employees would not be prosecuted under the criminal statute for disclosing such information under the Freedom of Information Act.

The fifth exemption has been argued over about as much as the one for 'trade secrets'. It protects internal government communications if they are 'deliberative'. The words of the Act are: 'inter-agency or intra-agency memoranda that are not available at law'. An English lawyer reading this might guess that it incorporates the ordinary law on what evidence the government can be compelled to produce in an ordinary law suit, very much like the House of Lords ruling in the 1979 *Waugh* case (see p. 105). In other words, if you couldn't get the document as evidence to use in an ordinary suit for damages, then you can't get it under the Freedom of Information Act.

The guess would be roughly right, but only roughly. The

exemption is important because it is the American attempt to deal with the common argument that disclosure of confidential advice would impair efficiency. To begin with, the exemption does not protect essentially factual material, such as statistics or laboratory studies. Also, the exemption will only protect documents containing confidential advice before a decision is taken. After the decision the advice must be made public on request. This is very similar to the similar provision in Swedish law, under which 'working papers' can be kept secret until the decision based on them is made (see Chapter 9). In a 1975 decision, the U.S. Supreme Court turned the 'candour' argument on its head, and suggested that later release of such 'pre-decisional' advice might actually encourage advisers to submit their recommendations. The advisers might be given credit if the agency relied on their advice.[14]

So the exemption only protects advice given before a decision based on the advice is taken. The latest decision of the Supreme Court rejected a request for policy directives about the sale and purchase of government securities.[15] The directives were released every month, but someone wanted them earlier. The court decided that they should not be released then because of the value of confidential advice in such matters, which they said was similar to the attorney–client privilege and executive privilege.

The sixth exemption protects personal information from general release if it would be a clearly unwarranted invasion of personal privacy. This does not mean that agencies can refuse an individual's access to the files on himself simply by saying that it would be an invasion of his privacy. It does mean that summaries of Air Force Academy ethics hearings would not be released, even with the names deleted.[16]

The exemption is the only one in which the reason for seeking the information is important. Otherwise, it is an essential principle of the Act that the right of access to government records is everyone's right, and that the purpose of the request is irrelevant. Because of the 'clearly unwarranted invasion of privacy' language, the courts balance the interests in getting the information against the interests in protecting personal privacy.

For example, they have refused to order disclosure of people who had registered their home-brewing activities with the tax authorities, as required by law, to a maker of wine-making kits who wanted to send them all invitations to try his product. [17]

The seventh exemption protects 'investigatory records compiled for law enforcement purposes'. This was heavily amended in 1974, partly because the Federal Bureau of Investigation had claimed that the earlier version protected nearly everything that they did, including their harassment of various political groups. Law enforcement files are now protected only if disclosure would cause any of six types of damage.

The six types of harm are: interference with enforcement proceedings (which justifies keeping investigations secret while they are 'active', but not after they are closed); depriving a person of a fair trial; unwarranted invasion of personal privacy (essentially a repetition of the preceding exemption); prejudicing confidential sources and information (only in criminal or national security investigations); disclosing investigative techniques; and endangering the safety of law enforcement personnel.

The most important case under this section held that a company which the National Labor Relations Board had accused of unfair labour practices could not see the statements of potential witnesses before the hearing. [18] The Supreme Court decided that release of such records before the hearing would create too much of a risk that there might be attempts at coercion or intimidation. The identity of confidential informants in criminal or national security investigations can be withheld, as can any information which might 'possibly threaten the safety of those involved'. [19]

The interpretation of this section is at the heart of a continuing campaign by the F.B.I. to have it changed. Congress has commissioned reports on its effect by the Comptroller General and the General Accounting Office, but they have not been particularly conclusive. It is clear that the F.B.I. resents the effect of both the Freedom of Information Act and the Privacy Act, and is more than willing to give accounts of anonymous informants who no longer inform because they fear disclosure. The examples remain anonymous, for reasons which seem quite plausible.

But they must be weighed against the documented malpractices of the F.B.I. in the recent past, which would never have been revealed if it had not been for a lawsuit under the Freedom of Information Act.[20]

The eighth exemption broadly protects records relating to the supervision of banks and other financial institutions. There were no cases interpreting it until fairly recently. Its use to withhold records relating to the enforcement of the Truth in Lending Act was upheld in 1978.[21]

The ninth, and last, exemption protects information about petroleum. Its inclusion at President Johnson's insistence has been described, and it has hardly been interpreted at all. The only reported case, which involved data furnished by natural gas companies to the Federal Power Commission, was simply sent back to the F.P.C. with instructions to think a bit more about the possibility of disclosure.[22]

The Privacy Act

This Act gives individuals the right to see dossiers kept on them by the federal government, which is one of the things that the Freedom of Information Act also does. Although the two laws both establish similar rights, they also do rather different things as well. The Freedom of Information Act gives the right to see many more records than just your own, and the Privacy Act also lays down a set of rules about the collection of information on individuals.

Although the two Acts overlap, they do not quite mesh, and it is a common complaint that Congress should have thought a little harder in 1974 when amending the Freedom of Information Act and passing the Privacy Act (although the Privacy Protection Commission decided in 1974 that they reinforced each other). To be on the safe side, requests to see personal files are usually made under both Acts in order to take advantage of the favourable provisions of each.

The F.O.I. Act covers all federal agencies, but the Privacy Act has two general exemptions that effectively protect all of the records of the Central Intelligence Agency, and many of the records of the F.B.I. and other criminal law enforcement agencies. One of the more important provisions of the Privacy Act is that it not only gives one the right to see one's file, but also to have it corrected. This right of correction is not included in the Freedom of Information Act. So in some cases of personal files held by a law enforcement agency, it might be possible to get a copy under the F.O.I. Act, but not to have it corrected under the Privacy Act.

The Privacy Act has not generated the same flood of lawsuits as the F.O.I. Act, partly because requests to see personal files usually go to court under the more generous provisions of the older of the two laws. As a result, there is very little judicial interpretation of the Privacy Act, leaving the bare words of the statute to tell what it means.

The Privacy Act is really a 'data protection' act. That is, it regulates the collection of information about individuals. It is different from most of the data protection laws that have been sprouting throughout western Europe in recent years in two important ways. It applies only to the federal government, and does not regulate commercial databanks (although these are subject to some other statutes). But it covers both manual and automatically processed records, unlike many of the laws in other countries which are directed at computer databanks.

It only gives individuals the right to see and correct records kept on them by federal government agencies. 'Corporate privacy' is largely a matter of the 'trade secrets' provision of the Freedom of Information Act. Also, in a bit of chauvinism, the statute only gives rights to U.S. citizens or aliens who are permanent residents. This contrasts with the F.O.I. Act, which apparently can be, and is, used by anyone from anywhere.

The Privacy Act also has a slightly restricted definition of records which fits its purpose. It only applies to a 'system of records' under which information about an individual can be retrieved. In other words, if an agency can get the information about an individual out of its files by using his name or some other information about him, he will generally have the right to see it too. If they can't, he can't.

Apart from the basic right of personal access, the Act mostly restricts agencies in collecting information about individuals and in passing it on to others inside the government or out of it. In asking individuals for information about themselves agencies must generally tell them what the government wants it for, and what will happen if it is not provided.

Government departments are not supposed to pass such information on to anyone else without the individual's consent, but there are a number of exceptions to this. Even if consent is not required before releasing the information to, for example, another government department, there must be a written record of such release.

The Act is enforced, like the Freedom of Information Act, through the federal courts. Individuals can sue to enforce any of the Act's requirements, such as the right to see and correct records, and they can also recover damages if they can show that they have been injured in some way by the agency's actions. Fines can also be imposed for failures to comply with the Act.

So far, there have been almost no significant legal cases reported under the Privacy Act. My own experience may give some idea of how the Act works, and its relationship with the Freedom of Information Act. Two requests were sent, both of which were accompanied by proof of identity. The first went to the F.B.I., which replied fairly quickly that they had no records under my name. The second went to the Department of Defense because there had been a security investigation which amounted to positive-vetting in connection with access to classified crypto-graphic material during military service. The reply, which came within a few weeks, was a bundle of photocopies (for which there could legally have been a copying charge). These were mostly reports of inquiries made by security agents in various corners of the United States. Only the names of the people interviewed had been deleted, as allowed under both the Privacy and Freedom of Information Acts. There was also a note, as required by the Privacy Act, that the file had been disclosed to the Civil Service Commission in connection with employment as a temporary civil servant. The reports were accurate about facts, and fair enough comment for the rest. It hardly seemed justifiable to file a statement of disagreement, let alone to demand any correction.

Other Legislation

The Federal Advisory Committee Act was the first federal open meetings act, passed in 1972. It was an attempt by Congress to open up the closed consultative system covering meetings between regulatory agencies and regulated industries.

Many meetings remain closed because of the interpretations that have been given to the exemptions under the Act. Notice of such committee meetings must be published in the *Federal Register*, and there are record-keeping requirements about minutes, conclusions, and reports considered. But the few cases which were taken to court resulted in fairly broad readings of the exemptions, and the Act was amended in 1976 to be as close as possible to the similar provisions of the Government in the Sunshine Act which was passed that year.

The Government in the Sunshine Act was passed in 1976 and went into effect in 1977. It only applies to agencies headed by a 'collegial' body of two or more members, most of whom are appointed by the President. There are more of these in the U.S. than in Britain, and they are designed to be relatively independent from direction by the President. They include over fifty bodies such as the Federal Trade Commission and the Securities and Exchange Commission, with a variety of regulatory, licensing, and quasi-judicial functions.

The Act generally requires that meetings of such bodies must be open to the public if they result in disposition of official agency matters. Meetings may be closed by a vote of the members citing one of the ten statutory reasons for private meetings, most of which are taken directly from the exemptions under the Freedom of Information Act.

Even if meetings are closed, the Act requires records to be kept. These are usually transcripts or recordings, although minutes may be kept in some cases. Such transcripts or minutes are records under the F.O.I. Act, and may later be the subject of disclosure requirements under that Act.

The Sunshine Act is still fairly new, and its application will depend on how the courts interpret the exemptions. Some fairly simple questions must still be answered, such as whether there is a right to photograph or record an open meeting. The Act does not say, and several agencies have adopted regulations limiting the use of sound recorders.

The 'Whistle-blowers' (Civil Service Reform) Act was passed in 1978. It is designed to protect civil servants from administrative retaliation if they disclose government wrongdoing or malpractice. The Act describes this as information which the employee reasonably believes shows 'a violation of any law, rule, or regulation' or 'mismanagement, a gross waste of funds, an abuse of authority, or a substantial and specific danger to public health or safety'.

Civil servants are not protected if the information they leak is specifically protected by law or required by Executive Order to be kept secret in the interest of national defence or foreign affairs. Otherwise the law prohibits action taken against them, including reduction in rank or transfers.

The enforcement system is different from those in the other U.S. open government laws. Instead of relying on individual legal actions, the law establishes a sort of 'ombudsman' in the Office of Special Counsel. The Special Counsel is appointed by the President with the Senate's approval, and serves a five-year term. The Office has considerable power under the Act, and can stop retaliatory government action against an employee, require agencies to respond to allegations, and initiate disciplinary action against officials who abuse their power in attempts at retaliation.

The 'whistle-blower' is not only protected when releasing information to the general public or to Congress. The Act also protects such disclosures if they are made to the Office of Special Counsel or to inspectors-general within government agencies.

The Act was passed after a series of incidents, many of them involving disclosures to Congressional committees, in which civil servants were later disciplined or transferred. One of the best-known was the case of a civil servant who was effectively demoted after telling Congress about the huge cost overruns in production of the C-5A aircraft for the Department of Defense.

Lessons from America

There have been three official British government missions to the United States to consider the Freedom of Information and Privacy Acts, as well as countless trips by journalists, academics, and pressure group activists. They have returned with impressions as varied as their backgrounds and interests. Some of the non-government researchers have come back with information which they could not get in this country, occasionally even getting British government records kept secret here.

The first official trip was made by the chairman of the Franks Committee, who concluded that government in the U.S. was not markedly more open than in Britain, whatever the legal differences. The others were made in 1975, when the then Home Secretary, Roy Jenkins, went to Washington with his political adviser, and in 1978, by two Civil Service Department officials. All that we know of Mr Jenkins's evaluation is in his 1975 Granada Guildhall lecture, and his decision not to introduce legislation similar to the Freedom of Information Act. The Civil Service Department visit was to carry out the study of open government overseas promised in the July 1978 White Paper on section 2 of the Official Secrets Act.

The Civil Service Department inquiry is worth considering in particular, if only because its results were published in April 1978, along with reports on law and practice in eight other countries. It is, in its own way, an example of open government, being released as a background paper to the Labour Government's Green Paper on such legislation. [23]

The report is generally accurate about the terms of the statutes considered. It is balanced in its presentation, but leaves little doubt that the visitors were less than convinced that Britain needed anything similar.

They attempted to determine who actually used the F.O.I. and

Privacy Acts and divided the searchers for information into five groups: individuals, corporations, public interest groups, the media, and foreign governments. But it is difficult to say who uses the laws most. The number of applications can be misleading because a single request, as for information about the Rosenberg case, can result in the release of over 150,000 pages. Also, the very basis of the F.O.I. Act makes it difficult to discover who is the real recipient of the information, and why.

The identities of the major users also vary from agency to agency, and have changed since the F.O.I. Act went into effect in 1967. The individuals seeking access to F.B.I. files include a mixed bag of prisoners, attorneys, academic researchers, journalists, and F.B.I. employees. The State Department found that up to 75 per cent of their workload on requests was, at times, on inquiries from historians. Corporations are said to account for most of the requests to the Food and Drug Administration and the Federal Trade Commission. Public interest pressure groups account for most of the information released by agencies such as the Nuclear Regulatory Commission. Although the press is not a major user, at least in the sense of making formal requests, it accounts for 20 per cent of the Nuclear Regulatory Commission requests.

The C.S.D. team was particularly interested in finding out how much the laws had cost. Their candid report is that nobody really knows, despite all the studies which have been made. The agencies, who are not fond of the legislation, reported that their costs regularly ran into millions of dollars. But the General Accounting Office, a subsidiary of Congress roughly equivalent to the Comptroller and Auditor General in Britain, concluded in June 1978 that many of the estimates were exaggerated. This report was not quoted by the C.S.D. visitors, although they did report one conclusion, from the Privacy Protection Study Commission, that some estimates had been high. In 1974 the Office of Management and Budget estimated that the Privacy Act would cost $100 million to begin, and $200–300 million per year for the first five years. Three years later the O.M.B. estimated that the actual start-up cost had been only about $29.5 million, with $36.6 million spent the first year.

Faced with such gross discrepancies, the C.S.D. study properly concludes that 'there will always be argument about the costs . . . and it seems unlikely that any more reliable estimates can be discovered'. When asked by the Minister of State for estimates of what similar British legislation would cost, a C.S.D. accountant replied that it depends on what the law requires, and it depends on how expenses are allocated. It is possible to increase the costs by including the expense of keeping and reviewing records, particularly if a law has retroactive effect, as the U.S. statutes do.

Turning from financial costs of the U.S. laws to other costs and benefits, the C.S.D. report shows that impressions depend even more on who is quoted. In its balanced way, the report gave about three times as much space to those who think the laws have been a bad thing to those who are in favour of them. After three paragraphs on the amount of time required, the concern of other countries and foreign companies about maintaining secrecy, and the F.B.I.'s well-known objections, there was one paragraph from the academics and lawyers favouring the Acts, whose 'views are illustrative of a general preoccupation in American society about openness . . . as well as a concern to know more about the policies and working of the government machine'.

Whether one sees the American experience as a praiseworthy experiment to be followed or as an aberration to be avoided depends very roughly on the observer's proximity to power. Even those who are most wholeheartedly in favour of open government can learn from the U.S. laws, however. Some of the problems in definition of national defence information, commercial confidentiality, and the relationship of disclosure laws to other secrecy statutes, for example, should have been foreseen by Congress in 1966. More accurately, many of them were foreseen, but were left to the courts for resolution. Also, some sort of 'small claims' enforcement procedure along the lines of appeals to the Ombudsman in Sweden might help in the administration of the Acts. But ultimately the evaluation of U.S. experience depends on whether one approves or disapproves of the results in particular cases, such as the release of letters warning about health violations sent to meat processors, reports on employment of minorities, reports on standards in nursing homes, lists of insecticides containing vinyl chloride and animal test data on an injectible contraceptive. [24]

Chapter Nine

The Scandinavian Way, and Other Efforts

'Why' (variously attributed to Lord Hailsham and Sir Keith Joseph) 'must it *always* be Sweden?' Whatever the subject, from auto safety to public administration, the Swedes always seem to be suggesting in their reserved way that other countries might benefit from their experience.

Sweden's open government system was established by the Freedom of the Press Act, which is part of the Constitution, in 1766. It was suspended during the absolutist reign of Gustav III, but restored in 1809. One illustration of how it works in its modern form was the case of John Stonehouse's letter to the Swedish Prime Minister in 1975. Stonehouse sought a way out of his troubles by asking for political asylum, and the letter was, like a large part of the Prime Minister's post, available for public inspection.

It was enough to prompt British head-shaking at this curious way of conducting the business of government. In a 1958 article Professor Nils Herlitz described a similar reaction to his attempts at explaining the Swedish open government system to foreigners. 'Whilst [the listener] shows the courtesy not to make any observations, it is obvious that he ponders a question. Is this man unable to express himself intelligibly in my language, so that I have misunderstood him? Or is he mad?' [1]

Not everyone is impressed, favourably or unfavourably, with the openness of Swedish government, though. The Franks Committee considered overseas law and experience in their 1972 report on section 2 of the Official Secrets Act, and found no 'support to the stark contrast, drawn by a few witnesses, between an obsessively secret system in this country and gloriously open systems in some other countries'. Presumably it was Lord Franks himself who included a similar comment in the Report of the Radcliffe Committee of Privy Councillors on Ministerial Memoirs in 1976. The report remarked that the 'wide-spread impression . . . that there prevails in Sweden an exceptional liberality of access for the inquirer . . . does not appear to be borne out by the facts'. [2]

The particular fact of the Stonehouse letter does show that there are at least some differences between law and practice in Sweden and in the United Kingdom, although it is hardly the most typical or the most important kind of example. If a Swedish Stonehouse wrote to the British Prime Minister it would be highly unlikely that the letter would be disclosed to the public. If it were, the disclosure would either be an illegal leak or an authorized discretionary disclosure.

But Lord Franks was right to observe that Swedish government is not entirely open. It may even appear to require extensive secrecy if one only looks at the provisions of the Secrecy Act. This is partly because of one fundamental difference between the Swedish and U.S. statutes in defining the kinds of records that are not available for public inspection. The Swedish exemptions are much more detailed than the U.S. ones. The U.S. law (see Chapter 8) relies largely on nine general provisions which may justify withholding records, leaving it up to the courts to interpret them in particular cases. The U.S. exemption which approaches the Swedish system is the provision for keeping documents secret when it is required by other statutes (of which there are about a hundred). Even that American exemption has been heavily qualified since 1976 (see p. 133).

The Swedish Freedom of the Press Act has only seven general exemption clauses (the last being a curious one for 'the protection of species of animals and plants'), but it also incorporates the highly detailed provisions of the Secrecy Act.

There is another fundamental difference between the U.S. and Swedish system which must be understood. Under American law, government information effectively falls into one of three general categories. Most government records must be made available on request. At the other extreme is information, mostly concerning national defence and some personal records, which is protected against disclosure by criminal penalties. In the middle is information which can be disclosed either by government discretion, or even leaked without criminal penalties.

Swedish law is, at first glance at least, simpler. There are only two categories of information: that in records open for public inspection, and that protected by the criminal law. But another provision of Swedish law allows for a great deal of leaking in practice. The Swedish Constitution provides what Americans would call a 'shield law' for journalists' sources. It is usually impossible for the government to prosecute, or even discover the identity of, a civil servant who leaks information to the press.

This is closely related to two essential provisions of the Freedom of the Press Act. The first is that only one person is legally responsible for what is published, usually the editor of a newspaper or the author of a book. The other is that a special kind of 'jury'* trial is required in legal actions under the Freedom of the Press Act.

Although the basic principles of the Swedish system are simple enough, the law is extremely complicated in important details. It is made more so by the new Secrecy Act, effective 1 January 1981, which even Swedish lawyers find somewhat difficult to interpret.

The general trend of the law recently has been to expand the scope of secrecy, and specifically to tighten up on unauthorized leaks by civil servants. This has been at least partly because of a leak about national security information in 1973. The leak led to a successful espionage prosecution in the case known as the 'I.B. Affair', and it aroused considerable political and legal controversy.

In considering the case it must be remembered that it did not involve legal questions under the public records system. The issue was not what information the government must make

---

* 'Jury' must be in inverted commas because such a body is very different from common law juries. The jury members are elected (by proportional representation) in their areas.

public under law, but what information could be made public by a civil servant without his going to gaol.

We are, in short, in whistle-blower land. The informant, Håkan Isacsson, did go to gaol, and so did two journalists. The case was roughly similar to the prosecution of Daniel Ellsberg in the U.S. for leaking the Pentagon Papers, the ABC case in Britain, and the *Ny Tid* prosecution in Norway. All three cases raised the same basic question under three similar laws: is it espionage to disclose information to a journalist in your own country rather than to a foreign power?

The I.B. trial was about the leaking of national security information, and is relevant for two reasons. The new secrecy law, which affects the public records system in Sweden, was at least partly prompted by the case. More immediately, some of the information related directly to the United Kingdom.

The information was about one of Sweden's security services, the 'I.B.' or 'Information Bureau'. Before 1973 I.B. had a record (or rather did not have a record) to make even the British security services envious: its very existence was unknown to the Swedish public and to the Parliament. Two journalists, Peter Bratt and Jan Guillou, found out about it and prepared a series of articles which were published in a journal called *Folket i Bild – Kulturfront*.

The articles gave detailed information about I.B. including the names of I.B. officials and addresses of I.B. offices. They also included information about cooperation between I.B. and the security services of other countries such as the U.S., the United Kingdom, and Israel. This was said to include assisting Israeli agents who broke into the Egyptian embassy in Stockholm.

Bratt also wrote a book with more detailed information on the organization.[3] The section on relations between I.B. and M.I.6 described several examples of cooperation between the security services. M.I.6 provided I.B. with a fortnightly summary of information gathered by the British, such as detailed reports on economic conditions in China. It also furnished I.B. with information about Swedes travelling to China from Hong Kong every month. In exchange I.B. replied to inquiries from M.I.6. These were not limited to British matters, and included reports on

Commonwealth citizens in Sweden from countries such as
Kenya, Nigeria, and Australia. There was also said to have been
a joint operation to burgle the South African Legation in
Stockholm. I.B. planned the operation for M.I.6, kept watch, and
even provided a key made by a lock expert working for the
Swedish secret police (Säkerhets Polis). Despite the prosecutions
there was no attempt by the government to suppress the book,
which was still available in bookstores two years later.

The journalists took legal advice before publishing, and were
told that charges might be brought against them under the
Freedom of the Press Act. But they felt that the information
justified the risk and went ahead. In particular they thought that
I.B. had shown political partiality by compiling files on left-wing
groups in Sweden, and that its cooperation with other security
forces had violated Sweden's neutrality.

It was clear that they could have been charged under the
Freedom of the Press Act, which then provided for offences
embracing 'publication of secret documents or the disclosure of
information which may threaten national security . . .'[4] But
under the Act they would have been entitled to a jury trial.
Also, only the editor could have been charged (or Bratt as author
of the book), and it would have been difficult to discover their
sources.

Instead they were charged under the espionage section of the
penal code. This provided for prosecution of 'a person, who,
with the intent of aiding a foreign power, without authorization,
obtains, transmits, gives, or otherwise reveals information . . . the
disclosure of which to a foreign power can bring harm to the
defence of the Realm'. The section also applied to 'a person, with
the intent just mentioned, [who] without authorization produces
or is concerned with a writing, drawing or other object containing
such information'. Section 23:4 further penalized 'anyone who
furthered it by advice or deed'. Anyone who 'induced another'
could be charged with 'instigation' or 'being an accessory'.

They were tried *in camera* and convicted. Guillou appealed, but
only succeeded in getting his sentence reduced from one year to
ten months. The Court of Appeal affirmed that they were

considered to have an implied intent to aid a foreign power under the espionage law. It also ruled that Guillou's crime was not so much in publication of the articles but in gathering the information for them. [5]

The verdicts were widely criticized. Justice Gustav Petrén, of the Supreme Administrative Court, said that the espionage statute was too vague. [6] The Press Ombudsman, an officer of the non-governmental Press Council, was critical of the identification of sources and the police search of the magazine's offices. [7]

One result was the establishment of a Royal Commission to consider changes to the Press Act. Their proposals were approved by two successive Parliaments with an intervening general election, as required for amendments to the Swedish Constitution. The anonymity of journalists' sources is now subject to three exceptions: (1) offences against the security of the State, such as espionage; (2) intentional handing over of a secret document; and (3) violation of a duty not to divulge information as provided for by another Act.

The I.B. affair was not the only reason for this change. The Swedish Constitution was in the process of being amended during the 1970s, and one effect was to make civil servants more free to divulge information than they had been thought to be under the old constitution. As a Ministry of Justice memorandum explains, prior to 1974 it was generally considered that civil servants had a duty of secrecy not only if there was a law specifically barring them from disclosing certain information, but even if there was no specific statute. The 1974 Constitution effectively made them more free to leak. They only had a legal obligation to keep information secret if there was a specific statute barring certain kinds of disclosure. The 1980 Secrecy Act, together with the 1976 amendments to the Constitution on identifying sources, tightens up the law on civil servants who divulge information in those documents which are to be kept secret. Effectively the law now provides for three kinds of government information. Most government documents are available for public inspection. If the documents are not open to the public, civil servants are still free to talk about their contents and be protected, especially by the rule on anonymity of sources. The exception to this freedom is in the third category of documents which are not to be given out or talked about.

Apart from this important restriction, the new Act does not go much further than the old one in specifying the kinds of information to be kept secret. There are some extensions, such as a provision for the secrecy of information held by school authorities. One important question remains to be answered. Information about corporations and individuals involved in public administration is generally not covered by the Act (although the Data Protection Act restricts computer-stored information on individuals). This involves the question of what commercial secrets should be protected by law, which is now being considered by yet another government committee.

The Act does specify time limits on disclosure of official documents. These are maximum periods, and documents may be made public earlier if there is no more danger to personal privacy. Documents containing personal information can be withheld for as long as seventy years, and documents with economic information can be withheld for twenty.

The equivalent of British 'Crown privilege' in legal cases is sharply restricted. Even if documents (and their contents) are protected from disclosure to the general public, they must usually be disclosed to the parties if they are relevant to a legal case or an administrative proceeding.

Sweden was one of the first countries to legislate in the field of data protection, preceded only by the fairly limited law passed by the German state of Hessen in 1970. In 1973 Sweden passed a comprehensive Data Act, which regulates all computerized files containing personal information, whether they are maintained by government or private bodies. Part of the public concern that produced the law came during the 1970 census.

The Act is enforced by an independent Data Inspection Board, and one of the basic requirements is that the D.I.B. must grant a licence for any automated system of personal files. Another basic requirement of the law is a broad right of personal access. Generally, any individual has the right to know what is in the computerized file kept on him, as well as a right to make sure that the information is correct and complete.

The Credit Information Act of 1974 and the Debt Recovery Act of the same year have similar provisions. The subject access provisions are very like those in the British Consumer Credit Act 1974. The Lindop Committee was fairly impressed by the Swedish legislation on data protection, although their recommendations were not quite so stringent on the sensitive subject of 'subject access', which is just where open government and data protection coincide.

Other Scandinavian countries have followed Sweden's example in both government information and data protection, although their open government statutes are much weaker. Finland was first, in 1951, with a public information law which is similar to Sweden's but different in two important ways. The first is that it is not a part of the constitution, and can be changed as easily as any other law. The second, far more important, is the method of specifying exemptions. Finland anticipated the U.S. law by giving a few general reasons to justify secrecy rather than the detailed provisions of the Swedish Secrecy Act. The law was not much used, and was thought by many to be too restrictive.

Norway took its time about imitating the open government system of Sweden (with which it was united until 1905). The law was finally passed in 1970, but only after a series of commissions and political battles somewhat like those in Britain. The battles started inside a commission on public administration set up in 1951. Its recommendations were unanimous when it reported in 1958, except for the open government proposal, which a majority approved in principle.

In the first half of the 1960s the Labour Government was criticized by opposition parties for secrecy, and responded by appointing another commission on the subject. This commission report in 1967 was unanimously against the idea of a disclosure law, but submitted a draft bill just in case. By that time Labour were out of office and free to criticize their opponents for secrecy. A bill was finally introduced and passed, but with no specific date for it to come into force. Labour had pushed for such a definite date, and could not back down when they gained office in 1971. So the law took effect that year.

The process ensured that all of the arguments had been heard several times before the law was finally passed. The fact that the bill was drafted by a committee which thought that it was a bad idea in the first place may account for some of its limitations. The Justice Department issued a memorandum interpreting the Act restrictively (rather like the first memorandum issued by the U.S. Attorney-General), including a comment that records could be denied to 'the mentally ill, inebriates, small children, rowdies, and slanderers'. [8]

There was already an Administrative Procedure Act, passed in 1967, which provided a kind of access to records. But it was limited to those who had some particular interest in proceedings. In other words, there was a 'need to know' test. Institutions that would be affected by a regulation had a right to be consulted on it, and individuals who were the subjects of a particular decision had fairly wide rights of access to relevant documents. This is very like both a similar provision in Swedish law and the U.S. Administrative Procedure Act of 1946 (before it was amended by the 1966 Freedom of Information Act).

The Norwegian law is more like the U.S. statute than the Swedish one in some ways. The exemptions are in very general terms, even more so than the U.S. equivalents. There is a massive loophole in sections 4 and 11, which permit the government to exempt classes of documents by decree. Also, section 4 permits administrative agencies to refuse access to documents if they would give an 'obviously misleading picture of the case'.

There are some other similarities between the U.S. and Norwegian laws. Both provide, in effect, for a large class of documents which can be disclosed by administrative discretion. The authorities are not required to make them available, but equally are not required to keep them secret. Another problem common to both laws is that members of the public must specify what document they want to see. At first, under both systems, it was difficult to know if the document existed, let alone what it was called, in order to ask for it. But both countries have gone some way towards remedying this by requiring lists and registers of documents to be made available. In one very important way the Norwegian and U.S. laws are different: the Norwegian law did not apply to any documents prepared before the law went into effect.

Norway, like Sweden and the U.S., has also adopted a separate law on 'data privacy'. So there are really three Norwegian laws under which an individual can get access to government documents. A 'party' to a case can get access to records under the Administrative Procedure Act; a 'data subject' can often see a file on him under the Data Protection Act 1978; and a member of the public can satisfy his curiosity (sometimes) under the Law on Publicity in Information.

Norwegian law on privacy has an even more detailed history than in Sweden. One possible reason for their delay in legislation (compared to Sweden) was that there was already a fair amount of law on the subject made by both the Parliament (Storting) and the courts. Violation of 'the peace of private life' had been a crime since 1899. In 1977 the Supreme Court held that a patient had a right to see hospital records whether or not he wanted to use the records in a malpractice suit (he could easily have got the records by actually filing the lawsuit first). [9]

After several commissions, committees, and fierce parliamentary battles, the Privacy Act (Personal Registers Act) became law in 1978, although its effective date was left open. As data protection laws go, it is one of the more sweeping ones. It covers personal information held both by government and by private companies. Although it is generally directed at computer databanks, it also applies to manual personal files held by government. And 'person', unlike the definition in the laws of several other countries, includes both people and companies. Limits are placed on the kinds of information collected, so that the list of people considered political 'radicals', kept by an Oslo bank and circulated to its clients, would be illegal. The law also establishes a near-absolute right of 'subject access' to files. This right is subject to exceptions: if disclosure would be dangerous to the subject's mental or physical health, and for statistical information which is not easily retrieved on an individual basis.

The new law is enforced by an independent Data Surveillance Service, and requires licensing of all personal registers by the D.S.S. The regulatory system is one of the broadest among data protection laws, but its effectiveness will be determined as much by the application as by the terms of the law.

Norway has also had its own version of the I.B. case in Sweden. In 1979 journalists connected with *Ny Tid*, a left-wing newspaper, were collecting information about police and security service surveillance. Unlike *FIB-Kulturfront* in Sweden, and more like the ABC defendants in Britain, they had not published anything when the police moved in. They were convicted, and the convictions were upheld by the Court of Appeal. Most of the information had been collected using what can be called the 'Campbell technique' (the C in ABC) of putting together bits from public sources. The appeal court held, just as the Swedish appeal court held in the I.B. case, that the very collecting of information was an offence against national security.

The Danish open government law (Law on Publicity in Administration) was passed in 1970 after a series of arguments in commissions and in parliament that were nearly as hard-fought as those in Norway. As in Norway, the result was much weaker than the Swedish model.

Denmark may be particularly relevant to the United Kingdom because its system of parliamentary democracy is very like that of Westminster. It does not follow the Swedish system of separating ministries as small planning bodies from large quasi-autonomous executive agencies.

Denmark started on the road to legislation, like Norway, with a government commission. They very nearly stopped there when the commission voted against such a law. The 1953 Constitution made no provision for public access to records. In 1957 another commission was appointed, and when they reported in 1963 they also recommended against legislation. But they included a draft bill anyway.

The Danish road towards a right of general access began, as the Norwegian, with a law giving parties to administrative cases the right to see relevant documents. [10] Much as in Norway, opposition parties urged a general disclosure law on the Social Democratic government, and introduced a bill in 1967. When the Social Democrats lost power in 1968, their opponents introduced such a bill (with some Social Democratic support). It was passed and became law in 1970. Its terms are even more restrictive than those in Norway. In particular, anyone requesting documents must identify them, and he will not even have the assistance of indices (as he does to some extent in Norway) to help him. The exemptions are very generally drawn, with the broadest being one which allows secrecy if it is 'required by the special character of the circumstances'. [11] The same section also allows the government to make final decisions about secrecy in designated areas.

The enforcement of the law is left largely to the Ombudsman, an office first established by the 1953 Constitution. In theory appeals to the courts could be made, but the broad language of the exemptions would make it very difficult for the courts to find that a refusal to disclose documents was unjustified in law. There are no separate administrative courts in Denmark, and no general Administrative Procedure Act. It is the closest to Westminster-style government of the Scandinavian countries, preserving ministerial responsibility (and discretion) and leaving judicial review of administrative action to the ordinary courts. Despite the relative weakness of the law, it was met with administrative opposition and arguments that it would require staff increases and would make government less efficient. It has not, according to the British Civil Service Department report.

The law was to be reviewed in 1974, but it has taken rather longer. The review was set up in 1973, and a draft 'open files' bill was presented in 1978. This would continue many of the provisions of the existing law. In particular, broad ministerial authority to decide against disclosure would be retained. The major change would be to establish 'mail registers' in government departments, very like those used in Sweden, so that inquirers would at least be able to have a better idea of what they were asking for. The 1970 law apprently has not been much used, and the Ombudsman spends about five per cent of his time on disclosure cases.

Data protection law has advanced more rapidly. Denmark

passed two laws on the subject in 1979, one (the Public Authorities Register Act) for government, and the other (the Private Register Act) for commercial databanks. Both are supervised by a Data Surveillance Authority. They apply only to computerized systems of personal information. The 'legal persons' question is treated rather differently than it is in some other countries. Government databanks are only regulated if they contain personal information. But commercial databanks are regulated if they contain information on individuals or on 'institutions'. There is no general right of 'subject access' to such records, but the Data Surveillance Authority may require such access in some cases. The laws are mainly directed at the accumulation and transfer of 'sensitive' personal information, such as religion, race, or political beliefs.

European Efforts

Pushed gently by the Scandinavians, some other European countries began seriously to consider legislation on the related subjects of open government and data protection. Despite the relationship between the two subjects, they have been considered almost entirely separately in Europe. People concerned about open government legislation tend to be civil servants, administrative law specialists, pressure groups, and some journalists. Those concerned with data protection tend to be those in and around the computer world, as well as some outside it who see potential uses of computer technology as a threat to civil liberties.

Pressure for some sort of open government legislation came mostly through the Council of Europe, a much larger and looser association of European states than the E.E.C. It is involved in the enforcement of the European Convention on Human Rights, by which the member nations of the Council of Europe are bound in varying degrees. Article 10 of that Convention, on freedom of expression, effectively was the peg for various diplomatic efforts to persuade European countries to be more open about how they ran their governments.

Slowly and diplomatically the Council began to take steps. The Consultative Assembly, which is the closest thing to a parliament the Council of Europe has, made a modest recommendation in 1970 to extend the rights guaranteed by Article 10 of the Convention 'to include freedom to seek information ... [with] a corresponding duty on public authorities to make information available on matters of public interest, subject to appropriate limitations'. [12]

The 'executive' of the Council of Europe consists of the foreign ministers of the member nations, known as the Committee of Ministers. They passed the recommendation along to a body officially known as the Committee of Experts on Human Rights. This committee considered the subject, and convened a 'colloquy' in Graz, Austria, in September 1976. It was all very low-key, with nothing so crude as voting on conclusions or recommendations (although one young Swede did suggest that).

It was mostly an occasion for presenting reports from various countries about how open they already were, or how they intended to do something about open government legislation in the future. The most significant report was inevitably from Sweden, presented by Bertil Wennergren, who had just finished serving as Ombudsman in charge of enforcing the Swedish open government law, and had been made a judge. Norway and Denmark were also represented and their laws were considered. Perhaps because it was the host country, Austria's rather weak law on the same subject was also described.

Reports from France and the Netherlands were more interesting. Both countries' representatives said that legislation on the subject was being prepared, and both countries have since turned their proposals into law. The United Kingdom was represented by two civil servants who said almost nothing, let alone present any report on the state of open government in Britain.

France's move towards open government legislation came as something of a surprise. Previously, government in that country had generally been considered to be at least as secretive as that in Britain, as well as being highly centralized. But M. Louis Fougères announced in Graz that the Conseil d'État had actually prepared two alternative open government bills. There had been some pressure for such legislation, mostly from sections of the press and the growing ecology movement, but in 1976 it was nothing near the pressure building up in Britain.

In February 1977 a French committee was set up not just to consider the subject, but also to take a slightly more active role in encouraging release of documents to the public. It reported in 1978, asking for its terms of reference to be amended to establish a general principle that documents should be available to the public. None of this was in the form of legislation, however. But legislation there was, and quickly. France's open government law was passed on 17 July 1978.

It was part of a package to improve relations between the bureaucracy and the general public. Apparently some astute French civil servants had decided that open government legislation was something of an international tide in public administration, and that it would be wiser to go along with, even to anticipate it, and present a government bill. Presumably it was one of the two prepared by the Conseil d'État which were already to hand. It may have helped that there was some literature on the subject in French and that France had been well represented at the Graz colloquy. In short, within the rather small world of senior public administrators in France, the idea had been considered seriously.

But it was hardly noticed at all until after the decree bringing it into effect was promulgated in December 1978. The French had certainly learned from foreign experience. The law established a general right of public access to administrative documents, subject to ten exceptions, and established a Commission to monitor the law and hear complaints from those refused access to documents. The exemptions were broadly worded, both in their similarity to the U.S. law and in keeping with the general character of statutes in European 'civil law' countries. The effectiveness of the law will depend very much on how the new Commission interprets the exemptions, even bearing in mind that such decisions will not have the effect of binding precedents like decisions of U.S. or British courts. Still, it was done slickly and quickly, and was hardly even noticed until an article was published in *Le Monde* early in 1979. It has at least given the open government campaigners a rather nice French term: *transparence administrative*.

The lack of attention given to the new open government law may have resulted from the attention being paid to data protection legislation. The data protection law which was passed in January 1978 had been preceded by quite a bit of publicity, at least in relative terms. There had been an outcry in 1974 over a plan called 'Safari' to establish what amounted to dossiers on everyone; there was an edict to stop the plan; and the 'Tricot Commission' was established to consider the subject and make recommendations. The Commission reported in 1975, and the 1978 law was based on its recommendations.

As a data protection law the French statute is comprehensive. It covers both the public and private sector, it includes both automated and manual files, and it has a strong independent enforcement body. Its major limitation is that it is only concerned with the data privacy of humans (although companies were included in the original proposal). The enforcement body, usually referred to as the 'National Committee' or C.N.I.L. (Commission Nationale de l'Informatique et des Libertés) has far more independence and power than the government originally intended.

Data protection attracts far more attention in France than open government. There have been books, articles, and major debates in the press and the National Assembly. The open government law, by contrast, was not the subject of much concern, and is coming into effect almost without comment.

The Netherlands also more or less made good on their prediction at the Graz colloquy that an open government law would be introduced. But, comparing the texts of the laws at least, it has been more cautious than France. Once again, the law was preceded by a committee, appointed in 1968, which in 1970 recommended a law establishing a right of access to official documents, complete with a draft bill. When the chairman of the committee became Prime Minister it gave the notion something of a boost. But by then the committee's proposal had been watered down considerably. When the law was passed in 1978 it had one particular feature distinguishing it from other laws on the subject: it established a right to 'information' rather than a right of access to 'documents'. In other words, it is an obligation to tell rather than to show.

The exemptions are worded in the most general of terms, excluding opinions or 'incomplete data'. There is a near-absolute exemption for commercial information furnished to government in confidence, along with other general exemptions for the usual subjects. These include a separate one for information that might 'endanger the unity of the Crown', which is distinguished from the security of the State. It does, however, have an independent review body in the Council of State. This body serves both as the supreme administrative court and an advisory body on proposed legislation. The open government law only came into effect on 1 May 1980, and it is far too early to determine how its rather flexible provisions will be applied.

Data protection, on the other hand, has not yet been taken to the stage of legislation in Holland, although it probably will be in the near future. It has been the subject of increasing controversy since the 1971 census, and a Royal Commission on computer privacy (the Koopmans Commission) reported in 1976. In short, proposals for a Dutch data protection law are very much in the stage of those in the United Kingdom: some sort of regulatory law for databanks is likely to be passed in the next few years, as much for commercial as political reasons. But the Dutch open government law, despite its emphasis on information rather than records, and its broad exemptions, probably goes further than any British government would now be willing to go, particularly in allowing an independent body to hear appeals.

Austria is almost the reverse of the Netherlands in rushing ahead with comprehensive data protection legislation, but lagging far behind with open government law (and apparently happy to remain so). Their open government system was described at the Graz colloquy in 1976. It is far less stringent than the Swedish or U.S. laws, and almost any British government would probably be happy to live with it. Briefly, the Federal Parliament passed a 1973 amendment to the Federal Ministries Act establishing their 'duty to inform'. But the duty is more a statement of good intentions than an establishment of any effective enforceable rights.

For one thing, the 'duty to inform' is qualified by the constitutional obligation of civil servants to keep information secret when it is in the 'interests of the administrative authority' or of parties concerned. The guidelines that have been issued to explain the duty to inform are at least as flexible as those under the Dutch law. Inquiries must be specific, and there is no duty to disclose information until after a tangible decision has been reached. Requests for information can be rejected if they would require evaluation or sifting of voluminous papers. And, like the Dutch law, there is no duty to allow inspection of documents at all, but only to communicate their contents. The one provision of the Austrian system, like the Dutch one, that could make it more effective is for appeals. A refusal to provide information under the 1973 law can be taken to the administrative courts. So the possible effectiveness of a broadly worded open government law will be up to them.

On data protection, however, the Austrians are going about as far as any other European country, and perhaps even further. The 1978 Data Protection Act proclaims broad principles, establishes an elaborate enforcement system, and sets up a timetable for phasing-in the law's various requirements. It protects information on both individuals and 'legal persons', and it covers both government and private sector databanks. It establishes an administrative Data Protection Commission and a larger supervisory Data Protection Council. Enforcement of the law will involve both the Data Protection Commission and the ordinary courts. There is a basic right of 'data subjects' to see information kept on them and to ensure that it is correct. Although the law is directed at databanks generally, most of its requirements are limited to automatically processed information.

The law is thorough and elaborate, but its real effect will depend on the regulations and how they are interpreted by the enforcement authorities. Regulations for public-sector data processors were being drafted during the summer of 1980 for submission to the Data Protection Commission. In this field, Austria is well beyond Britain, where the Lindop proposals are still being leisurely considered.

Things have not quite stood still at the Council of Europe since their Consultative Assembly made a recommendation in 1970. In February 1979 the Assembly got round to approving an outright resolution calling on all member nations to introduce open government laws.

There has also been at least one case in which a would-be leaker or whistle-blower has complained to the European Commission of Human Rights. In 1969 an anonymous German civil servant said that he had been disciplined for attempting to write an article which supposedly would reveal maladministration in his department. [13] The report of the case is not very revealing, and there is a hint that it was something of a half-hearted effort. In any case, it did not even pass the very first barrier for such complaints, and was declared inadmissible. The facts he intended to reveal, said the Commission, were 'an official secret' and he did not have any right to reveal them under Article 10 of the European Convention on Human Rights.

There is, of course, another European body which can make rules which bite more directly on member countries: the E.E.C. But the Human Rights Convention is only a part of E.E.C. law in a very indirect and slowly developing way. However, in 1973 a Danish member of the European Parliament did ask both the E.E.C. Commission and its Council if they had any plans to introduce rules on public access to administrative records. Both bodies said no. [14]

More Like Us: Canada, Australia, and New Zealand

At the time of writing none of these three Commonwealth countries had a national (as distinct from provincial or state) open government law. But they had already given the subject much more serious consideration than the United Kingdom, and it is very likely that Canada and Australia, at least, will soon have national Freedom of Information Acts.

Canada was the first of the three to start taking a serious interest in the subject, and it began with Scandinavian influence rather than from the U.S. Coincidentally, though, it was in 1966, the year when the original U.S. Freedom of Information Act was passed, that a Canadian professor began to write on the subject. Donald Rowat, professor of political science at Carleton University, Ottawa, had already established himself as an authority on the Scandinavian ombudsman system, and it was his Nordic experience that he drew on. [15] There was a 1969 official report of a Task Force on Government Information, which quoted the Rowat article and was much in favour of greater openness, but didn't go so far as to recommend any sort of open government legislation. Canadian government was still very much in the British tradition, only mutated into federalism. It had, and still has, an Official Secrets Act which is almost identical to the one in Britain, and the Franks Committee cited this in their 1972 report as evidence that British law on government information was not particularly restrictive. Canada did not get round to introducing a general thirty-year rule on archives until 1969, following Britain by two years.

Professor Rowat was not the only Canadian who took an early and serious interest in the subject. A Conservative Member of Parliament, Gerald Baldwin, started introducing freedom of information bills regularly. The first were ordinary private member's bills, and they suffered the usual fate of such bills in Westminster-style parliaments. But in 1973, when he was House Leader of the Opposition, one of his bills made it to the committee stage. It was referred, along with government guidelines for the release of documents to M.P.s to a Standing Joint Committee of the Senate and House of Commons.

The Committee was jointly chaired by Gerald Baldwin and Senator Eugene Forsey, and in 1974 they went to work. They started calling witnesses, including ministers and senior civil servants, studying the U.S. law, which was then in the process of being strengthened, and generally got the government to take them seriously. The government responded first with the 'Wall Report' in June 1975. This was a report (*The Provision of*

Government Information) prepared by an officer of the Privy Council. It was liberal in its recommendations about disclosure of information, but the government was not willing to endorse any U.S. or Swedish-style disclosure law.

During the 1970s Canada was watching the Watergate scandals unfold to the south, and soon had its own only slightly less dramatic revelations about the Royal Canadian Mounted Police, which led to an Official Secrets Act prosecution. Perhaps it was partly because of proximity to the United States that government information law became a respectable political issue in Canada a few years before similar attention began to be paid in Great Britain. The Consumers' Association published a report on government secrecy, newspaper and academic articles began to appear, and in June 1977 the federal government published a Green Paper on the subject, *Legislation on Public Access to Government Documents* (nearly two years before the British government managed its equivalent). The Green Paper was very like the later British one, although the arguments were more detailed. It went much further than the British document in spelling out the sort of subjects that might be justifiable exceptions to any declared policy, or even law, on disclosure of government documents. It attempted a realistic estimate of what the U.S. Freedom of Information Act had cost. Perhaps most important, it gave some serious attention to the crucial question of who would decide disputed cases. Being Green rather than White, it did not reject outright alternatives to leaving the final decision with the relevant minister, but it clearly did not favour judicial review, and seemed inclined to have some sort of Parliamentary Information Commissioner.

In August the Canadian Bar Association responded with a specially commissioned response to the Green Paper. [16] Just as the Law Society in Britain was later to do, this favoured a right of appeal to the courts against refusals to disclose information, although the Canadian publication was rather more detailed and fiercely argued.

One of the advantages of a federal system is that the provinces or states serve as laboratories where new and interesting laws can be tried out. Before the federal government even published its

Green Paper in June 1977, the province of Nova Scotia had
passed its own Freedom of Information Act in May. It was
followed by a Right to Information Act in New Brunswick in
1978. Ontario did not jump into legislation so quickly, but it
established a Commission on Freedom of Information and Individual Privacy in March 1977. One of the Commission's main
functions so far has been to publish a series of monographs on
various aspects of its related subjects. One of these was written by
Professor Rowat and published in November 1978. [17] It is still
probably the most thorough and up-to-date survey of law and
practice in countries with laws or serious proposals on the
subject.

On the related subject of data protection Canada acted fairly
quickly, and along the lines of the U.S. 1974 Privacy Act. Part IV
of the Canadian Human Rights Act came into effect in 1978, and
established a right of 'subject access' for people to see files held on
them by government departments, with exceptions similar to
those in U.S. law. A Privacy Commissioner is in charge of
enforcing disclosures, although there is still a final power for a
minister to refuse disclosure, with no appeals to the courts.

The Parliamentary Standing Committee published its report[18]
in June 1978, and it generally lined up with the Canadian Bar
Association in criticizing the Government's Green Paper. The
report favoured more limited exemptions, and a two-stage system
of enforcement, with initial appeals to an information commissioner and an ultimate power for the courts to order disclosure.

Despite all this, the British Civil Service Department reported
in April 1979 that there was 'no noticeable public clamour' for
such legislation. But they did comment drily that the report of the
MacDonald Commission on allegations against the Royal
Canadian Mounted Police and the Security Service might 'well
have an influence on public attitudes', and that this might also
result in changes to the Official Secrets Act.

Then in July 1979 the Conservative Government headed by
Joe Clark came into office with a specific pledge to pass a
Freedom of Information Act very much like that outlined by the

Standing Committee. However, Mr Clark's government did not make it the very first item on its legislative agenda, and the bill had not passed when the government fell a few months later. The return of Pierre Trudeau's government was not based on any sort of specific pledge to pass an open government law, but nevertheless a fairly stringent open government bill was introduced by the government during the summer of 1980.

Australia

Australia is much like Canada, in a general constitutional sense, with Westminster-style parliamentary government superimposed on a federal system. The idea of a Freedom of Information Act came slightly later to Australia, but many of the elements were the same. Once again there was an active politician and an academic specialist. The difference was that the politician was Gough Whitlam, who promised a Freedom of Information Act when his Labour Government came to power in 1972. It was not, however, his only or even one of his main interests. The basis for his election promise was a book written by one of his assistants. [19] The book ran through examples of Australian government secrecy and recommended a law generally modelled on the U.S. Freedom of Information Act.

Once in office, the government set up an inter-departmental committee to consider the subject. The committee duly reported in 1974, endorsing American-style legislation. [20] But no bill had been introduced when the Labour Government fell, or was pushed, from power in the constitutional crisis of 1975. The proposal had, however, gained enough momentum for the new Liberal-Country Government to reconvene the same committee. In 1976 the committee produced another report, with the same title. By that time the open government lobby had grown, and writing on the subject had begun to proliferate. The Royal Commission on Australian Government Administration had commissioned a study of access laws. The Commission produced its own report in 1976, with a minority statement from one of the Commissioners, Mr Paul Munro, who argued for a U.S.-style law which would be much tougher than what the government had in mind.

What the government had in mind was presented to Parliament in 1978 in two bills, the Freedom of Information Bill 1978 and the Archives Bill 1978 (which would finally establish a thirty-year rule there). By this time academic interest had been aroused, and a critical article by Professor John McMillan had appeared. [21]

So, by the time the government got round to introducing a relatively weak bill on the subject, there was a stronger alternative (the Munro minority report from the Royal Commission had included a draft bill), academic criticism, and a fairly well-organized Freedom of Information Legislation Campaign Committee.

The bill as introduced was subject to criticism on several points. The exemptions from disclosure were broadly worded, and in several of them (such as national security, international relations, federal/state relations) the minister's decision would be final. There was also a broad clause giving authority for regulations to exempt any class of documents from the bill. About the only thing that opponents seemed to approve of was the right of appeal to the Administrative Appeals Tribunal in some cases.

On the related subject of privacy and data protection, there is no federal legislation at all. In 1976 the Law Reform Commission was asked by the federal Attorney-General to prepare a report on privacy, with legislative proposals. Its terms of reference are roughly similar to those of the Lindop Committee in Britain, and it could recommend wide-ranging data protection legislation to regulate databanks in both the public and private sectors.

As in Canada, the states have also been active in studying the issue and preparing legislation. The state of New South Wales established a commission which published a report in November 1977 strongly recommending a public access law. [22] New South Wales had already legislated on data protection with their Privacy Committee Act in 1975. In the state of Victoria the Labour Party introduced a freedom of information bill drafted by John McMillan, who has become more or less the Rowat of Australia.

So Australia may be the first in this Commonwealth group actually to enact a freedom of information law, but it will be a fairly weak one, perhaps somewhere between Denmark and Holland on a relative scale. Of course the timing and content of any legislation in Canada and Australia depends on the determination of the governments, and the strength of opposition from their own back-benchers.

New Zealand

In New Zealand the interest in open government legislation so far has been specifically academic. One of the few comparative articles in the world on the subject was published in the *New Zealand Law Journal* in 1977.[23] It was, however, written by the Australian law professor, John McMillan. The government took the first step of establishing a committee to look into the whole subject.

More has been done in data protection, however. Public concern seemed to start, as it does in many countries, with a census. After the 1971 census there was considerable criticism in the press, and one law journal article on the subject.[24] It became an issue in the 1972 election which brought Labour to power, and there was a pamphlet called *Your Right to Privacy*.

In 1976 an Act was passed establishing a Privacy Commissioner for the Wanganui Computer Centre, which is a New Zealand combination of the Swansea motor vehicle computer and the Police National Computer in Britain, along with holding many other kinds of records. The first Commissioner, Mr James Wixted, has been appointed to serve for five years. He has a fairly broadly defined ombudsman job to investigate complaints, and 'subject access' can be refused if it 'would be likely to be detrimental to the administration of justice'.

New Zealand also established a Human Rights Commission in 1977, which has very general investigatory powers to see that the International Covenants on Human Rights are being complied with. About the only activity involving information, or anything else, that the Commission cannot inquire into is the operation of the Wanganui Computer Centre, which is considered to have been taken care of.

Chapter Ten

Lessons from Other Lands

There have been three related international trends in the last couple of decades. First came the ombudsman system, establishing some sort of independent office to investigate complaints by individuals against bureaucracies. This necessarily involved disclosure of government information in two ways. Any sort of ombudsman worth the name must have the power to see government files in order to carry out a proper investigation; and the sanction in most ombudsman systems is largely that of publicity, usually a report from the ombudsman that there has been maladministration, and that something should be done about it.

The second trend has been for data protection legislation. This has mostly been directed at computer-stored information on individuals, from a fear that governments (and private bodies) would use new technology to collect too much information on people. The general pattern of such legislation has been to establish limits on collection of such information, establish an independent enforcement body, and sometimes to give individuals the right to see and correct information held on them.

It is only in the last 'subject access' aspect of data protection legislation that it overlaps the third general trend of legislation giving citizens legal rights of access to government records. This notion is being taken up in more and more countries, and the brief review of international developments in this book only attempts an accurate summary up to the summer of 1980.

Most of the reasons for these developments have been suggested already. The growth of bureaucracy, often for very good reasons, has meant that individuals' lives are increasingly affected by administrative decisions. Assisted by electronic technology, governments have accumulated more and more information, both about individuals and on important questions of public policy. Public access to the information in government records is one important way both of protecting individual rights and providing democratic checks on bureaucratic excesses.

There have also been common elements in the application of these trends in various countries. There are usually academics writing up their comparative research, pressure groups that would like to have such laws in their own countries, parliamentarians, and often some press interest.

Once the process begins, it feeds on itself. In the academic world the growth of literature is exponential. There are now shelves of books and hundreds of articles on ombudsman systems. Data protection literature is catching up quickly. Comparative work on open government is still in a fairly early stage, with several articles and a few books. But writing about secrecy and open government in particular countries has understandably grown far more rapidly. There are now a fair number of articles, pamphlets, and books on secrecy in Britain, although it hardly compares with the mass of literature in the United States.

Governments have rarely taken up any of these ideas on their own initiative, for the obvious reason that they all represent restrictions on the exercise of government power. It takes an astute politician or civil servant to anticipate such a trend and do something about it before legislation becomes inevitable.

The British reaction to the open government trend has mostly been to dismiss it as being merely trendy, and something that could safely be ignored. It was James Fawcett, professor of law at King's College London and President of the European Commission on Human Rights, who once said that the usual British reaction to a description of how anything is done differently elsewhere is simply to say 'how funny'.

A less flippant response is to explain that other countries may feel the need for such laws because they do not have the system of ministerial responsibility and Parliamentary Questions to ensure accountability of government at Westminster. Both of those institutions have already been considered in Chapter 4 but it is worth noting what two academics who have done comparative research on the subject say. Professor Rowat, in his study prepared for the Ontario Commission, derides the 'spurious argument that a right of appeal to the courts [against refusals to disclose information] will interfere with ministerial responsibility to Parliament'. Such a right, he continues,

increases rather than interferes with ministerial responsibility because it prevents the Ministers from permanently hiding information for personal or partisan advantage. And from a broader point of view, a strong access law forces them to release more information about all of the activities for which they are responsible, thus giving Parliament, and through it the public, a better basis for controlling government.

A South African who studied government secrecy in Britain, the U.S., and his own country, is similarly sceptical:

It is questionable that secrecy is a necessary corollary to the rule that the Minister should take responsibility for departmental actions in Parliament, and, in any event, secrecy frequently enables the Minister to evade responsibility by confusing those who are ignorant of the real facts and background to government actions.[1]

The British Labour Government's 1979 Green Paper considered that a statutory right of access to records could 'affect adversely and fundamentally the accountability to Parliament . . .' It is true that such a law would affect ministerial accountability fundamentally, because it would make questioning of how a department was run more informed. The principal adverse effect would be on the ability of ministers to withstand such informed criticism by bland reassurances or simple refusals to answer.

There are some specific lessons to be learned from the experiences of other countries with open government laws of varying stringency. Professor Rowat describes two that are particularly relevant to Britain. The first is that while it is possible, as in Sweden, to have a strong tradition of openness 'without the wheels of government grinding to a halt', countries without that tradition require a radical change in law, practices, and attitudes. In order for the practices and attitudes to change, as in the United States, 'such a law will not succeed unless it contains strong provisions for its enforcement'. The second is that under a parliamentary system, 'the government will resist sponsoring a strong law because this will limit its own powers and because it finds the present system of discretionary secrecy so much to its own advantage'.

He then goes on to outline what he thinks are the essential features for a successful open government law. There are three basic characteristics: disclosure as the rule rather than the exception; narrowly-defined exceptions justifying secrecy; and effective enforcement through appeals against secrecy to some independent arbiter. Professor Rowat adds two more requirements. He thinks that such a law must also 'facilitate full and easy public access, for instance by not limiting requests to specific documents (as in Denmark and Norway) or to citizens with a personal interest in a case, and by requiring public registers of all documents and low fees for searches and copies, with the fees waived if the request is for a public purpose'. He elaborates on the requirement for narrow and specific exemptions from disclosure, with provisions for limiting the time for which they can be kept secret, permitting earlier release, and requiring 'nonsecret parts of documents to be released'. His enforcement requirements would include specific time limits for replying to requests, requiring reasons for refusals, and penalties for noncompliance. And he feels that the independent arbiter must ultimately be the courts.

The British Civil Service Department report[2] came to rather different conclusions from those of Professor Rowat. Of course it was a balanced and factual report, with the conclusions, or at least the possibilities, expressed in the Green Paper which it accompanied. But it is fairly clear what was considered impractical in the countries studied. The U.S. pattern was particularly to be avoided, mostly for those very aspects which Rowat thinks important. America was the exception to the general pattern they found of moving towards more open government 'one cautious step at a time'. The U.S. laws on freedom of information and privacy had 'given rise to many anomalies, anxieties, and administrative headaches and cost, which is greatly increased by the large amount of litigation'. As for time limits on dealing with requests, the U.S. '10-day limit has often proved to be unattainable, and likewise the 20-day limit to judge an appeal'.

In Canada and Australia, the C.S.D. team found that 'involvement of third parties, whether the courts or quasi-judicial bodies such as an ombudsman or a tribunal in assessing the merits of ministerial decisions on disclosure is held to represent a weakening of this [ministerial] accountability to Parliament, with the complementing danger of politicizing the courts or other body'. The Canadian government may certainly have 'held' this, but it was not the conclusion of other Canadians such as Professor Rowat or the Canadian Bar Association.

As if to show that a modern democracy could function efficiently and disclose all the necessary information without any legal compulsion, the C.S.D. report included a section on the Federal Republic of Germany. There, a minister receiving requests for information might 'in theory . . . refuse to answer but in practice replies are forthcoming and comprehensive'. There was found to be 'little pressure for more openness in government in the F.R.G. and no plans for introducing any legislation on the subject'.

Generally, the C.S.D. report was a thorough job of research. The summaries of the laws and proposals were largely accurate, and if there was a certain selectivity in quoting those who thought that the U.S. law had gone too far, cost too much, and caused too much trouble, or that ministerial responsibility in Commonwealth countries would be damaged by disclosure laws involving the courts, it probably reflects the fact that civil servants are more inclined to accept the views of other civil servants than those of outsiders. It was something like a judicial summing-up to a jury: one might think that such laws were a good idea, but on the other hand many reasonable and responsible people did not much care for them. There was a pervasive scepticism about the whole idea. But that attitude is not at all limited to civil servants or to ministers.

Questions about the desirability of open government legislation do not all come from those who wish to defend the *status quo*. Even those who wholeheartedly feel that people should know more about how they are governed are not quite convinced that a statutory right of access to government records would have much effect.

E. P. Thompson, the historian, expressed his reservations in an introduction to *Review of Security and the State 1978*.[3]

That is, if some Freedom of Information Act commands that there shall be public access to this and that category of document, then the state within the State will simply seal off this information in new ways: they will either assume, in their obscurity, the right to 'weed' the papers, or they will take care that certain decisions never appear in documents at all, or they will find an even more simple recourse. Thus the White Paper on the Official Secrets Act makes immense play upon the question of which categories of classified documents should come within its provisions – should these be TOP SECRET, or SECRET, or DEFENCE-CONFIDENTIAL, or whatever? But of course, whatever decision is come to, this tank will be able to seal itself in the easiest possible way, by a simple motion of re-classification, in which all that top people do not wish the public to know is placed within the inviolable category.

The conclusion, that 'whatever act is passed, our public servants will find a way around it', is similar to the observation by the then Home Secretary, Merlyn Rees, in the House of Commons (19 July 1978) that secrecy is a 'self-sealing tank'. And there is something in it. In the United States the requirements of the Freedom of Information Act were certainly resisted and evaded after it went into effect in 1967. It was to deal with such evasive tactics that Congress greatly strengthened the Act in 1974, over-riding the veto imposed by President Ford.

To some extent, Thompson's objections are not so much against the principle of open government legislation (which he does support) as warnings to those who draft and enforce such laws. Taking his last objection first, what is to prevent officials from re-classifying documents in some 'inviolable category'?

The question has serious implications both for public records laws and for those which punish unauthorized disclosures of some kinds of information. As explained earlier, the two are different, although often confused. Public records laws say that government documents are to be made available to the public unless they are in a category exempt from disclosure under the statute. Some, but not all, documents which are exempt from such mandatory disclosure are also protected from unauthorized disclosure by criminal penalties.

For both types of law, there is an answer to Thompson's question: it is to set up machinery so that 'top people [who] do not wish the public to know' do not have the final word. For public records statutes, Swedish and U.S. experiences provide two alternative models. In both systems citizens may appeal against a civil servant's refusal to disclose a particular document.

In Sweden appeals usually go either to the Ombudsman or the Supreme Administrative Court. In the United States they are made to the federal courts. In both countries there is ample evidence that reasons given by officials for keeping documents secret are not routinely accepted. Both countries have spelled out in their legislation what reasons can justify secrecy of particular records, with Sweden doing so in rather more detail than the United States. Their common characteristic is that appeals may be taken to an arbiter who is independent of the government machine.

The safeguard in criminal prosecutions is similar in principle. Before someone is imprisoned for an unauthorized disclosure of information which, for example, allegedly would cause 'serious injury to national defence' there should be some evidence that the information actually was injurious. There are problems about the extent to which such evidence can be presented in court without defeating the whole object of keeping the information secret. But the powers of the courts to hold *in camera* hearings should be adequate to deal with them. The alternative of accepting a ministerial certificate is too close to gaoling people by administrative fiat.

Under a public records law what is to stop officials from destroying documents to keep them from public view? In one sense, it depends on the law's requirements about maintaining records. In another, it depends on the ultimate effectiveness of legal sanctions.

There has been some discussion in this country, mostly among historians, about the existing system of departmental 'weeding' of files before they are transferred to the Public Record Office. The Wilson Committee is now considering a more organized way of deciding what should be kept and what discarded. The new technology of microfiche storage and computer access may help to solve the problem.

But there remains the problem of the official who destroys a document which the law says should be kept and made public. One partial answer is that open government legislation should provide sanctions against those who disregard a legal obligation to maintain records for public access. Sweden has such sanctions, at least against civil servants who refuse to disclose documents that should be public under the law. The United States Congress established a similar system in 1974. Both measures are to combat the natural secretiveness of bureaucracies, expressed bluntly by a sign in the information office of the U.S. Federal Bureau of Investigation: 'When in doubt, blot it out.'

It is even more difficult to deal with those who 'take care that certain decisions never appear in documents at all'. Swedish experience seems to confirm that some kinds of information are regularly given over the telephone rather than being put on paper because of their law. Usually, this involves personal references for civil servants.

Not much can be done about such evasion, but in itself it provides a partial remedy for one danger which public records and data protection laws are supposed to guard against. The problem with inaccurate information in personal dossiers is largely that it is a matter of record rather than of a transient conversation. As such it acquires a semi-factual status, and may be acted on by people who know nothing of the original circumstances. There is still a difference in the capacity for harm of derogatory statements in conversation and the same statements written down, and it should be kept in mind when drafting public records legislation.

But the particular case of derogatory information in personal dossiers was probably not what Thompson had in mind. What sort of record would be kept, for example, of clearly illegal actions by public officials, especially under a system of public access to government records?

The case of the Nixon tapes comes quickly to mind, and illustrates some of the problems and perhaps some of the solutions. One aspect is the tendency to assume that those engaged in maladministration, to put it at its lowest, are peculiarly efficient. Part of this efficiency is an assumed ability to do without the usual reliance of other organizations on records of what is done and what is decided.

Of course those who plan a burglary will be more cautious about recording their actions than those who are engaged in more acceptable forms of official action. But despite their caution, such conspirators are no better than the rest of us in carrying out a complicated plan without some sort of record.

The point is that some records of government decisions will usually be made, however indefensible the actions they lead to, and we should not assume that all of them will be efficiently destroyed. The reasons vary from the simple requirements of efficient execution to personal pique. They are even more likely to be made and kept when the actors think that they are doing the right thing. After all, Cabinet minutes began in this country when the press of business made it difficult to recall exactly what had been decided. Until it was too late Richard Nixon thought that the White House tapes (suitably edited by him in retirement) would enhance his reputation as a statesman.

It is unlikely that any future U.S. President would make such recordings, but history's loss was democracy's gain. Under the U.S. Freedom of Information Act, even in its post-1974 form, such tapes would almost certainly be exempt from compulsory disclosure. But that does not mean that they would necessarily remain secret.

An earlier section suggested that the law on government information can do three things. It can be protective, by punishing unauthorized disclosures; it can be neutral, neither punishing disclosures nor requiring them; or it can encourage openness by requiring public access. Most legal systems have laws of all three types. But there are intermediate categories, and the Nixon tapes illustrate one of them.

Some records may be exempt from general public disclosure and still be required to be given to certain people for particular purposes. The constitutional issue around the Nixon tapes was not whether they were for general public scrutiny, but whether they could be withheld from the Special Prosecutor investigating the crimes we now call the Watergate affair. The decision of the Supreme Court was that they could not be kept from the prosecutor. In this country the closest legal equivalent is the doctrine of Crown privilege. The courts rather than the Crown now determine whether the public interest justifies keeping information secret.

But the interests balanced are different from those under public records legislation. Such laws assume that there is a general value in the public's knowing how they are governed, to be weighed against values such as national defence and personal privacy.

What Is to be Done

The need for radical and stringent legislation to restrain the habit of secrecy and replace it with a presumption of openness extends even to the order of considering legislation. This requires a break with the tradition established by the 1972 Franks Committee, repeated by successive governments since, and summed up in the comment of the Civil Service Department report that the usual way of going about such things is to 'first decide what information must be kept secret before deciding to open wider doors to official information'.

This attitude not only reflects a basic assumption that secrecy is the more important value, and openness a concession to be made later; it also presents a very specific legislative tactical advantage to those who wish to ensure the greatest possible secrecy and limit disclosure to government discretion. That was done in the committee stage of the Freud bill, as described in Chapter 11. The government managed to persuade the committee that they should first consider the part of the bill which dealt with criminal penalties for unauthorized disclosure, then deal with the bill's open government provisions (reversing the original structure of the bill). *New Society* commented on this by saying that the bill would distribute government information among three 'baskets', in the jargon of Helsinki. [4] Most records would be in the public basket, available for inspection and copying to anyone. The second would be for discretionary disclosure through briefing, leaking, or even whistle-blowing. Public access would not be legally required, but the records or their contents could be disclosed without legal penalties. The third basket would be the strongbox, for information which really deserved criminal penalties to protect its secrecy.

The strongbox was the only part of the Freud bill that the front-benchers liked at all, and they wanted it to contain just about anything that the government of the day wanted kept there. The effect, if they had succeeded, would have made 'the other two baskets pretty empty, or perhaps just filled with chaff'.

To avoid this trap, discussion of open government legislation should begin with the assumption that there should be a general enforceable right of public access to government records. It immediately raises rather complicated questions of defining both 'government' and 'records'. Most of the open government bills in Britain vary even on these basic definitions.

The Freud bill applied only to central government, while the bill adopted by the Labour Party's National Executive would have included local authorities, nationalized industries, and a wide range of other bodies with public functions. It is a subject for some legislative compromise, but institutions of national and local government would seem to be the very minimum for an effective open government law in Britain. And legislative draftsmen should be aware that in Sweden the requirements of their disclosure law are sometimes avoided by hiving off various activities into what are nominally corporations with majority government ownership, and that there have been more recent attempts in the United States to avoid the Freedom of Information Act in the same way. [5]

Once 'government' is defined, however arbitrarily, what are 'government records'? A fairly simple working definition is any recorded information in the possession or under the control of 'government'. This would include everything from handwritten notes to electronically stored items. It is far broader than the Swedish definition, which is effectively limited to papers officially recorded or received by departments (although this has recently been extended to their electronic equivalents). The question of 'working papers' containing 'advice' is better dealt with as a possible exemption to the rule of disclosure than at the basic stage of definition. The U.S. definition is fairly broad, but it has been held not to include physical objects, such as those collected as evidence in the Kennedy assassination case.

The standard objections to such a definition vary widely, and are not always consistent. Civil servants are likely to say, yet again, that they won't write anything down if it's going to be a public record while they are still around to be criticized for it. This 'candour' argument has already been considered in other chapters. To some extent it can be provided for by limited exemptions from immediate disclosure for purely advisory memoranda. But there is also a strong argument that government writers might be more careful about giving advice if it was recorded, not just for an overtired minister to glance at and initial, but for possible wider public scrutiny.

Some historians argue that making such records generally available now would diminish the quality and quantity of material available to future historians. We all have particular interests to be protected, but it is perhaps worth remembering that government records are not made solely, or even primarily, for the purpose of providing as much raw material as possible for later students of how we are governed today.

Occasionally candid civil servants will object to open government proposals on the realistic ground that they have enough trouble finding things in the files themselves, and that it would be impossible to dig out documents just because some outsider wanted to see them. But the Civil Service Department report observed that 'access regimes often force government to improve its system of records whilst at the same time changing an official filing system into a public library'. In a very mundane way this illustrates the argument that public scrutiny of government records can actually improve, rather than impair, efficiency.

There are also related questions about what should be written down and when it should be destroyed. A common observation is that one effect of possible public exposure would be a rush to the shredding machines in Whitehall. To some extent the argument simply ignores the reality of any large organization. Records must be kept, and, if the experience of such previously secretive and supposedly efficient bodies such as the Crown Agents is anything to go by, public scrutiny is likely to be as much an incentive to better record-keeping and general efficiency as the opposite.

The present system by which records are indexed, retained, and possibly destroyed appears to be rather *ad hoc* at best. The Wilson Committee is the first attempt since the Grigg Committee's effort in 1954 to inquire into the process and make recommendations. The proposals may turn out to be as significant for any system of open government as for the benefit of historians.

Once there is a workable definition of what a 'government record' is, and of the system by which they are to be retained, retrieved, and possibly discarded, how should the law provide for public access to them? The very same technological advances that the Lindop Committee saw as potential dangers to the security of personal information will also make it very much easier to index, store and retrieve records of a more general sort.

Professor Rowat felt that one of the lessons from other countries was that a system of public registers of government documents was necessary for an effective law. This has certainly been true in the United States, where bureaucrats regularly evaded the requirements of the Freedom of Information Act until 1974 by playing guessing games with requesters. The 1974 amendments introduced an indexing system which has improved the ability of citizens to discover what documents are on hand so they will know what to ask for.

An example illustrates how the system works now in at least one U.S. agency. The Consumer Product Safety Commission maintains a database of accident investigations involving particular products. A simple request for a list of investigations involving British products quickly produced a computer print-out. Most of the accidents were clearly not caused by product failures. However, one particular British-made bicycle had turned up often enough for the Commission to investigate it further and take action. The example not only shows how a system of public access to records can be made easier by technology, but also how such access can relate to everyday concerns such as consumer product safety. It did not reveal a British government secret, however, because the relevant departments here knew nothing about it.

If there is to be such a system of, in the C.S.D.'s terms, turning official files into a public library, the first question is whether it is to be retrospective. In other words, if the present thirty-year rule on records is, for most of them, to be turned into a now-rule, is it only to apply to records created from this day forward? Some of the bureaucratic horror at the idea of retrospection is a reflection of the slightly informal system by which records are now kept. If only because of the cost of sorting through the miles of old-style shelves, a system of phased retrospection is probably the most sensible. Departments already have enough trouble getting their archives to the Public Record Office after thirty years. But this is in part because of the combination of no general rules at all and some ludicrous ones that the 'weeders' are working under. One of the rules, which has only now been slightly adjusted to reality, is that the British security services ceased to exist at the end of the Second World War. Because of this rule, until now, every document that even referred to M.I.5 or 6 was sorted out and kept back.

What records should be exempted from compulsory disclosure? American and Swedish experience points the way, but one very important distinction must be made first. A document that is exempt from disclosure is not necessarily one which is protected by criminal sanctions. Returning to the three-baskets metaphor, much of the information in such documents, and the records themselves, would be subject to discretionary disclosure. In other words, many of them could be handed over or their contents revealed by briefing or leaking without criminal penalties being imposed on anyone.

Documents containing policy advice would probably be the best example of such 'leakable' material. Diplomatic information that might cause embarrassment or strained relations, as in the nineteenth-century cases in Chapter 3, would be another. The law should recognize that governments regularly disclose such information through briefings when it is to their advantage, and they should not be able to put people in gaol for doing it when disclosures are embarrassing to them. There is, as Roy Jenkins commented in his 1975 Guildhall lecture, enough civil service discipline to keep most of such information secret as it is. Many would argue that there is too much, and that statutory protection along the lines of the U.S. 'Whistle-blower' Act of 1978 might be considered to protect leakers of some kinds of information.

What else should be exempt from disclosure? 'Commercial secrets' are commonly exempted, even to some extent in the United States (under the fourth exemption for 'trade secrets', and contrary to the C.S.D. assertion that U.S. law did not exempt commercial secrets). But there must be a balancing test or this would simply amount to handing over a government classification stamp to corporations. The test applied under U.S. law (see pp. 134–5) is about right, exempting commercial information from disclosure if it would result in substantial harm to a company's competitive position.

Personal information should also be exempt from general disclosure if it would amount to an invasion of personal privacy. But this should not be a reason for refusing to disclose such information to the person concerned. That must be justified, if at all, by some other principle such as ensuring that law enforcement is not impaired. And some form of data protection law should also be enacted to control the collection of personal information and its use within government.

Who Decides?

There must be effective enforcement machinery for an open government, and if there is only an appeal to ministers the whole exercise is nothing more than a statement of good intentions. It is far too easy for ministers in any country to confuse national security with their own security in office to let them have the final word.

Once that principle is established, there is a bewildering variety of judges, ombudsmen, and special panels of one sort or another to choose from, all attempts to find some arbiter who is independent of the government of the day and who can be relied upon to care at least as much about the value of public knowledge as the convenience of private government. The various solutions in other countries have been described. The most practical solution might well be a combination of an Information Commissioner and the possibility of ultimate appeal to the courts. But the choices must be made carefully. Until recently, the British 'ombudsman', the Parliamentary Commissioner for Administration, has been a straight government appointment, with almost no prior consultation in the House of Commons. And although there have been a few encouraging recent signs that some English judges are looking more sceptically at claims for government secrecy (see Chapter 6), there are also signs that some of them still frown on any disclosure that might result in 'captious or ill-informed criticism', as Lord Reid put it in *Conway v. Rimmer*.

But what about the strongbox? What should be done with someone who leaks information that really does cause some sort of indefensible damage? First of all, there are the hard cases of espionage. Section 1 of the Official Secrets Act should be replaced by a real espionage statute. This should be restricted to exactly what the marginal note to section 1 says: 'penalties for spying'. 'Spying' is, very roughly, communicating or attempting to communicate information to a foreign power when it is likely to cause serious damage to national defence, and with the intent of causing such damage. It should be for the prosecution to prove the elements of the offence, as it must do in most criminal cases. Simply to call someone a spy, particularly in times of international tension, arouses such intense emotions that it should not be left open to infer intent to damage the country's national defence from general circumstances. That effectively puts the burden on the accused to prove his innocence, and it should not be allowed.

Information likely to cause such serious damage as to warrant espionage prosecution should be carefully protected by proper classification. And this classification should be subject to safeguards. In an espionage prosecution involving disclosure of classified information the minister's certificate that the classification was proper should not be the final word. The judge and jury should be allowed to consider whether the information really merited the classification. And ministers should not be allowed, as the Conservative Protection of Official Information Bill would have done, to apply what would amount to retrospective classification: certifying that information in unclassified or even public documents would damage national defence. Both the Conservative and Labour bills would have gone even further, though. They would have made it an offence to communicate anything at all, without authorization, about security and intelligence. If such information is vital to national defence it should be properly classified. It should not be left for journalists and people in general to be threatened away from the entire subject, particularly when it includes surveillance directed as much at Britons with different political views as it is against foreign agents.

Other 'Leaking' Crimes

There are other kinds of official information that deserve legal protection against unauthorized disclosure, apart from information covered by a new espionage law. But there are not many of them, and protecting them by criminal penalties deserves careful consideration.

Anthony Mathews, the South African academic, commented that 'there seems to be in British official circles a feeling of reverence for the criminal law and a widespread belief in its desirability and efficacy'. Almost every new British statute, including some which have provisions for disclosure of information such as the Health and Safety at Work Act 1974, also contains criminal penalties for the unauthorized disclosure of information. This is based on a reflex assumption that leaking is one of the worst things a civil servant can do, and it must always be a crime.

It is not, and the law should be changed to acknowledge that. Criminal penalties for unauthorized disclosures of various kinds of official information should be limited to those which cause, or are likely to cause, a particular kind of damage to a protected interest. Even if information is exempt from automatic disclosure under some sort of open government law, leaking it should not necessarily be a crime.

This means that most of the other sixty-one statutes which Franks found with criminal penalties for unauthorized disclosures (expanded to eighty-nine by 1980) should be repealed and replaced with as few criminal laws as possible. This would avoid legal tangles like those in the United States, where the Supreme Court finally decided that the Freedom of Information Act was subject to the restrictions of about a hundred older statutes on unauthorized disclosure. It was a legislative oversight, and Congress took care of it with an amendment to the original Act in 1976.

The statutes which Franks described as measures to protect the confidences of the citizen were almost entirely directed at protecting commercial confidences. The distinction between personal and corporate privacy has already been discussed (pp. 123–6), and it is possible to wonder why the criminal law needs to be used so much, despite the emotive term of 'industrial espionage' often used.

There is already quite an adequate body of law on corruption, used recently, to punish civil servants who use official information for private gain, and their accomplices as well. The damage done by unauthorized disclosures of commercial secrets is financial damage, and it is regularly assessed in cases for civil damages.

The law on 'trade secrets' in Britain is civil law, a judge-made branch of the 'law of confidence' already discussed. The Law Commission has made thorough proposals for establishing this as a statutory tort, with provisions for a defence that a breach of confidence might be in the public interest. The protection of commercial information in government hands should not be the subject of criminal statutes, apart from the existing law on corruption. The law on trade secrets should apply to government as well as industry, no less and no more.

A few of the statutes counted by Franks did use criminal penalties to protect the confidences of citizens rather than companies. In short, they were very limited 'data protection statutes'. But prosecutions under them seem to be extraordinarily rare. When a firm of private detectives used various ruses to get personal information from government departments and other institutions, the sanction which the authorities attempted to apply was to prosecute for 'conspiracy to effect a public mischief', an extension of the law of conspiracy which the House of Lords ultimately rejected.

Personal privacy, here in the limited sense of 'data privacy', deserves legal protection, but the protection should be more in the form of civil damages than a criminal prosecution. The Lindop Committee recommended such a right as a part of their comprehensive scheme for data protection, and the Law Commission made another proposal for civil damages to be awarded when a breach of confidence amounted to an invasion of privacy. The criminal law should only be involved in protecting the personal privacy of some government files to the limited extent that Lindop proposed.

Information about law enforcement is an obvious subject for exemption from compulsory disclosure. But that exemption should be narrowly drawn, if only to avoid making the police a law unto themselves. And criminal penalties for leaks of information about law enforcement should be even further limited. For example, a postman was prosecuted in 1967 under section 2 of the Official Secrets Act for leaking information which was used in a mail robbery. The prosecution was probably justifiable (the trial was held *in camera*), but not necessarily under that Act. Any replacement statute should limit criminal penalties for leaking of law enforcement information to cases in which the effect of the leak is to aid in the commission of a crime or impede its detection.

All of this is based on the assumption that there is a positive value in public knowledge about government, and that only in hard cases such as espionage, corruption, or use of official information in aid of crime should criminal penalties be imposed for leaking. There are more than enough forces for secrecy, including administrative ones, as it is. In a more open society, the law should provide a positive right of access to most records, leaking should be tolerated as much as briefing is practised (and perhaps even protected in some cases), and the criminal law reserved for really serious cases. But this is far more radical than most of the proposals put forward thus far to change the law.

During the winter of 1977–8 all of these questions were discussed and argued over in a series of meetings held under the auspices of the Outer Circle Policy Unit, a non-partisan pressure group. The Unit was drafting a model bill to follow a pamphlet on open government, and some points were left open or vague, partly from the realization that it was, after all, only a hypothetical exercise. The draft bill which emerged was a cautious compromise in some ways, at least by comparison with some laws in other countries. But a few months later the same arguments were being made again, and with rather more intensity, because the venue was no longer the Unit's office at Cambridge Terrace in London, but Committee Rooms Nine and Twelve of the House of Commons.

Chapter Eleven

Opening British Government

Britain does not now have a general open government law, and is not likely to get one in the near future. But in the spring of 1979 Parliament came very close to passing such a law. The private member's bill introduced by Clement Freud, Liberal M.P. for the Isle of Ely, had completed most of its stages in the House of Commons when the Labour Government lost a vote of confidence in the last week in March. The Freud bill was scheduled for final consideration on the floor of the House of Commons the following week. When Parliament was dissolved the bill lapsed along with most other pending legislation.

The story of how the proposal got that far is an interesting one, and not just because it indicates what is likely to happen again in future. It is also a rather neat illustration of how, in well under a decade, the notion of such a law progressed from being a crank's dream to a respectable proposal for legislative change which came close to succeeding. It shows how an idea arrives, and may help generally to understand better the chancy, lurching way Britain goes about making important changes in its way of government.

It did not follow the pattern of most legislation. It was not a central element in any party's election campaign; it was not recommended, or even seriously considered, by any Royal Commission or Departmental Committee; the Law Commissions were not, and have not been, asked to consider it as a subject for possible law reform; it certainly was not one of those proposals that civil servants occasionally come up with on their own initiative.

It was, appropriately, a project begun by outsiders, particularly by pressure groups that wanted to influence government, but which had not achieved or been drawn into the 'closed consultative status' described by Professor Finer in *Comparative Government*. It was also suggested by some academics, especially those who had done comparative research.

There had been earlier concern about secrecy in government, and a few specific changes had been made. A committee under Sir Oliver Franks was appointed in 1955 to consider administrative tribunals and public local inquiries. When the commission reported in 1957 it recommended that the inspectors' reports on which ministerial decisions were made should be regularly published. The commission was '. . . impressed by the need for some further control beyond that which Parliament, in theory, though not always in practice, can exercise. There is no doubt that publicity is in itself an effective check against arbitrary action.'

The recommendation went against established law and practice. A House of Lords decision in 1911 had clearly protected the confidentiality of inspectors' reports. (The report in question was on the mundane question of whether a house had been made unfit for human habitation by damp.) Any publication would, the Lords said, 'cripple the usefulness of these inquiries', and impede 'that frankness which ought to obtain among a staff accustomed to elaborately detailed and often most delicate and difficult tasks'.

Similar arguments that publicity would inhibit candour and be impractical were put to the Franks Commission in the 1950s by Dame Evelyn Sharp, the Permanent Secretary at the Ministry of Housing and Local Government, who was later to play a major role in the *Diaries* of Richard Crossman. Publication of reports that might run to over a hundred pages would delay decisions, she argued, and it would be 'embarrassing' for the recommendations to be published.

Despite the Committee's proposal there was no provision for making reports public in the legislation which followed in 1958. But the recommendation was put into effect anyway by the Ministry of Housing and Local Government. It may have been an illustration that, at least in specific areas, pressure short of law can lead to slightly less secrecy in administration.

It was also in 1958 that the 'fifty-year rule' for historical archives was established by the Public Records Act. At the time it was seen as a major step towards disclosure for historians, and had been recommended by the Grigg Committee on Departmental Records in 1954. After pressure from historians this was reduced to thirty years by a 1967 amendment to the Act (although it must be remembered that there is still wide administrative discretion to keep records back for much longer periods).

The Report of the Fulton Committee on the Civil Service in 1968 concluded that public administration was 'surrounded by too much secrecy' and that 'the public interest would be better served if there were a greater amount of openness'. Their proposal that 'the Government should set up an inquiry to make recommendations for getting rid of unnecessary secrecy in this country' was not really taken up, although the slim White Paper 'Information and the Public Interest' published by the Labour Government in June 1969 was officially declared to be the result of such an inquiry.

It is always difficult to trace the origins of slogans, but the first major political figure to call for more 'open government' seems to have been Edward Heath, in a 1969 House of Commons debate. In any case, the 1970 Conservative manifesto included a promise to 'eliminate unnecessary secrecy concerning the workings of government, and to review the operation of the Official Secrets Acts'. Although she did not use the phrase, Margaret Thatcher had taken a small but firm step to make local government more open ten years before with her private member's bill for admission of the press and public to local authority meetings.

The revival of Conservative interest in open government in 1970 may have been more than coincidental with the *Sunday Telegraph* Official Secrets Act trial, which had been initiated by a Labour Attorney-General, and which concerned information which was embarrassing to the Wilson Labour Government. But the Franks Committee on section 2 of the Official Secrets Act went to some pains to explain that their appointment was the result of the Conservative election promise rather than the trial.

Although they referred to the Fulton proposal in the introduction to their own report, the Committee (chaired by the same Oliver Franks who led the earlier commission in 1955–7) strictly interpreted the terms of reference as limited to section 2 of the Official Secrets Act. That did not stop one witness, Professor H. W. R. Wade, Q.C., of Oxford, from suggesting modestly that they might still consider recommending legislation along Swedish or U.S. lines which could 'positively assist the public to obtain information about government'. Professor Wade may have picked up the idea in the course of writing *Legal Control of Government* [1] with an American professor of administrative law. At least the book was critical of 'the difficulties which British law puts in the way of the ordinary citizen trying to obtain or use information in government hands'.

The Committee gave Professor Wade a rather hard time when he made his argument to them in person. In the final report the Committee said his suggestion was 'interesting' but 'raised important constitutional questions going beyond our terms of reference'. In any case, they were not at all persuaded that British government was particularly more secretive than any other.

Until 1972 official secrecy was seen almost entirely in terms of the Official Secrets Act. The National Council for Civil Liberties had campaigned for the reform or abolition of section 2 of the Act at least since 1939. There had only been hints here and there that something other than removal or restriction of the Official Secrets Act penalties might be necessary to make government more open. The Grigg, Franks (1956), and Fulton Reports had considered some other aspects, and modest steps had been taken in the particular fields of archives, some inspectors' reports, and local government meetings.

What little interest there was in generally opening up government by legislation was largely limited to a few academics with American experience. Apart from Professor Wade, William Birtles, a London University law lecturer who had spent a year with the American Civil Liberties Union, wrote a *Public Law*

973 criticizing the Franks proposals and outlining an
nment law modelled largely on the U.S. Freedom of
n Act. [2]

The American example of Ralph Nader inspired Charles
Medawar to establish two related British groups, the Public
Interest Research Centre and Social Audit, in 1972. The first issue
of the *Social Audit* journal appeared in June 1973, with an article
on 'The Politics of Secrecy/The Secrecy of Politics' by myself.
Some journalists with American experience were impressed by
the example of the U.S. law, and articles about it began to appear
occasionally. Pressure groups such as the National Council for
Civil Liberties and Friends of the Earth began to argue for
legislation to require disclosure of government information. But
government heavy-handedness brought the subject to public
attention as much as efforts by pressure groups.

In the autumn of 1972 the *Sunday Times* published a leaked
memo about plans to cut railway services. The reporter who
wrote the story remarked that the Official Secrets Act was not
used against that sort of leak; but a few weeks later it was. Police
descended on the offices of the *Railway Gazette*, which had passed
on the memo to the *Sunday Times*, and spent several hours going
through their files on the basis of a search warrant under the
Theft Act. Finding nothing, they proceeded to the *Sunday Times*,
where they solemnly cautioned the editor that his publication had
breached the Official Secrets Act. There were allegations of
telephone-tapping and threats against a *Railway Gazette* employee,
which were carefully turned aside without being denied, but no
further action was taken.

Apart from a desultory 'take-note' Commons debate on the
Franks Report in June 1973, little more attention was given to the
issue. There was nothing about it in any of the manifestos for the
February 1974 election. But there was a fairly explicit promise in
the Labour manifesto for the October election that same year.
The origin of the pledge to 'replace the Official Secrets Act by a
measure to put the burden on the public authorities to justify
withholding information' is a small case study in how party
policy sometimes gets made. There were probably only a few

Labour M.P.s who understood that this meant something like a U.S.-style Freedom of Information Act.

Some of them, in particular Tony Benn and John Grant, had been members of a Labour Party study committee which produced a report called 'The People and the Media' in June 1974. Although the report was most controversial for its proposals on broadcasting, it had about a page recommending a 'Freedom of Information Act' along Swedish lines.

The proposal was probably not the subject of any debate, or perhaps even of any discussion, when the 1974 autumn election manifesto was hammered out between the National Executive of the Labour Party and the leadership of the Parliamentary Labour Party. If it had been even partly understood by most of them it almost certainly would have been toned down or even dropped. It was a stick that the open government campaigners would use again and again on the shoulders of Labour Home Secretaries and Prime Ministers until 1979.

Roy Jenkins, then the Labour Home Secretary, grasped the implications quickly, probably after an explanation by his political adviser, Anthony Lester, Q.C. Soon after the autumn Labour victory, he took the slightly unusual step of going to the United States with the specific purpose of considering U.S. legislation on two related subjects: privacy and freedom of information. Some of his briefings were arranged outside the usual embassy channels. Lester got in touch with Ronald Plesser, a lawyer who had headed Ralph Nader's Freedom of Information Clearinghouse and was general counsel to the Privacy Protection Study Commission, and two days of meetings with the Washington Freedom of Information/Privacy community were held. There were also discussions with Justice Department officials and others who were apprehensive both about the new 1974 Privacy Act and the 1974 amendments strengthening the Freedom of Information Act.

Before he left on his Washington trip, Jenkins produced a White Paper on Computers and Privacy, which may have been a signal about which of the two related subjects he thought was more ready for legislation. On his return there were unofficial

dicating that he did not think a U.S.-style Freedom of
1 Act was right for Britain. He confirmed this in his
Guildhall lecture, commenting that he did not think
that .... hole process of decision-making' should be 'carried out
under a public searchlight'. The extent to which he did argue in
Cabinet for liberalizing the disclosure of official information
cannot be known until the relevant Cabinet minutes are made
public in 2005. But in November 1978, long after Jenkins had
gone to the E.E.C. and Lester back to the Bar, a letter from
Lester to *The Times* hinted that the Home Secretary had at least
pressed for some changes. But he was much more active in
starting the process towards legislation on privacy, appointing the
Lindop Committee on Data Protection and Privacy in July 1976.

At about the time Jenkins and Lester were off to Washington,
around Christmas 1974, there was another heavy-handed use of
the Official Secrets Act by the police. While searching houses of
political activists they came across a Ministry of Defence manual
marked 'Restricted' (the lowest possible classification, and one
which Franks said should be abolished). Two people were
charged under section 2 of the Official Secrets Act, and one spent
ten days in Brixton Prison before the charges were dropped.

In 1975 the Scientologists entered the scene. When the 'All-
Party Committee for a Freedom of Information and Privacy Act'
was formed, it was something of a surprise. Many of the M.P.s
involved had not expressed much interest in the subject before,
and a great deal of work was being done by what seemed to be
full-time activists. Almost all of them were Scientologists.
Although they did not announce their affiliation, they did not
deny it when they were questioned directly.

Why the Scientologists? And who were (and are) they exactly?
They claim to be a religion, and have achieved official recognition
of that status in some countries. Scientology evolved from
'dianetics', a theory developed in the late 1940s and early 1950s
by L. Ron Hubbard, an American science-fiction writer who is
still effectively their leader. They are, to put it mildly, controversial. The movement grew rapidly and internationally
during the 1950s and 1960s, and was subject to government

investigation and restrictions in several countries. In the United States the Food and Drug Administration said the Scientologists were breaking various legal restrictions on medical practice and medical devices; the Internal Revenue Service disagreed with their claim to be exempt from taxation as a religious body. They, in turn, claimed to be the victims of an international conspiracy involving psychiatrists, the F.B.I., the C.I.A., and Interpol.

In the United Kingdom the sect was particularly active, and established a world headquarters at Saint Hill Manor, East Grinstead during the 1960s. But in 1968 two restrictions were imposed on their activities: aliens were to be refused permission to enter the country for purposes of training or employment as Scientologists; and L. Ron Hubbard was not to be allowed into the country under any circumstances. Richard Crossman later commissioned an inquiry into Scientology by Sir John Foster, Q.C. The report was critical of the group, but also suggested that the immigration ban should be lifted. Its validity under E.E.C. law was later upheld by the European Court of Justice, but it was finally lifted in 1980.

One of the characteristics of Scientology is litigiousness, and the movement is wealthy enough to finance about as many legal actions as it wants to bring (it is a major financial investment to be 'trained' as a Scientologist). The group was particularly active in going to court under the U.S. Freedom of Information Act because it thought that disclosure of government documents would reveal the conspiracy against it. They were equally ready to take legal action in Britain against 'Entheta' (criticism of Scientology) and 'Suppressive Persons' who made such criticisms. As a 1971 memo from the Scientology *Guardian World Wide* put it: 'Legal U.K. has been in courts more often than the rest of the Scientology world combined. They have won more cases and lost more cases than anywhere else . . . The losses did not hurt us, and the successes established an iron-clad ethics presence which has probably prevented more Entheta than we will ever know about . . .'

The reasons for their involvement in campaigning for an open government law were clear. The British restrictions on alien

Scientologists and on their leader were the result of a world-wide conspiracy against them. If government records were made open they would surely reveal that this conspiracy was based on false information, and the restrictions would then be lifted. So they set about getting a Freedom of Information Act.

They set about it with characteristic energy and a fair amount of money. Arthur Lewis, Labour M.P. for the London constituency of North-West Newham, was the first chairman of the All-Party Committee. The committee's staff, including Lewis's secretary, the press secretary, the legal adviser, and the medical adviser, were Scientologists. Money was available for secretarial help, printing of glossy brochures, holding conferences, and making a campaign film.

It was about a year before their participation in the campaign became generally known. Some groups, such as the National Council for Civil Liberties, Social Audit, and Mind (the National Association for Mental Health) were aware of the connection, and generally kept away from the Committee's campaign. N.C.C.L. and Mind had had a few conflicts with the Scientologists in the past (in Mind's case going as far as the courts). But such normally well-informed people as Harold Evans, editor of the *Sunday Times*, did not know, and he was persuaded to be a main speaker at a day-long conference sponsored by the Committee in Westminster Hall in April 1976. The next day news of their involvement was out, and most of the newspaper and radio coverage was about the Scientology connection rather than the subject of the meeting.

Their participation was not welcomed by most of the original open government campaigners. Some simply had no time for Scientology, thinking its 'theology' spurious, its structure autocratic, and its methods suspect. Others took a pragmatic view that the respectability of a legislative proposal would not be enhanced if it were supported by a group which many people regarded with suspicion.

But the Committee certainly succeeded in getting attention for the idea of a Freedom of Information (and Privacy) Act, even if the attention was not always favourable. Petitions were gathered from passers-by in High Streets, anyone who had said or written anything on the subject of secrecy was approached for recruitment, and press releases poured out. The first open government bill actually presented to Parliament was drafted by the All-Party Committee's legal adviser, drawing heavily on the U.S. Freedom of Information and Privacy Acts, but also incorporating some provisions from Scandinavian legislation. It was introduced in 1977 by Tom Litterick, then Labour M.P. for Birmingham Selly Oak.

The subject of open government began to attract more serious attention from a number of organizations, and a lobbying coalition was formed at the beginning of 1977 by the Outer Circle Policy Unit, which had been formed the previous autumn with a grant from the Rowntree Social Service Trust. Its chairman was Mark Bonham Carter, and the director was James Cornford, a former professor of politics at Edinburgh University. Active lobbying soon was divided more or less between the 'respectables' of the Outer Circle coalition and the more strident Scientologists working with the All-Party Committee. Of course they were both working for the support of the same M.P.s in order to get a bill passed, and many of the M.P.s maintained connections with both groups. The two factions cooperated occasionally, but the relationship between them was, and remains, an arm's-length one.

But they were not the only ones writing about and even lobbying for some sort of open government legislation. In 1977 the Royal Institute of Public Administration published a pamphlet by Ronald Wraith. *Open Government: the British Interpretation* criticized government secrecy, but felt that openness would be better achieved through administrative discretion than by legislation. In July of the same year the Outer Circle produced a pamphlet of its own, outlining its proposals for legislation, which were to be published the next year as a draft bill.

1977 was the year when open government legislative ideas reached adolescence, if they had not quite come of age, in Britain. The House of Commons had two bills before it, although there clearly would be no legislative time for their serious consideration.

Besides the Litterick bill there was another introduced by Ronald Atkins, M.P.

There had been other legislative efforts to require disclosure of specific kinds of government information, some more successful than others. The Industry Act 1975 had provisions which could force companies to provide information to government, and even allow for further disclosure by government to trade unions. It was weakened by many amendments, but there was one straightforward public information amendment which was forced through by Dr Jeremy Bray, a Labour back-bencher. Confidential Treasury economic models and forecasts not only had to be made available on request, but there was also a public right to use the computer on which they were maintained, on payment of an appropriate fee.

The Control of Pollution Act 1974 had several complicated provisions aimed at creating public registers of consent orders for waste-dumping, water pollution, and air pollution. But these were riddled with loopholes, and the enforcement agency which had been most severely criticized for secretiveness, the Alkali Inspectorate, managed to evade almost completely any legal requirement to be more open about how it did its job.

The Health and Safety Act 1974 also had guarded provisions for telling employees about hazards at work, and even for possible regulations allowing the general public to know about industrial processes that might affect their health. Two other statutes had already established rather different 'rights to know' for consumers and employees. The Consumer Credit Act 1974 had provided a clear right for anyone to get copies of personal reports held by credit reference agencies, with the Office of Fair Trading as a quasi-judicial enforcement body. This was the sort of 'subject access' later considered in more general terms by the Lindop Committee on Data Protection and Privacy. The Employment Protection Act 1975 had a fairly weak provision for disclosure of information by employers to trade unions.

These were piecemeal attempts to require greater openness in specific areas, and most of them had serious defects, either in broadly worded exemptions or in the machinery for enforcement.

But they did provide examples of how openness might be achieved by small steps, just as the Local Government Act 1972 had contained some public records requirements along with the 'open meetings' provisions introduced long before by Margaret Thatcher. In April 1977 the London Borough of Hillingdon's conviction for violating this provision was upheld on appeal. The climate was clearly changing, with attempts at open government amendments to the Devolution Bill, and the beginnings during the summer of 1977 of a draft open government bill within the Labour Party itself.

But the Labour Government lagged behind. The Queen's Speech in the autumn of 1975 had announced that 'proposals will be prepared to amend the Official Secrets Act 1911 and to liberalize the practices relating to official information'. This probably was an indication of what Roy Jenkins had more or less decided to do about the subject. 'Proposals' meant a Green or White Paper rather than a bill. Open government legislation along U.S. lines simply was not on, but there could be some sort of statement that the government would generally be more open about things in future.

The whole subject of secrecy law was seen as eminently deferrable. The 1975 Crossman *Diaries* decision was something of a disappointment, but a Committee of Privy Councillors could be trusted to come up with something sensible. The Radcliffe Committee did that in January 1976. In effect, it was felt that Crossman had been a maverick anyway, and the best way to stop a recurrence of his behaviour was to be a bit firmer about letting people like him into the insiders' club in future.

There was, from the viewpoint of most civil servants and ministers, a serious political miscalculation in 1976 in deciding to put off any legislation on government information. The Franks proposals were still generally considered to be about right as a 'reform' of the discredited Official Secrets Act. 'Open government' legislation was still very much a fringe idea. However the promise had slipped into the manifesto, it could be declared to have been fulfilled by a fairly cosmetic sort of policy statement. A Franks bill could be got through easily enough, and a liberalized version of the 1969 White Paper could take care of the 'open government' side. But there were no votes in it, and other matters were pressing. It could wait.

The promise in the 1975 Queen's Speech was carried out as little and as late as possible. The 'proposals' amounted to a statement by the Home Secretary in the Commons on the very last day of Parliament in the autumn of 1976. There was a new Prime Minister, James Callaghan, and the new Home Secretary, Merlyn Rees, was very much his man.

Rees had managed Callaghan's campaign for election by the Parliamentary Labour Party as the successor to Harold Wilson. Roy Jenkins, badly defeated in the contest, had gone off to Brussels. There was a new ministerial Cabinet Committee called GEN 29 to consider government secrecy law, and it was chaired by the Prime Minister himself. Whether out of sheer conservatism or a distaste for any Jenkinsite reformist notions, Callaghan let it be known that the Official Secrets Act was fine as it stood.

But it was not so fine for dealing with the leak in June 1976 of Cabinet information about delaying a child benefit scheme. The author of the article was soon identified as Frank Field, director of the Child Poverty Action Group (later to join the Outer Circle group, and to become a Labour M.P. himself in 1979). Despite an emergency debate, a leak inquiry, and a police investigation, the leaker was not prosecuted. Callaghan then confirmed to the Commons that, although it was true that he had been opposed to any change in the Official Secrets Act, he was converted: he wanted to reform the Act to make it 'more effective'.

By the time Merlyn Rees made his statement to the Commons in autumn 1976 it was too late to get the modified version of Franks into law without a great deal of trouble, and the trouble might have taken the form of demands for an open government bill along with it. The Rees criminal law proposals were more liberal than Franks in some ways, but more strict in others. The open government pledge was for more Green Papers, and James Callaghan promised, on 24 November 1976, a 'modest change' to publish more background material to them.

The Labour Government was losing its majority, and the announcement in November 1976 that Philip Agee and Mark Hosenball were to be deported (see Chapter 3) made some Labour back-benchers more rebellious than usual, even about things presented as serious matters of national security. Then in February 1977 Aubrey, Berry, and Campbell were arrested under the Official Secrets Act. After that, nothing the government did about secrecy legislation was likely to be easy, and nothing was.

During the summer of 1977 there was an effort to do something about open government, but the attempt itself was flawed by secrecy. The Head of the Home Civil Service, Sir Douglas Allen, sent a memorandum to Civil Service Permanent Secretaries on 6 July. In future they were to prepare papers so that as many as possible might be made public. Facts and the advice based on those facts were to be segregated, so that the factual parts could be released.

It was his final act as a model civil servant, doing his best to provide the government of the day with what was necessary to carry out manifesto commitments. He became Lord Croham, and went off to the Bank of England. The circular was leaked rather quickly. There were hurried conferences within the Civil Service Department, and it was even suggested that an embarrassingly candid explanation of the memo's purpose to avoid the 'formidably burdensome' provisions of a possible Freedom of Information Act could be deleted before releasing the memo officially.

The Croham Directive, as it became known, might have been forgotten if it had not been for Peter Hennessy, Whitehall correspondent of *The Times*, who was taking it very seriously. He started asking departments what they were doing about it, and he kept on asking them. Writing about which departments had released what, making up league tables of secrecy and openness, writing letters demanding background papers under the Croham Directive and printing whatever replies he got . . . he was clearly becoming obsessive on the subject. He was also talking to James Cornford, and taking an active part in the detailed preparation of the Outer Circle's draft bill.

The winter of 1977–8 was proving difficult for the government. On the criminal law side, the ABC case was going badly long before it actually came to trial. On the open government side Hennessy and others were keeping up the pressure. Something finally had to be done, and responsibility was divided between the Home Office, which would handle 'reforming' the Official Secrets Act, and the Civil Service Department, which would handle the open government side. The conventional wisdom was, and still is, that the criminal law side comes first: get straight who can go to gaol for leaking what, then consider possible measures about open government. The Home Office got to work on turning the Franks proposals, with the modifications that Rees had announced in 1976, into a White Paper. The Civil Service Department, now under Sir Ian Bancroft, weren't doing very much, although they did have an open government man. The Croham memo was enough, and anything further would naturally come well after whatever was done about the Official Secrets Act.

The Outer Circle coalition was pressing ahead, preparing a draft bill that would cover both reform of the criminal law on official information and provisions for open government. The membership was a shifting group of lawyers, pressure-group activists, journalists, and M.P.s. At one time or another their meetings included people from the National Council for Civil Liberties, the Consumers' Association, Child Poverty Action Group, Social Audit, the editor of *New Society*, and many others. At the end of May 1978 they held a weekend conference at Ware in Hertfordshire. The draft bill was presented, and there were fierce arguments.

There was some polite competition between the Outer Circle effort and the draft bill which was working its way through the Labour Party. One of the points of disagreement on the open government side was on where to appeal against secrecy. The Outer Circle favoured some combination of an ombudsman and the courts. The Labour version started out with judicial review, but that was quickly replaced by an independent panel. Labour distrust of the judges runs deep.

Justice (the British section of the International Commission of

Jurists) had appointed a panel of their own, which included three former permanent secretaries. When their proposal was published as a pamphlet in summer 1978 it was no surprise that it favoured a moderate, flexible approach to open government, with a minimum of legislation. A code of conduct for more openness, with the most general of exceptions, could be enforced by complaints to the Parliamentary Commissioner for Administration.

In July 1978 the Outer Circle's draft bill was published. Almost simultaneously the Home Office White Paper on reform of section 2 of the Official Secrets Act was released.[3] It was, more or less, as expected. The criminal provisions followed the Franks/Rees recommendations about the information to be covered, with ministers to have the final word about what information was or was not to be protected by criminal penalties. As for open government, reference was made to the Croham Directive and Green Papers, and there was a promise that they would have a look at how such things were ordered in other lands. As for open government *legislation*, that unfortunate pledge in the second 1974 manifesto, the government had 'an open mind'.

Merlyn Rees got some stick in the Commons about all that. The ABC defendants were still facing possible fourteen-year prison sentences under section 1 of the Act, and many Labour M.P.s supported them strongly. And what did he mean by 'an open mind' on open government legislation? That was when the Home Secretary gave a short public lecture in political realities to Robert Kilroy-Silk, telling him that there probably weren't more than two or three people in his constituency who cared anything about the issue.

Then the newspapers started asking for more. After all, the Croham Directive had said that background papers to policy decisions should generally be made available, at least the factual parts. Surely the White Paper on the Official Secrets Act was such a policy decision, so where were the background papers? The reflex civil service reaction was to say that they were confidential communications from foreign governments. A bit of checking with those foreign governments showed just the opposite. All the documents obtained from Canada, the United States, Sweden, and Australia were freely available in those countries, and all of their titles eventually appeared in *The Times*.

The reaction to the White Paper was enough to convince the government that it should do its best to forget about the whole subject. Labour had only been staying in office by an 'arrangement' with the Liberals anyway. The Liberals had gently been exercising the little influence they had by urging open government legislation, with yet another pamphlet.[4]

The 'arrangement' with the Liberals came to an end. Everyone was expecting an autumn election and official information law was the least of their worries. Whatever they did would cause trouble, and nothing they did would gain votes. Then James Callaghan announced that Labour would soldier on with a minority in the House of Commons. The vetting of the jury in the ABC trial came out, and the trial was started all over again. The 'espionage' charges had to be dropped and the defendants effectively got off. The *New Statesman* published the Prime Minister's memo explaining why everything about Cabinet Committees had to be kept secret, most importantly because letting anything out 'would be more likely to whet appetites than to satisfy them'.

As if to indicate that open government was now a legitimate issue, the influential Ditchley Foundation held a weekend conference in November, and the consensus was that it might be time to try going even beyond the Croham Directive.

But for the Government, the whole subject was to be put aside as long as possible. The ABC fiasco would be forgotten after a while, and the subject would be left to cool off, at least until after the election. There was nothing that actually required the Government to become involved in the whole business again. Then Clement Freud drew first place in the ballot for private members' bills, and introduced the Outer Circle bill.

The Parliamentary system for private members' bills is a minor exception to the rule in Westminster-style parliamentary democracy that legislation is government legislation. The government of the day must have the confidence of a majority in the House of Commons, and in normal times it expects and is expected to use that majority to pass whatever laws it thinks are necessary for the business of government. The spring of 1979 was not a normal time in Parliamentary terms, however. The Parliamentary Labour Party did not have an overall majority, and it had only managed to defeat a motion of no-confidence by making promises to various minority parties.

But it was still the government, and it still controlled the Parliamentary timetable, even if it had to be cautious about the contents of its own legislation. The arrangements for private members' bills provide that a certain number of Fridays are set aside for debating bills introduced by M.P.s who are not Ministers of the Crown. At the beginning of each session M.P.s draw lots to determine who will get those Fridays. Usually only private members' bills introduced by the first six to ten lucky members have any chance of becoming law, and then only if the government gives tacit support or remains neutral.

The Litterick bill had been introduced under the 'ten-minute' rule, so called because only that much Parliamentary time is allowed for a speech to introduce it. Ronald Atkins had drawn fifteenth place in the 1977 ballot, which was much too far down the list for his bill to have any chance of being debated.

It was bad luck for the Government that Clement Freud drew first place and chose the Outer Circle bill. He looked round for something worthy which had enough back-bench support to have a reasonable chance of succeeding. Richard Wainwright, who shared an office with him, was a trustee of the Rowntree Trust, which funded the Outer Circle. So the Outer Circle and Clement Freud were properly introduced, and it was that bill which he decided to put forward.

The first real debate on any legislation in the House of Commons is on a bill's second reading, and that was set for 19 January 1979 on the Freud bill. Freud had two immediate jobs. He had to prepare a persuasive speech with which to introduce the bill, and he had to round up at least a hundred M.P.s to be in the Commons that Friday afternoon in case the Government decided to try killing it then and there. He did both skilfully. In his speech he was in turn witty (what were, he asked, the 'dark secrets of the White Fish Authority' on which Parliamentary Questions could not be tabled?), scathing, and reassuring for those who might think the bill was an assault on national security thought up by a bunch of dangerous lefties. He summoned up all the skills honed in countless 'Any Questions' broadcasts. He also summoned up more than enough supporters, calling in political debts and relying on old friendships. Jeremy Thorpe appeared in the House for the first time since the Minehead committal hearing, just in case his support was needed.

In the event, it was not. Although a vote might have been called it is more likely that the Government had already decided to let it pass for the time being. Merlyn Rees was harried and distracted (it was a winter of even more industrial discontent than usual). This was a very complicated subject, the Government had plans well in hand to do something about it, perhaps the Freud bill might be considered as a sort of 'Green Paper' for discussion. Conservative and Labour back-benchers all had their innings, from Hugh Fraser reminiscing about the *Sunday Telegraph* trial to Jeff Rooker describing the problems he had in discovering the subjects on which an M.P. couldn't submit Parliamentary Questions. The Conservative front-bench was represented by Sir William Percival, who made a short speech about who should approve prosecutions under any new official secrets law.

The bill was unopposed, there was tea in one of the Commons rooms afterwards, and the bill's various supporters were pleased and relieved. The hard part in the bill's committee stage was still to come, and it would be trickier than any of them anticipated.

Second-reading debates are about the general principle of a bill, with detailed, line-by-line consideration left to the committee stage. (It is possible for a bill to go through all of its stages – first reading, second reading, committee, third reading, and report – in a single day on the floor of the House of Commons, as was done with the 1911 Official Secrets Act.) The Freud bill had a proper committee stage by a standing committee of the House sitting in one of the smaller chambers upstairs. But it was only the usual sort of committee stage in the most formal sense. Most legislation is prepared by Parliamentary draftsmen for government departments, and introduced by ministers who are briefed by civil servants. Most legislation is also on clear party-political lines, and the Opposition M.P.s have their own researchers to brief them and prepare amendments.

The shape of committee rooms reflects this pattern. They are laid out like miniatures of the Commons chamber itself, with facing rows of benches for the government and opposition members. The Chairman of the committee, like the Speaker in the House, sits at one end in the centre, with a box behind and to the right for the civil servants who observe and occasionally pass notes to ministers as tricky points come up.

In normal times the committee goes through the bill, with the minister explaining the clauses, the opposition arguing for their amendments, and everyone voting more or less along party lines. Party discipline is less strict in committee than it is in the Commons itself, and can usually afford to be. Committee amendments that would have any serious effect on government legislation are usually removed when the bill is returned to the floor of the House.

But private members' bills are exceptional by definition. Usually they deal with matters of law reform considered to be either too routine or too sensitive altogether for a government to introduce. Many private members' bills are on subjects such as the death penalty, homosexuality, or abortion, which are emotionally loaded, but not terribly complicated in legislative terms.

The Freud bill was on an unusually complicated subject for a private members' bill. It was an attempt to change an essential part of the whole machinery of government. Some of the complexity has been demonstrated in the previous chapter and the one on U.S. law. On the criminal law side, there were complicated questions about classification, authorization, disclosure, receipt, and many others. On the open government side there were equally difficult questions about defining records, setting out the exemptions, and providing machinery for enforcement.

The government's initial decision not to oppose the Freud bill on its second reading may have been based on the assumption that the bill could hardly get through all its stages before a spring election was called, and it was better to avoid unnecessary fuss. (They turned out to be right about a spring election, although they could hardly have anticipated the circumstances.) But when the committee stage began it was clear that there had been some hard thinking about the bill. If things were handled just right, the bill might even be turned to government advantage. The tactics were to take the criminal penalties part of the Freud bill and beef them up with amendments until they were the same as the Franks/Rees proposal, then throw away the open government parts except for a declaration of good intentions.

There were incipient divisions in the Freud ranks, and they could be exploited. Party loyalty could be invoked gently, without actually using the whip. The Freedom Association and the Tribune Group were rarely on the same side about anything, and it could be tactfully pointed out that such unlikely alliances could look equally strange to constituencies and to party leaders. It could have worked, and almost did on some details.

After an initial procedural defeat the Freud team settled down to the punishing grind. Committee meetings were held on Tuesday and Thursday mornings. The stacks of government and Conservative front-bench amendments were available on Mondays. James Cornford and his team spent hours going through the amendments looking for the innocent-looking clauses that could emasculate the bill. Explanatory memoranda were written up and distributed to committee members.

The first government speaker was Brynmor John, a Welsh barrister who was Minister of State at the Home Office. He understood every nuance in the bill, despised it, and made little attempt to conceal his frequent anger and contempt. The Home Office civil servants in the box behind him were appropriately silent, except to whisper occasionally or pass a note. They had done their work already, beavering away at the bill since it was published in December, drafting the stacks of amendments that would turn it into what was wanted.

Cornford and his counter civil servants at the other end were rather busier. They had commandeered the box usually used by

the press, where they rapidly shuffled through the piles of amendments and notes on them made the day before. It was surprising
that the bill survived as relatively unscathed as it did. The
Cornford effort progressed from notes on the effect of amendments and advice on how to vote, to notes for speeches and,
finally, to full drafts of speeches for M.P.s. The printed record of
the committee proceedings reproduces the speeches and arguments made, along with the votes, but it does not include the
hurried whispered conferences, the frantic hand signals, the
committee members slipping out to another committee and
racing back at the shout of 'division', arriving just before the
doors were locked and looking for a signal on how to vote before
their names were called. And getting different signals from
different people.

After their initial success, the Home Office did not gain much
ground. Brynmor John left the committee room after making it
clear that the defeated government amendments would be reintroduced when the bill returned to the floor of the House of
Commons. His Home Office civil servants slipped out of their
box, and were replaced by another team from the Civil Service
Department.

The Minister of State from the Civil Service Department,
Charles Morris, was more conciliatory. He explained that he was
all in favour of open government; it was only the methods and the
expense that concerned him. The back-benchers were still very
far from being a disciplined team, and there were disagreements
on several of the provisions. On the final amendment the
committee voted narrowly against appeals to the courts from
secrecy decisions.

The committee stage was over. Charles Morris came down to
the Cornford bench and shook hands all round. There would be a
few weeks' pause before the next stage on the floor of the House of
Commons.

The battle was far from won. Government amendments would
probably be reintroduced in the Commons, the bill might be
starved of Parliamentary time, it might even be mutilated in the
House of Lords. The next stage was set to begin on 6 April

when the Freud bill would return to the floor of the Commons.

Outside Parliament a B.B.C. documentary was being made, and the National Council for Civil Liberties rushed out a pamphlet. The Civil Service Department was completing the survey of open government in other countries which had been promised in the White Paper the summer before, and a Green Paper on open government was being prepared. On Wednesday, 28 March, there was a meeting between the bill's supporters and Charles Morris with his advisers at the Civil Service Department. It was filmed, in part, by the B.B.C. crew. Although it was later reported that there was authorization to negotiate a compromise over the bill, no offers were made. The smell of impending defeat was drifting across from Westminster to Horse Guards Parade, and the meeting was a polite debate. It was the first direct exchange between the team advising Freud and the civil servants advising the Minister. On the civil service side it was clear who had done the homework. Senior civil servants repeated the old platitudes. Others could argue specific points; they knew how legislation worked in other countries, even if they did not particularly like it.

The Labour Government lost the vote of confidence. Before Parliament was officially dissolved the Green Paper on Open Government and the background Civil Service Department report were published on Friday, 30 April. The N.C.C.L. got copies that morning, and released its own pamphlet at noon. It was all something of a sideshow, because the general election was on.

The Labour Green Paper suggested a code of conduct about open government, but was vague about whether Parliament should be involved in drafting it, and vaguer still about how it would be enforced. The background study was a thorough, if sceptical, survey of law and practice in nine countries. They had learned a lesson from the summer before. Everything was published, including the names of people they had talked to.

The Labour manifesto contained a more guarded promise on open government than in 1974, but it wouldn't matter for several years. The Conservative manifesto said nothing at all on the subject, and the Conservatives won with a solid enough majority to get almost anything through.

The 'anything' was the Protection of Official Information Bill. It was tougher than the Franks/Rees combination that Labour had in mind, and tougher even than the proposals made by the Conservative front-bench during debates on the Freud bill. Prosecutions would be brought by the Attorney-General, and by him alone. In the committee stage of the Freud bill, Sir Michael Havers had suggested that the Security Commission might advise on such prosecutions, but now he was Attorney-General, and nothing more was said about the Commission.

The 1979 bill, like the 1911 bill, was introduced in the House of Lords. But there was now an articulate open government lobby which went into action again. The government bill was bitingly criticized in the Lords by peers such as Lord Wigoder. It was widely rumoured that the Thatcher Government would stand for no nonsense about the bill; that it was to be out of the Lords before Christmas, and through the Commons as quickly as possible. This might have been possible, with vigorous whipping, but Andrew Boyle's book, *The Climate of Treason*, was published, and, as has been mentioned in a previous chapter, the former Keeper of the Queen's Pictures was later named as a one-time Soviet spy. The Boyle book would have been a crime under the new bill, and that was reason, or excuse, enough to withdraw the bill.

Inclement Prospects

A comparative study of government secrecy published in 1978 (*The Darker Reaches of Government*) described the climate for open government law in Britain as being 'simultaneously clement and inclement' and the Thatcher Government was distinctly chillier towards the idea than even Callaghan had been.

1980 began with yet another pamphlet on the subject, a Fabian tract by Trevor Barnes, a B.B.C. journalist who had spent a year in the United States.[5] He advocated legislation in stages to open British government. First would come a statutory instrument to implement the Croham Directive, then a Preliminary Official Information Act establishing a code of practice slightly more stringent than the one proposed by Justice and enforced by a separate Information Ombudsman, and finally a more or less fully-fledged Freedom of Information Act after three or four years. The independent arbiter in this last Act would be a new sort of body, composed of two judges and three M.P.s. The criminal law would be reformed, and section 1 of the old Official Secrets Act would be replaced by a proper Espionage Act.

The Times resumed publication just in time for the Blunt affair, and Peter Hennessy resumed his badgering of Whitehall to release more information of the less exciting sort. During the year-long suspension of the newspaper Hennessy had been working with a post-graduate student at Cardiff, Colin Bennett, on a 'Consumers' Guide to Open Government', published by the Outer Circle in March 1980. Much of this was a detailed audit of how much had actually been released under the Croham Directive, with end-of-term marks for openness given out to departments.

It was nearly the end of the Croham Directive, although it survived in modified form. The new Prime Minister confirmed that it was still policy, but the monitoring of its application by the Civil Service Department was dropped. [6] The Home Secretary had told the National Council for Civil Liberties the summer before that there would be no open government legislation, and probably no code of conduct either.

Shortly before that the Prime Minister had sent a letter drafted by her Principal Private Secretary to all Secretaries of State. Although it was classified 'Confidential', something of its contents was revealed to *The Times* and it was explained by the new Minister of State at the Civil Service Department in the House of Commons on 20 June 1979. It was predictable: legislation to provide a public right of access 'would not be appropriate' and a code of practice 'would be open to many of the same objections'. They would, however, be as open as possible about releasing background papers.

The Hennessy–Bennett guide in effect urged everyone to keep

up the pressure. 'The great lesson for inquirers seeking to penetrate Whitehall is not to take "no" for an answer. When baulked, quote the Croham Directive, the Public Records Acts and the Establishment Officers' Guide at the "gatekeepers" who refuse access. Always make them justify their refusals, preferably in writing.'

The Public Records Act, by section 5(1), does make it possible for documents to be made public after a period 'either longer or shorter' than thirty years. The Establishment Officers' Guide (which itself was only published in part in the 1976 Commission on Standards of Conduct in Public Life) says that 'the need for greater openness in the work of Government is now widely accepted'. It also says that any disclosures must 'be such as will neither prejudice national security; create the possibility of embarrassment to the Government in the conduct of its policies; nor bring into question the impartiality of the Civil Service'.

In short, all of these 'tools' for opening up government are the usual statements of good intentions, with control over disclosures to be absolutely discretionary. The Establishment Guide, by juxtaposing the reasons for secrecy, was remarkably like the testimony of a government witness in the *Sunday Telegraph* case, when he explained that 'embarrassment and security are not really two different things'.

So there would be no open government law, nor even a code of practice of any kind. On the criminal side the more respectable-looking Protection of Official Information Bill would be put aside, and the country would carry on under the old Official Secrets Act for a while. As for leakers, British Steel tried very hard to get the courts to help it track down people who showed embarrassing documents to the press.

But the open government campaigners were getting hardened. They had countless variations on the Freud bill available, usually introduced and printed under the ten-minute rule, just in case. They were putting down disclosure amendments to every bit of important legislation that came along.

More books on government secrecy were being written, including one by David Leigh of the *Guardian* and another from the

National Consumer Council. The idea of open government had very nearly been acepted even though there was disagreement on details and government resistance.

Public opinion was changing, and a substantial majority of those questioned in a 1980 B.B.C. survey favoured a British Freedom of Information Act. It was, and is, a matter of time and effort before that is translated into law.

Postscript

The Thatcher Government is more decisive about open government legislation than its Labour predecessors: it is firmly opposed to it. Frank Hooley, Labour Member for Sheffield Heeley, drew third place in the ballot for private members' bills for the 1980–81 session and introduced a bill substantially the same as Clement Freud's. Flouting the convention that private members' bills are allowed a second reading, the Government used the 'payroll vote' (all ministers, and Parliamentary private secretaries) to kill the bill.

There were other developments in the field of government information during the autumn of 1980 and spring of 1981, few of them in the direction of greater openness. The officially secret A-Codes, guidelines for supplementary benefits, were replaced by a more open system. But concern about secrecy, or rather privacy, and social security was aroused by a report in *The Times* that computerized information on vehicles and drivers was being used for social security investigations.

The British Government signed the Council of Europe Data Protection Convention, but with no immediate prospect of legislation to implement it. (One defect of the Convention is that there is no procedure by which complaints can be made that Britain is failing to comply with its obligations.)

Other countries continued to take the related subjects of data protection and government information more seriously. The Netherlands passed a data protection statute. In Canada, the Trudeau government's plans to enact a relatively strong open government law were only delayed by the controversy over a new constitution. The Australian Freedom of Information bill was so watered down by the government that the open government lobby opposed it almost unanimously. The Danks Committee in New Zealand endorsed the principle of open government legislation.

Britain continued the familiar ritual of leak inquiries which led nowhere. The courts became involved in official information questions in two controversial cases. After Granada Television was ordered to name the British Steel 'mole' who had leaked embarrassing papers, British Steel dropped the case and the re-tired employee came forward voluntarily.

Some of the documents on prison control units, the disclosure of which is described on page 106, were made public. But the solicitor who showed them to a journalist after they had been read out in open court was held in contempt by the Court of Appeal. Lord Denning was particularly scathing, suggesting that the documents should never have been made available at all, even for the limited purposes of litigation.

In Britain, freedom of information made its way onto the political agenda as a serious issue, albeit rather far down. Conferences were held and resolutions passed, but it became clear that legislation would take a change of government, and probably a coincidental scandal or two. As a Swedish delegate to a 1976 conference in Austria tactfully put it, in this area there are developed countries and less developed ones.

Notes

Chapter 2

1. Itzhak Galnoor (ed.), *Government Secrecy in Democracies*, Harper & Row, New York, 1977.
2. Civil Service Department, *Disclosure of Information: A Report on Overseas Practice*, H.M.S.O., 1979.
3. S. E. Finer, *Comparative Government*, Pelican Books, 1974.
4. *Report from the Select Committee on Parliamentary Questions* (H. C. 393), H.M.S.O., 1972, p. 20
5. G. Almond and S. Verba, *The Civic Culture*, Princeton University Press, Princeton, N. J., 1963.
6. *New Statesman*, 15 December 1972, p. 900.
7. Peter Laurie, *Beneath the City Streets*, 3rd ed., Panther, 1979.

Chapter 3

1. *Departmental Committee on Section 2 of the Official Secrets Act 1911* (Cmnd 5104), H.M.S.O., 1972, para. 88.
2. *Chandler v. Director of Public Prosecutions* [1964] 3 All E. R. 142.
3. *Lewis v. Cattle* [1938] 2 All E.R. 368.
4. Tony Bunyan, *The Political Police in Britain*, Julian Friedmann, 1976.

Chapter 4

1. See Medawar, 'Parliamentary Questions and Answers', *Social Audit*, 1980.
2. *Sunday Times*, 12 December 1971.
3. *Report from the Select Committee on Parliamentary Questions* (H.C. 393), H.M.S.O., 1972.
4. *Labour Weekly*, 18 January 1980.
5. *Sunday Times*, 16 March 1980.
6. *Guardian*, 29 and 30 January 1980.
7. *The Times Higher Education Supplement*, 7 and 14 March 1980.
8. *Report of Inquiry into Vehicle and General Insurance Company* (H.L. 80, H.C. 133), H.M.S.O., 1972.
9. H.C. 393, op. cit.
10. *Guardian*, 12 February 1980.
11. 'Danger of a Freudian Slip', *New Society*, 15 February 1979.

Chapter 5

1. Jeremy Tunstall, *The Westminster Lobby Correspondents*, Routledge & Kegan Paul, 1970.
2. *Report of the Committee of Privy Councillors* (Cmnd 3309), H.M.S.O., 1967, p. 145.
3. *The 'D' Notice System* (Cmnd 3312), H.M.S.O., 1967.
4. *The New York Times v. Sullivan*, 376 U.S. 254 (1964).
5. *Report of the Committee on Defamation* (Cmnd 5909), H.M.S.O., 1975, para. 215.

Chapter 6

1. *Beloff v. Pressdram* [1973] 1 All E.R. 241.
2. *Hubbard v. Vosper* [1972] 1 All E.R. 1023.
3. *Attorney-General v. Jonathan Cape* [1975] 3 All E.R. 484.
4. Hugo Young, *The Crossman Affair*, Hamish Hamilton and Jonathan Cape, 1976.
5. Cmnd 6386.
6. *Duncan v. Cammell Laird* [1942] 1 All E.R. 874.
7. *Conway v. Rimmer* [1968] 1 All E.R. 874.
8. *R. v. Lewes Justices* [1973] A.C. 388.
9. *Crompton Amusement Machines v. Commissioners of Customs and Excise (No. 2)* [1973] 2 All E.R. 1169.
10. *D. v. N.S.P.C.C.* [1977] 1 All E.R. 589.
11. *Norwich Pharmacal v. Commissioners of Customs and Excise* [1973] 2 All E.R. 943.
12. *F. Hoffman La Roche & Co. A.G. v. Department of Trade and Industry*, The Times Law Report, 18 April 1975. (Most of these cases are considered at length by Jacob in 'Discovery and the Public Interest', *Public Law*, 1976.)
13. *Burmah Oil v. Bank of England* [1979] 2 All E.R. 461.
14. *Science Research Council v. Nasse, Leyland Cars v. Vyas* [1979] 3 W.L.R. 762.
15. *Waugh v. British Railways Board* [1979] 2 All E.R. 1169.
16. *The Times*, 1 February 1980.
17. *Guardian*, 7 March 1980.
18. *Distillers Co. (Biochemicals) Ltd v. Times Newspapers Ltd* [1974] 3 WLR 728.
19. R. Woodward and W. Armstrong, *The Brethren*, Secker & Warburg, 1979.
20. *New York Review of Books*, 7 February 1980, pp. 3–8.
21. Cmnd 3121, 1966, para. 40.
22. *Guardian*, 16 August 1980.
23. *R. v. Socialist Worker* [1975] 1 All E.R. 142.

Chapter 7

1. *Report of the Committee on Privacy* (Cmnd 5012), H.M.S.O., 1972.
2. *Report of the Data Protection Committee* (Cmnd 7341), H.M.S.O., 1978.

Chapter 8

1. *Environmental Protection Agency v. Mink*, 410 U.S. 73 (1973).
2. *Department of Air Force v. Rose*, 425 U.S. 352 (1976).
3. *Vaughan v. Rosen*, 523 F.2d 1136 (1975).
4. *N.L.R.B. v. Sears, Roebuck & Co.*, 421 U.S. 132 (1975).
5. *Hawkes v. I.R.S.*, 467 F.2d 787 (6th Cir. 1972).
6. *Robertson v. F.A.A.*, 422 U.S. 255 (1975).

7. *Tax Analysts v. I.R.S.*, 505 F.2d 350 (D.C. Cir. 1974).
8. *Pierce & Stevens Chemical Co. v. C.S.P.C.*, 585 F.2d 1382 (2d Cir. 1978).
9. *Philippi v. C.I.A.*, 546 F2d 1009 (D.C. Cir. 1976).
10. S. E. Finer, *Comparative Government*, Pelican Books, 1974.
11. *Consumers' Union v. Veterans' Administration*, 301 F. Supp. 796 (S.D.N.Y. 1969) appeal dismissed, 436 F.2d 1363 (2d Cir. 1971).
12. *National Parks & Conservation Association v. Morton*, 498 F.2d 765 (D.C. Cir. 1974).
13. *Chrysler Corporation v. Brown*, 99 S.Ct. 1705 (1979).
14. *N.L.R.B. v. Sears, Roebuck & Co.*, 421 U.S. 132 (1975).
15. *Federal Open Market Committee v. Merrill*, 99 S. Ct. 2800 (1979).
16. *Department of Air Force v. Rose*, 425 U.S. 352 (1976).
17. *Wine Hobby U.S.A. v. I.R.S.*, 502 F.2d 133 (3d Cir. 1974).
18. *N.L.R.B. v. Robbins Tire & Rubber Co.*, 98 S.Ct. 311 (1978).
19. *Maroscia v. Levy*, 569 F.2d 1000 (7th Cir. 1977).
20. *Stern v. Richardson*, 367 F.Supp. 1316 (D.D.C. 1973).
21. *Consumers' Union v. Heimann*, 589 F.2d 531 (D.C. Cir. 1978).
22. *Pennzoil v. F.P.C.*, 534 F.2d 627 (5th Cir. 1976).
23. Civil Service Department, *Disclosure of Official Information: A Report on Overseas Practice*, H.M.S.O., 1979, and *Open Government* (Cmnd 7250), H.M.S.O., 1979.
24. *Wellford v. Hardin*, 444 F.2d (4th Cir. 1971).
    Chrysler Corporation v. Brown, 99 S.Ct. 1705 (1979).
    Schechter v. Richardson; Hricko v. Train; Health Research Group v. H.E.W.: unreported because information released after suits filed. Summarized in *Litigation under the Amended Freedom of Information Act*, appendix p. 182 (4th ed., ed. Christine Marwick, Center for National Security Studies, Washington, D.C., 1978).

Chapter 9

1. Nils Herlitz, 'Publicity of Official Documents in Sweden', *Public Law*, 1958.
2. Cmnd 6386, para. 35.
3. P. Bratt, *IB och Hotet mot Vår Säkerhet* (IB and the threat to our security), Gidlunds, Stockholm, 1973.
4. Freedom of the Press Act, Chapter 7, article 3.
5. Svea Hovrätt, DB 37, 195/74.
6. 'IB Affären: De Viktiga Frågorna' (The IB affair: the important questions), *Svenska Dagbladet*, 3 December 1973.
7. L. Gröll, *Press Law and Press Ethics in Sweden*, 1975.
8. Justice Department Orientation Booklet, p. 8.
9. Rt 1977. s. 1035.
10. Law on Party Access in Administration, 1964.
11. Section 2 (para. 2(4)).
12. No. 582, 1970.
13. *X v. Federal Republic of Germany*, no. 4274/69, *Yearbook* 11, p. 782.
14. *Bulletin of the European Parliament*, 1973–4, no. 30/73, pp. 9f.; *Official Journal of the European Communities*, no. C114, 27 December 1973, p. 11, and no. C22, 7 March 1974, p. 12.
15. D. Rowat, 'The Problem of Administrative Secrecy', *International Review of*

Administrative Sciences, vol. 32, no. 2, 1966, pp. 99–106; 'How Much Administrative Secrecy?', *Canadian Journal of Economics and Political Science*, vol. 1, no. 4, November 1975.

16. T. M. Rankin, *Freedom of Information in Canada: Will the Doors Stay Shut?*, Canadian Bar Association, 1977.

17. D. Rowat, *Public Access to Government Documents: A Comparative Perspective*.

18. *Fifth Report, Joint Standing Committee on Regulations and Statutory Instruments, Third Session, Thirtieth Parliament*, Supply and Services Canada, 1978.

19. J. Spigelman, *Government Secrecy: Political Censorship in Australia*, Angus & Robertson, Sydney, 1972.

20. Attorney-General's Department, *Report of Interdepartmental Committee, Proposed Freedom of Information Legislation*, Australian Government Publishing Service, Canberra, 1974.

21. John McMillan, 'Freedom of Information in Australia: Issue Closed', *Federal Law Review*, no. 8, 1977.

22. Review of New South Wales Government Administration, *Interim Report: Directions for Change*, N.S.W. Printer, Sydney, 1977.

23. John McMillan, 'Making Government Accountable: A Comparative Analysis of Freedom of Information Statutes', *New Zealand Law Journal*, 1977.

24. F. M. Auburn, 'Computers and Privacy', *New Zealand Law Journal*, 1972.

Chapter 10

1. Anthony Mathews, *The Darker Reaches of Government*, University of California Press, Berkeley, 1978, p. 181.

2. Civil Service Department, *Disclosure of Official Information: A Report on Overseas Practice*, H.M.S.O., 1979.

3. Published by Julian Friedmann, p. xvii.

4. 'Danger of a Freudian Slip', *New Society*, 15 February 1979.

5. A thorough comparison of all bills introduced is contained in House of Commons Reference Sheet 79/1.

Chapter 11

1. B. Schwartz and H. W. R. Wade, *Legal Control of Government*, Clarendon Press, 1972.

2. W. Birtles, 'Big Brother Knows Best', *Public Law*, 1973.

3. Cmnd 7285.

4. Liberal Party, *Public Access to Official Information*, 1978.

5. Trevor Barnes, 'Open Up', Fabian Tract no. 467, 1980.

6. Commons Written Answer, 23 October 1979.

Bibliography

Agee, Philip, *Inside the Company: C.I.A. Diary*, Penguin Books, 1975.

Aitken, Jonathan, *Officially Secret*, Weidenfeld & Nicolson, 1971.

Almond, G., and Verba, S., *The Civic Culture*, Princeton University Press, Princeton, N.J., 1963

Anderson, Stanley, 'Public Access to Government Files in Sweden', 21 *American Journal of Comparative Law* 3 (Summer 1973).

Barker, A., and Rush, M., *The Member of Parliament and His Information*, Allen & Unwin, 1970.

Barnes, J. A., *Who Should Know What? Social Science, Privacy and Ethics*, Penguin Books, 1979.

Barnes, Michael, 'The Right to Know: The Dangers of Secrecy in Industry', *The Listener*, 2 May 1974, p. 559.

Barnes, Trevor, *Open Up: Britain and Freedom of Information*, Fabian Society, 1980.

Benn, Tony, *Arguments for Socialism*, Jonathan Cape, 1979; Penguin Books, 1980.

Berger, Raoul, *Executive Privilege: a Constitutional Myth*, Harvard University Press, 1974.

Birtles, William, 'Big Brother Knows Best', *Public Law*, 1973.

Boyle, Andrew, *The Climate of Treason*, Hutchinson, 1979.

Bradshaw, K., and Pring, D., *Parliament and Congress*, Constable, 1972.

Bratt, Peter, *IB och Hotet Mot Vår Säkerhet* (IB and the threat to our security), Gidlunds, Stockholm, 1973.

Breach of Confidence, Law Commission Working Paper No. 58, 1974.

Bunyan, Tony, *The Political Police in Britain*, Julian Friedmann, 1976.

Burney, Elizabeth, *J. P.: Magistrate, Court, and Community*, Hutchinson, 1979.

Campbell, Dennis, 'Free Press in Sweden and America', 8 *Southwestern Law Review* 61.

Campbell, Enid, 'Public Access to Government Documents', 41 *Australian Law Journal* 73 (1967).

Castle, Barbara, *The Castle Diaries*, Weidenfeld & Nicolson, 1980.

Chapman, Leslie, *Your Disobedient Servant: the Continuing Story of Government Overspending*, Penguin Books, 1979.

Civil Service Department, *Disclosure of Information: a Report on Overseas Practice*, H.M.S.O., 1979.

Cohen, Stan, and Taylor, Laurie, *Prison Secrets*, National Council for Civil Liberties and Radical Alternatives to Prison, 1978.

Computers and Privacy, Cmnd. 6353, H.M.S.O., 1975.

Computers: Safeguards for Privacy, Cmnd. 6354, H.M.S.O., 1975.

Confidential Information, Scottish Law Commission Memorandum No. 40, 1977.

Cox, Barry, *Civil Liberties in Britain*, Penguin Books, 1975.

Cross, Harold, *The People's Right to Know*, Columbia University Press, New York, 1953.

Crossman, Richard, *Diaries of a Cabinet Minister* (3 vols.), Hamish Hamilton, 1975, 1976, 1977.

Denning, Lord, *Report in the Light of Circumstances Surrounding the Resignation of the Former Secretary of State for War, Mr J. D. Profumo*, Cmnd. 2152, H.M.S.O., 1963.

Dorsen, N., and Gillers, S. (eds.), *None of Your Business: Government Secrecy in America*, Viking Press, New York, 1974.

Dresner, Stuart, *Open Government: Lessons from America*, Outer Circle Policy Unit, 1980.

Dworkin, Ronald, 'Open Government – or Closed?', *New Society*, 24 June 1976, p. 680.

Evans, Harold, 'The Half-Free Press', *The New Review*, January 1976, p. 3.

'Executive Privilege and the Press', *New Law Journal*, 6 February 1975, p. 122.

Faulks, Mr Justice, *Report of the Committee on Defamation*, Cmnd. 5909, H.M.S.O., 1975.

Finer, S. E., *Comparative Government*, Penguin Books, 1970.

Fox, Larry, *Freedom of Information and the Administrative Process*, Ontario Commission on Freedom of Information and Individual Privacy, 1979.

Franck, T., and Weisband, E. (eds.), *Secrecy and Foreign Policy*, Oxford University Press, 1974.

Franks, Lord (chairman), *Report and Evidence of the Committee on Section 2 of the Official Secrets Act 1911* (4 vols.), Cmnd. 5104, H.M.S.O., 1972.

Franks, Sir Oliver (chairman), *Report of the Committee on Administrative Tribunals and Inquiries*, Cmnd. 218, H.M.S.O., 1957.

Freedom of Information Bill 1978: Explanatory Memorandum, Australian Parliament, 1978.

Fulton, Lord (chairman), *The Civil Service: Report of the Committee*, Cmnd. 3638, H.M.S.O., 1968.

Galnoor, Itzhak (ed.), *Government Secrecy in Democracies*, Harper & Row, New York, 1977.

Griffith, J. A. G., *The Politics of the Judiciary*, Fontana, 1977.

Haines, Joe, *The Politics of Power*, Jonathan Cape, 1977.

Halperin, Morton, and Hoffman, Daniel, *Top Secret: National Security and the Right to Know*, New Republic Books, Washington, D. C., 1977.

Harman, Harriet, and Griffith, John, *Justice Deserted: the Subversion of the Jury*, National Council for Civil Liberties, 1980.

Heclo, Hugh, and Wildavsky, Aaron, *The Private Government of Public Money*, Macmillan, 1974.

Herlitz, Nils, 'Publicity of Official Documents in Sweden', *Public Law*, 1958.

Hewitt, Patricia (ed.), *Computers, Records, and the Right to Privacy*, Input Two-Nine, 1979.

Hewitt, Patricia, *Privacy: the Information Gatherers*, National Council for Civil Liberties, 1977.

Holm, Nils Elschou, 'The Danish System of Open Files in Public Administration', *Scandinavian Studies in Law*, 1975.

Home Office, *Reform of Section 2 of the Official Secrets Act 1911*, Cmnd. 7285, H.M.S.O., 1978.

Information and Public Interest. Cmnd. 4089, H.M.S.O., 1969.

Jacob, Joseph, and Jacob, Robin, 'Confidential Communications', *New Law Journal*, 6 February 1969, p. 133.

Jacob, Joseph, 'Discovery and the Public Interest', *Public Law*, 1976.

Jacob, Joseph, and Jacob, Robin, 'Protection of Privacy', *New Law Journal*, 13 February 1969, p. 157.

Jacob, Joseph, 'Some Reflections on Government Secrecy', *Public Law*, 1974.

Jenkins, Roy, 'Government, Broadcasting, and the Press', Granada Guildhall Lecture, 1975.

Jones, Marjorie, *Justice and Journalism*, Barry Rose, 1974.

Jones, Mervyn (ed.), *Privacy*, David & Charles, 1974.

Justice (British Section of the International Commission of Jurists), *Freedom of Information*, 1978.

Kellner, Peter, and Lord Crowther-Hunt, *The Civil Servants: an Inquiry into Britain's Ruling Class*, Macdonald and Jane's, 1980.

Kernaghan, Kenneth, *Freedom of Information and Ministerial Responsibility*, Ontario Commission on Freedom of Information and Individual Privacy, 1978.

Lamont, Norman, 'The Treasury and the Cult of Secrecy', *Sunday Times*, 7 December 1975, p. 16.

Laurie, Peter, *Beneath the City Streets* (3rd ed.), Panther, 1979.

Liberal Party, *Public Access to Official Information*, 1978.

Lindop, Sir Norman (chairman), *Report of the Committee on Data Protection*, Cmnd. 7341, H.M.S.O., 1978.

Lucas, J. R., *Democracy and Participation*, Penguin Books, 1976.

McMillan, John, 'Making Government Accountable – a Comparative Analysis of Freedom of Information Statutes', *New Zealand Law Journal*, 1977.

Madgwick, Donald, and Smythe, Tony, *The Invasion of Privacy*, Pitman, 1974.

Marchetti, Victor, and Marks, John, *The C.I.A. and the Cult of Intelligence*, Coronet, 1976.

Margach, James, *The Anatomy of Power*, W. H. Allen & Co., 1979.

Margolis, Michael, *Viable Democracy*, Penguin Books, 1979.

Marwick, Christine (ed.), *Litigation Under the Amended Federal Freedom of Information Act* (4th ed.), Center for National Security Studies, Washington, D.C., 1978.

Mathews, Anthony, *The Darker Reaches of Government: Access to Information about Public Administration in the United States, Britain, and South Africa*, University of California Press, 1978.

Miller, Arthur, *The Assault on Privacy: Computers, Data Banks, and Dossiers*, University of Michigan Press, 1971.

Morgenthau, Hans J., *Truth and Power*, Pall Mall Press, 1970.

Murdoch, Laurel, and Hillard, Jane, *Freedom of Information and Individual Privacy: a Selective Bibliography*, Ontario Commission on Freedom of Information and Individual Privacy, 1979.

O'Higgins, Paul, *Censorship in Britain*, Thomas Nelson & Sons, 1972.

Open Government, Cmnd. 7250, H.M.S.O., 1979.

O'Reilly, James T., 'Government Disclosure of Private Secrets under the Freedom of Information Act', *The Business Lawyer*, July 1975, p. 1125.

Outer Circle Policy Unit, *A Consumers' Guide to Open Government: Techniques for Penetrating Whitehall*, 1980.

Outer Circle Policy Unit, *An Official Information Act*, 1977.

Outer Circle Policy Unit, *Official Information Bill*, 1978.

Page, Bruce, Leitch, David, and Knightley, Philip, *Philby, the Spy Who Betrayed a Generation*, Sphere, 1977.

The People and the Media, Labour Party Discussion Paper, 1974.

Peters, Charles, and Branch, Taylor, *Blowing the Whistle: Dissent in the Public Interest*, Praeger, New York, 1972.

Phillimore, Lord Justice (chairman), *Report of the Committee on Contempt of Court*, Cmnd. 5794, H.M.S.O., 1974.

Pincher, Chapman, *Inside Story: a Documentary of the Pursuit of Power*, Sidgwick & Jackson, 1978.

'Public Right to Know?', *New Law Journal*, 9 October 1976, p. 965.

Radcliffe, Lord (chairman), *Report of the Committee on Ministerial Memoirs*, Cmnd. 6386, H.M.S.O., 1976.

Radcliffe, Lord (chairman), *Report of the Committee of Privy Councillors Appointed to Inquire into 'D' Notice Matters*, Cmnd. 3309, H.M.S.O., 1967.

Parliamentary Questions, Report of Select Committee on, H.C. 393, H.M.S.O., 1972.

Policy Proposals for Freedom of Information Legislation, Report of Interdepartmental Committee, Australian Parliamentary Paper No. 400, 1976.

Privilege in Civil Proceedings, 16th Report of the Law Reform Committee, Cmnd. 3472, H.M.S.O., 1967.

Rankin, T. Murray, *Freedom of Information in Canada: Will the Doors Stay Shut?*, Canadian Bar Association, 1977.

Rourke, Francis E., *Secrecy and Publicity: Dilemmas of Democracy*, Johns Hopkins Press, Baltimore, 1961.

Rourke, Francis E. (ed.), 'Symposium: Administrative Secrecy, a Comparative Perspective', *Public Administration Review*, January 1975.

Rowat, Donald (ed.), *Administrative Secrecy in Developed Countries*, International Institute of Administrative Sciences, Macmillan, 1979.

Rowat, Donald, 'The Problem of Administrative Secrecy', *International Review of Administrative Sciences*, 1966, pp. 99–106.

Rowat, Donald, *Public Access to Government Documents: A Comparative Perspective*, Ontario Commission on Freedom of Information and Individual Privacy, 1978.

Sampson, Anthony, *New Anatomy of Britain*, Hodder & Stoughton, 1971.

Schwartz, B., and Wade, H. W. R., *Legal Control of Government*, Clarendon Press, 1972.

Secrecy, or the Right to Know?, The Library Association, 1980.

Sedgemore, Brian, *The Secret Constitution: an Analysis of the Political Establishment*, Hodder & Stoughton, 1980.

Shils, Edward A., *The Torment of Secrecy*, William Heinemann, 1956.

Sieghart, Paul, *Privacy and Computers*, Latimer New Dimensions, 1976.

Smiley, Donald, *The Freedom of Information Issue: a Political Analysis*, Ontario Commission on Freedom of Information and Personal Privacy, 1978.

Smith, Robin Callender, *Press Law*, Sweet & Maxwell, 1978.

Spigelman, Jim, *Secrecy: Political Censorship in Australia*, Angus & Robertson, 1972.

State Research, *Review of Security and the State*, Julian Friedmann, 1979.

Street, Harry, *Freedom, the Individual and the Law*, Penguin Books, 1973.

Sweden, Constitutional Documents of, and *Amendments*, Swedish Riksdag, Stockholm, 1975, 1978.

U.S. Department of Justice, *Attorney-General's Memorandum on the 1974 Amendments to the Freedom of Information Act*, U.S. Government Printing Office, Washington, D.C., 1975.

Vaughan, Robert, *Explanation of Federal Freedom of Information Act, Privacy Act, and Advisory Committee Act*, Prentice-Hall, Englewood Cliffs, N.J., 1979.

Vinge, P. G., *Experiences of the Swedish Data Act*, Federation of Swedish Industries, Stockholm, 1975.

Wacks, Raymond, *The Protection of Privacy*, Sweet & Maxwell, 1980.

Wallace, James H., Jr., 'Proper Disclosure and Indecent Exposure: Protection of Trade Secrets and Confidential Commercial Information Supplied to the Government', *Federal Bar Journal*, vol. 34, p. 295.

Wennergren, Bertil, 'Civic Information – Administrative Publicity', *International Review of Administrative Sciences*, vol. 36, 1970, p. 243.

Westin, Alan, and Baker, Michael, *Databanks in a Free Society*, Quadrangle Books, New York, 1972.

Whale, John, *The Politics of the Media* (2nd ed.), Fontana, 1980.

Wiggins, J. R., *Freedom or Secrecy*, Oxford University Press, 1964.

Williams, David, *Not in the Public Interest*, Hutchinson, 1965.

Wraith, Ronald, *Open Government: the British Interpretation*, Royal Institute of Public Administration, 1977.

Wynn, H. P., 'Freedom of Statistical Information', *Journal of the Royal Statistical Society*, vol. 141, part 1, 1978.

Young, Hugo, *The Crossman Affair*, Hamish Hamilton and Jonathan Cape, 1976.

Young, J. B. (ed.), *Privacy*, John Wiley & Sons, 1978.

Younger, Kenneth (chairman), *Report of the Committee on Privacy*, Cmnd. 5012, H.M.S.O., 1972.

Table of Cases

Index